ADVOCACY GROUPS AND THE ENTERTAINMENT INDUSTRY

ADVOCACY GROUPS AND THE ENTERTAINMENT INDUSTRY

Michael Suman, Senior Editor

Gabriel Rossman, Assistant Editor

Prepared under the auspices of the Center
for Communication Policy,
University of California, Los Angeles

Westport, Connecticut
London

Library of Congress Cataloging-in-Publication Data

Advocacy groups and the entertainment industry / Michael Suman, senior ed., Gabriel
Rossman, assistant ed. ; prepared under the auspices of the Center for Communication Policy,
University of California, Los Angeles.

    p. cm.

    UCLA Center for Communication Policy, along with the American Cinema Foundation
and the Center for the Study of Popular Culture, hosted a conference on Advocacy
Groups and the Entertainment Industry on Feb. 9, 1997.

    Includes bibliographical references and index.

    ISBN 0–275–96885–5 (alk. paper)

    1. Mass media—Political aspects—United States—Congresses. 2. Mass media—Social
aspects—United States—Congresses. 3. Social advocacy—United States—Congresses. I.
Suman, Michael, 1958– II. Rossman, Gabriel, 1977– III. UCLA Center for Communication
Policy.

    P95.82.U6A36   2000

    302.23—dc21   99–088623

British Library Cataloguing in Publication Data is available.

Library of Congress Catalog Card Number: 99–088623
ISBN: 0–275–96885–5

First published in 2000

Praeger Publishers, 88 Post Road West, Westport, CT 06881
An imprint of Greenwood Publishing Group, Inc.
www.praeger.com

Printed in the United States of America

The paper used in this book complies with the
Permanent Paper Standard issued by the National
Information Standards Organization (Z39.48–1984).

10 9 8 7 6 5 4 3 2 1

Copyright Acknowledgment

Portions of chapter 8 in this volume are reprinted with permission from *Media Law*. Copyright © 1995
by The Bureau of National Affairs, Inc., Washington, DC 20037. For copies of BNA Books publications
call toll free 1–800–960–1220.

Contents

Acknowledgements   vii

Introduction   ix

Part I: Articles by Advocates

1. The Harvard Alcohol Project: Promoting the "Designated Driver"   3
   Jay A. Winsten
2. Principles for Effective Advocacy from the Founder of Action for
   Children's Television   9
   Peggy Charren
3. Using Soap Operas to Confront the World's Population Problem   13
   Irwin Sonny Fox
4. A Catholic Look at the Entertainment Industry   19
   William A. Donohue
5. The Proactive Strategy of GLAAD   23
   William Horn, as interviewed by Gabriel Rossman
6. Strategies of the Media Action Network for Asian Americans   29
   Guy Aoki
7. How Church Advocacy Groups Fostered the Golden Age of
   Hollywood   37
   Ted Baehr

Part II: Articles by Lawyers

8. Influencing Media Content Through the Legal System: A Less
   Than Perfect Solution for Advocacy Groups   43
   Rex S. Heinke and Michelle H. Tremain
9. Public Policy Advocacy: Truant Independent Producers in a
   Federal City Fixated on a "Values Agenda"   53
   Mickey R. Gardner

Part III: Articles by Academics

10. Gatekeeping in the Neo-Network Era   65
    Michael Curtin
11. What Is an Advocacy Group, Anyway?   77
    Thomas Streeter
12. Hostile and Cooperative Advocacy   85
    Gabriel Rossman
13. Advocacy Groups in the Age of Audience Fragmentation:
    Thoughts on a New Strategy   105
    Robert Pekurny
14. Interest Groups and Public Debate   115
    Michael Suman

Part IV: Articles by Industry Representatives

15. Advocacy Groups Confront CBS: Problems or Opportunities?   125
    Carol Altieri
16. Dealing with Advocacy Groups at ABC   131
    Alfred R. Schneider
17. Television and Pressure Groups: Balancing the Bland   139
    Lionel Chetwynd

Part V: Epilogue

18. A Millenarian View of Artists and Audiences   145
    Nicholas Johnson

Selected Bibliography   159
Index   163
About the Editors and Contributors   173

Acknowledgements

We would like to thank Marde Gregory, Jeff Cole, and Phoebe Schramm for their assistance and support. Marde has been a constant source of intellectual and emotional encouragement. Jeff, as the director of the UCLA Center for Communication Policy, has provided steady, sound, and inspired leadership that has made this book, as well as others, possible. Phoebe has been a continual fount of editorial wisdom. We constantly sought her invaluable advice on matters of grammar, punctuation, syntax, and wording. She also helped ferret out errors that we failed to detect by carefully reading over the whole manuscript at the end of the editing process.

In addition, Michael Suman would like to thank his parents, Glenn W. Suman and Doris J. Koehler Suman, for their constant love and support.

Gabriel Rossman would also like to thank his parents, Steven Kirby Rossman and Ruth Ann Rossman, for their encouragement.

Introduction

On February 19, 1997, the UCLA Center for Communication Policy, along with the American Cinema Foundation and the Center for the Study of Popular Culture, hosted a conference on advocacy groups and the entertainment industry. This book is an outgrowth of the debate that occurred at that meeting.

The UCLA Center for Communication Policy periodically hosts conferences on controversial issues in the mass media. We aim to bring together leading figures from academia, the media industries, and other relevant groups and organizations to discuss the issue at hand. The first such conference we hosted was the Information Superhighway Summit, which featured Vice President Albert Gore, FCC Chairman Reed Hundt, and the chief executive officers of practically every major film studio and communications technology company in America. Another notable conference was held in June 1995 and focused on religion and prime time television. The February 1997 topic was the nature and extent of the influence of advocacy groups on the entertainment industry and the effect this influence has on society in general.

A select group of participants from the conference was chosen to make contributions to this book. Some additional scholars and experts were also contacted to submit chapters. The writers, all national figures prominent in their respective fields, are a varied lot and provide a great diversity of viewpoints on the issue.

This book is divided into four major sections, framed by this prologue and an epilogue. The first part features articles by representatives of media advocacy groups. Jay Winsten, director of the Center for Health Communication at the Harvard School of Public Health, discusses his successful campaign to introduce a new social concept, the designated driver. He explains how, with the cooperation of the Hollywood studios and television networks, the Center for Health Communication promoted a new social norm, that is, that drivers should not drink, through public service announcements and plot lines. Peggy Charren writes about her experiences as founder of Action for Children's Television (ACT). She describes the values that guided her and 12 strategies she developed which made ACT a successful organization. Irwin Sonny Fox, senior vice president of Population Communications International, explains how his organization, in cooperation with local authorities and talent throughout the world, develops soap operas to confront the world population problem. He discusses how population control messages can be created in an entertaining and culturally relevant way for maximum effect. William Donohue, president and CEO of the Catholic League for Religious and Civil Rights, argues that Catholics are treated unfairly by the entertainment industry. He suggests that this is primarily a consequence of a largely secular and liberal Hollywood uncomfortable with the traditional sexual morality of the Catholic Church. William Horn, assistant director of entertainment media at the Gay and Lesbian Alliance Against Defamation (GLAAD), describes the history and tactics of his organization in an interview with Gabriel Rossman. He credits general social trends toward tolerance, as well as his organization's nonantagonistic, proactive strategies for fostering increasingly positive media portrayals of lesbians and gay men. Guy Aoki, cofounder and past president of Media Action Network for Asian Americans (MANAA), describes how the image of Asian Americans has been distorted by the entertainment industry. Through detailed accounts of campaigns waged by his organization, he explains how it monitors and responds to the mass media. Ted Baehr, chairman of the Christian Film and Television Commission and publisher of *Movieguide*, explains how between 1933 and 1966 church-affiliated advocacy groups successfully promoted wholesome entertainment. With the demise of these groups there was a proliferation of sex, violence, and other objectionable content. Baehr's office was created to restore the "golden age" of film that existed in the middle of this century.

The second part of this book is composed of articles by attorneys specializing in communications. Rex Heinke and Michelle Tremain, partners at the law firm Gibson, Dunn, & Crutcher, argue that the courts are an increasingly inhospitable place for advocacy groups seeking change in the media. This is because of the formidable requirements of defamation suits, the government's limited ability to censor film, the courts' refusal to compel government broadcasters to air particular programming, the demise of governmental rules regarding balanced presentation of issues in the broadcast media, and the total lack of similar rules for newspapers. Michael Gardner, an attorney who manages a communications law firm in Washington, D.C., observes that such "values"-oriented legislation as television content labels and educational broadcast standards imposed during the Clinton administration have impinged upon the industry's First Amendment freedoms. Similarly, deregulation has diminished the diversity of the industry by fostering a consolidated marketplace and mega-corporations. He urges the creative elements within the television industry that are confronted with this dangerous environment, especially independent production houses, to take an active role in lobbying against government action that is contrary to their, and indeed by extension the nation's, interests.

The third part of this book features articles by academics. Michael Curtin, associate professor of communication and culture at Indiana University, argues that television has changed dramatically over the last two decades. Today corporate executives exercise a decreasing amount of control over an increasingly diverse menu of programming. This situation has created uncertainty for the corporate executives and opportunity for advocacy groups. He explains how this opportunity can be realized only if advocacy groups understand the logic of the new media era, especially how the gatekeeping practices of the media have changed, and help make the populace aware of the new options available to them. Thomas Streeter, associate professor of sociology at the University of Vermont, asks the question, "What is an advocacy group?" In part his answer is historical: he explains how advocacy groups compose an institution that can be understood in terms of the history of the relationship between business and government in the 20th century. In part his answer is theoretical: he argues that advocacy groups embody a particular vision of democratic politics in contemporary America. He concludes that advocacy groups are important, although limited, vehicles for affecting change in the world of the mass media. Gabriel Rossman, a graduate student in sociology at Princeton University and assistant editor of this book, analyzes advocacy groups by comparing them to two idealizations, the hostile outsider group and the cooperative insider group. Through use of ethnographic data and content analysis he demonstrates the differences between these two sorts of groups and shows why, due to deeply entrenched ideological conflict with the media elite, many hostile groups are incapable of making the transition to proactively cooperating with the media. Robert Pekurny, assistant professor of communication at Florida State University, argues that the mass media have changed significantly over the last several decades, and this has altered the task facing advocacy groups. He describes how negative tactics, such as boycotts and letter-writing campaigns, have never been successful, and this is even more the case in the current world of mega-media corporations and audience fragmentation. He explains how advocacy groups, to be effective, must deal directly with the creative personnel who have become increasingly important to media corporations. Michael Suman, research director of the UCLA Center for Communication Policy and senior editor of this book, argues that all too often interest groups do more harm than good, especially by being overly sensitive and too narrowly focused on their own concerns. Instead of leading or participating in public debates on significant issues, they often instead work to prevent, stifle, and distort these discussions. He also identifies important economic considerations within the television industry that are working against the open and robust debates over significant social issues that he favors.

The fourth part of the book is composed of articles by representatives of the entertainment industry. Carol Altieri tells of her experiences working within the practices and standards division at CBS. She discusses which strategies advocacy groups have used and then explains how these groups could be more effective given the nature of the television industry and the pressures with which it must deal. Alfred Schneider, long-time head of policy and standards for ABC, describes encounters with advocacy groups during his 35-year tenure in the industry. He describes his experiences with a wide variety of advocacy groups, giving especially detailed attention to the actions of anticommunists, homosexual rights groups, and conservative Christians opposed to sex and violence. He shows how the network has responded to advocates, for example, by creating standards manuals, and how some of these advocates also have attempted to use the influence of advertisers on the networks. Lionel Chetwynd, a writer, director, and producer of film and television, argues that technological changes have led to ever greater battles over audience share. This has given advocates greater power as they can potentially persuade viewers not to watch a particular program. In this environment, network programmers are constantly trapped between liberal forces typically aligned with the creative community and conservative forces which more often conduct national campaigns which threaten a show's viewer or advertising base. In response, programmers play it safe by presenting bland shows that are internally balanced so as to offend no one.

Nicholas Johnson, a former FCC commissioner who now teaches at the University of Iowa, concludes the volume with an epilogue in which he offers an overview of the issue and tries to make sense of the variety of viewpoints offered by the book's authors. He reviews some of the advocacy strategies discussed by the authors and concludes with an idea for the establishment of a council to which individuals and organizations could take their complaints about the media.

In sum, this book offers the wide-ranging viewpoints of a select group of media advocates, media lawyers, academics, and entertainment industry representatives on the important public policy issue of how advocacy groups affect the entertainment industry.

I

Articles by Advocates

The Harvard Alcohol Project: Promoting the "Designated Driver"

Jay A. Winsten

How effective are projects that rely on mass communication strategies to promote healthy behaviors? One of the best documented examples is the National Designated Driver Campaign. Launched in November 1988, the campaign was spearheaded by the Harvard School of Public Health's Center for Health Communication in partnership with all the major Hollywood studios and the leading television networks.

The campaign was initiated because the movement against drunk driving had lost momentum by the mid-1980s. In the early 1980s, Mothers Against Drunk Driving (MADD), other activist organizations, and government agencies achieved tremendous success placing the drunk driving issue on the public and media agendas. Annual alcohol-related traffic fatalities declined substantially during this period. However, by 1985, the activities of these organizations—while still critically important—were no longer fresh and newsworthy, and media attention turned to other issues. When media coverage fell off drastically, progress in reducing fatalities ground to a halt. Indeed, annual alcohol-related traffic fatalities increased in 1986 and then remained unchanged through 1988. Clearly, there was a need for a fresh new idea to recapture public and media interest and rejuvenate the anti-drunk driving movement. The designated driver concept, invented in the Nordic countries, filled that role.

The Center for Health Communication was attracted to the designated driver concept for several reasons. From a marketing perspective, it offers a very simple media message—an essential requirement for working effectively through mass communication. However, the concept's simplicity is the tip of an iceberg; beneath the surface lies enormous complexity. The designated driver concept promotes a new social norm, a new social expectation, that the driver does not drink any alcohol; lends social legitimacy to the non-drinking option; encourages people to plan ahead when they are going out for the evening; and places the issue of driving-after-drinking on the interpersonal agendas of couples and small groups. In addition, the concept enjoys broad public support, engenders no opposition from economic interests, and asks for only a modest shift in behavior (that is, it is not anti-alcohol).

The Center viewed the designated driver concept as one component of a comprehensive strategy for reducing alcohol-related traffic fatalities. Since traffic crashes are but one of several adverse consequences of abusive drinking, the Center devised a message promoting three distinct social norms related to alcohol: If you choose to drink (reinforcing the social legitimacy of nondrinking), drink only in moderation (addressed to the driver's companions), and choose a designated driver who doesn't drink at all (promoting the norm that no drinking is acceptable before driving).

The Center initially organized a statewide designated driver campaign in Massachusetts in 1986 in partnership with Westinghouse-owned WBZ-TV and the Massachusetts Restaurant Association. Then, in 1988, the Center set out to demonstrate how a new social concept, the "designated driver," could be rapidly diffused throughout American society via mass communication, catalyzing a fundamental shift in the nation's social norms relating to driving-after-drinking. The Center's national communications strategy included three components: news, advertising, and entertainment programming.

NEWS

The Center viewed each news story reporting on the campaign as a well-placed "public service announcement" for the designated driver concept. The Center's public relations effort generated extensive national news coverage, including a front-page story in *The New York Times*,[1] an editorial applauding the campaign in *The New York Times*,[2] a special four-minute report on "ABC's World News Tonight with Peter Jennings,"[3] major stories in the *Washington Post*[4] and the *Los Angeles Times*,[5] and favorable editorial commentary and news coverage in many other newspapers, national news weeklies, and television newscasts. Also drawing extensive press attention were two special Center initiatives: a community-based designated driver campaign on Martha's Vineyard[6] and a restaurant-based designated driver promotion at Boston's Hard Rock Cafe.[7]

ADVERTISING

At the Center's request, the ABC, CBS, and NBC television networks promoted the designated driver concept for several years through network-produced and network-sponsored public service announcements (PSAs). In peak periods, these were broadcast as often as 10–20 times per week, including frequently in prime time. For example, CBS ran four annual mini-campaigns, each consisting of a cluster of about seven prime time PSAs, leading up to Memorial Day, Independence Day, and Labor Day, and in early December. ABC and NBC clustered their designated driver messages in December. With support from the National Association of Broadcasters, radio and television stations in many local media markets also broadcast frequent designated driver PSAs. In addition, at the

Center's initiative, it became a tradition for the President of the United States to be featured in a designated driver PSA on network television each December.

ENTERTAINMENT PROGRAMMING

The campaign broke new ground when television writers agreed to insert drunk driving prevention messages, including frequent references to the use of designated drivers, into the scripts of top-rated shows such as "The Cosby Show," "Cheers," and "L.A. Law." Short messages, embedded within dialogue, were casually presented by characters who served as role models within a dramatic context, thereby facilitating social learning. The National Designated Driver Campaign represented the first successful effort to mobilize the Hollywood creative community on such a scale, using dialogue in prime time entertainment as a health promotion technology. With introductions arranged by Frank Stanton, former CBS president, and Grant Tinker, former NBC chairman, Center staff held meetings with over 250 executive producers, senior producers, and chief writers from all the leading prime time shows. In addition, the boards of the Screen Actors Guild and the Writers Guild of America, West endorsed and promoted the campaign. During four television seasons, beginning with the 1988–1989 season, more than 160 prime time programs included subplots, scenes, dialogue, or (in over 25 instances) entire 30-minute or 60-minute episodes supporting the campaign, with audiences numbering to 45 million. Many programs subsequently were rebroadcast, either as network reruns or in syndication, greatly amplifying the campaign's exposure.

In its early years, the designated driver campaign received an estimated $100 million each year in donated network airtime—adequate for promoting a major new product in the commercial sector. The Center's goal was to package and market a new product to the American public—the "designated driver."

The campaign soon became transformed into a national movement. A broad range of prominent individuals (e.g., former Surgeon General C. Everett Koop[8]), government agencies (e.g., the National Highway Traffic Safety Administration[9]), national organizations (e.g., Mothers Against Drunk Driving[10]), professional sports leagues (e.g., Major League Baseball[11]), major corporations (e.g., State Farm Insurance[12]), and leading police departments (e.g., the California Highway Patrol[13]) endorsed and promoted the designated driver concept.

Fueled by this overall national effort, the designated driver concept became so deeply embedded in American life and language over a three-year period that by 1991 the term was included in the *Random House Webster's College Dictionary*.[14] The campaign's dramatic impact on awareness, acceptance, and the usage of the designated driver concept was documented in national public opinion polls conducted by the Gallup Organization, the Wirthlin Group, and the Roper Organization.

In 1989, Gallup found that 67% of adults had noticed the designated driver messages on network television.[15] In 1990, Wirthlin found that 89% of respondents in the country were familiar with the designated driver program and gave it an average favorability rating of 81 on a 100-point scale; the designated driver program rated higher than all other programs and industries measured. Among parents of children 13–18 years of age, Wirthlin found that 97% were familiar with the designated driver program and gave it an average favorability rating of 82. Among young adults 18–24, 97% were familiar with the designated driver program and gave it an average favorability rating of 88. By way of comparison, in a separate Wirthlin survey rating individuals, Mother Teresa scored highest with an average favorability rating of 84.[16]

The most detailed survey data have been collected by the Roper Organization in studies of U.S. adults conducted in 1989 and 1991. Roper's 1991 findings, with selected comparisons to those of 1989, are highlighted below:

1. Ninety-three percent of Americans characterized the designated driver concept as an "excellent" or "good" idea (71 %, excellent; 22%, good). Among all drunk driving prevention strategies, U.S. adults gave their strongest endorsement to the use of designated drivers.[17]
2. Thirty-seven percent of U.S. adults had themselves refrained from drinking in order to be a designated driver at least once in their lifetime, up sharply from 29% in 1989.[18]
3. Fifty-two percent of U.S. adults younger than 30 had been a designated driver,[19] up from 43% in 1989.[20]
4. Forty-six percent of drinkers had been a designated driver,[21] versus 35% in 1989.[22] Fifty-one percent of frequent drinkers had been a designated driver, versus 36% in 1989.[23] Roper observed: "This indicates that it is not just the non-drinkers in a group who offer to be designated drivers, but that drinkers voluntarily refrain on occasions, and the concept is being implemented by this key group."[24]
5. Thirty-five percent of drinkers had been driven home by a designated driver, versus 28% in 1989.[25] Fifty-four percent of frequent drinkers had been driven home by a designated driver, versus 43% in 1989.[26]
6. Sixty-one percent of politically and socially active adults ("influentials") had been a designated driver, versus 45% in 1989.[27]
7. Fifty percent of executives and professionals had been a designated driver, versus 36% in 1989.[28]
8. Forty-six percent of union members and 41% of blue collar workers had been a designated driver, versus 33% and 34%, respectively, in 1989.[29]

Roper observed, "Considering how relatively new the concept of the designated driver is, the sustained growth and support of the idea is [sic] impressive."[30] Roper concluded, "The designated driver concept is fast becoming ingrained in the nation's psyche. . . . The designated driver system has likely saved many young lives: among those under 30, a majority have been [a designated driver]."[31]

What was the campaign's impact on alcohol-related traffic fatalities? When the campaign began in late 1988, annual fatalities stood at 23,626. By 1992, annual fatalities had dropped sharply to 17,858.[32] This represented a four-year decline of 24%, compared to 0% change in the three years just prior to the campaign. A variety of factors were responsible for the decline. Based on the extensive polling data, the Center concluded that the campaign made an important contribution to the downward trend in fatalities.

In June 1993, the U.S. Center for Substance Abuse Prevention joined with the National Highway Traffic Safety Administration to issue an official policy statement endorsing the designated driver concept within a comprehensive framework for addressing alcohol-related problems.[33] The agencies' *Statement on Designated Drivers* observed, "By encouraging drivers to remain alcohol-free, the designated driver [concept] both promotes a social norm of not mixing alcohol with driving and fosters the legitimacy of the non-drinking role. Moreover, the concept of no alcohol for the driver is more stringent than current state driving under the influence (DUI) laws permitting some alcohol for drivers." The joint statement stressed the need to promote moderation for the driver's companions and concluded as follows: "Policy: The use of designated drivers by the public and designated driver programs by servers of alcoholic beverages is encouraged for those over age 21."

NOTES

1. R. Rothenberg, "TV industry plans fight against drunken driving," in *The New York Times*, August 31, 1988, p. A1.

2. "Designating the driver," editorial in *The New York Times*, January 17, 1989, p. A24.

3. "ABC's World News Tonight with Peter Jennings," September 26, 1989.

4. C. Hall, "TV's pledge against drinking drivers," in *The Washington Post*, September 1, 1988, p. B1.

5. N. Finke, "TV series join crusade to curb drunk driving," in the *Los Angeles Times*, November 25, 1988, p. V1.

6. L. Walters, "Designating a driver, island ad campaign sells sobriety," in *The Christian Science Monitor*, September 12, 1990, p. 12.

7. Associated Press, "A drive is pressed for sober drivers, concept of designated driver catches on as old habits change in society," in *The New York Times*, December 31, 1989, p. 1:22.

8. M. Cimons, "Everett Koop, the former Surgeon General examines the nation's health," in the *Los Angeles Times*, February 23, 1992, p. M3.

9. National Highway Traffic Safety Administration (NHTSA), "Secretary Skinner pledges continued fight against drunk driving at White House '3D Week' briefing," press release of NHTSA 33–89 (Washington, DC: U.S. Department of Transportation, 1989).

10. Mothers Against Drunk Driving (MADD), "Responsible marketing and service of alcohol," position statement (Dallas, TX: MADD, 1990).

11. National Highway Traffic Safety Administration (NHTSA), "Techniques for effective alcohol management: 1990 progress report" (Washington, DC: Office of Alcohol and State Programs, NHTSA, U.S. Department of Transportation, 1991).

12. State Farm Insurance Companies, "Be a good neighbor, be a designated driver," a kit (Bloomington, IL: State Farm Insurance Companies, 1991).

13. Department of California Highway Patrol, "A compendium for the implementation of the designated driver program," designated driver program guidebook (Sacramento, CA: Office of Public Affairs, 1992).

14. *Random House Webster's College Dictionary* (New York: Random House, 1991), p. 366.

15. Gallup National Poll, unpublished, 1989.

16. Wirthlin National Survey, unpublished, 1990.

17. The Roper Organization, "Roper Reports," 91–3,1991, pp. 19–20.

18. The Roper Organization, "Roper Reports," 91–3,1991, pp. 19–20.

19. The Roper Organization, "A special report to Anheuser-Busch by the Roper Organization," 1991, pp. 24–26.

20. The Roper Organization, "The social climate for drinking: A Roper analysis prepared for the House of Seagram," 1990, p. 25.

21. The Roper Organization, unpublished data, 1991.

22. The Roper Organization, "The social climate for drinking: A Roper analysis prepared for the House of Seagram," 1990, p. 25.

23. The Roper Organization, unpublished data, 1991.

24. The Roper Organization, "The social climate for drinking: A Roper analysis prepared for the House of Seagram," 1990, p. 25.

25. The Roper Organization, "DWI: Public holds business more accountable," in *The Public Pulse*, December 1991, p. 6.

26. The Roper Organization, unpublished data, 1991; The Roper Organization, "The social climate for drinking: A Roper analysis prepared for the House of Seagram," 1990, p. 25.

27. The Roper Organization, unpublished data, 1989; unpublished data, 1991.

28. The Roper Organization, unpublished data, 1989; unpublished data, 1991.

29. The Roper Organization, unpublished data, 1989; unpublished data, 1991.

30. The Roper Organization, "A special report to Anheuser-Busch by the Roper Organization," 1991, pp. 24–26.

31. The Roper Organization, "DWI: Public holds businesses more accountable," in *The Public Pulse*, December 1991, p. 6.

32. National Highway Traffic Safety Administration, "Traffic Safety Facts 1995" (Washington, DC: NHTSA, U.S. Department of Transportation, September 1996), p. 32.

33. U.S. Center for Substance Abuse Prevention, U.S. National Highway Traffic Safety Administration, statement on designated drivers, June 1993.

Principles for Effective Advocacy from the Founder of Action for Children's Television

Peggy Charren

When I think back to how I got to be who I am, I am reminded of something John Kennedy said when asked how he became a hero. He replied, "It was involuntary. They sank my boat!"

My career as a child advocate was also largely involuntary. I started Action for Children's Television (ACT) because I couldn't find adequate daycare after my second daughter was born. I decided to close my small business running children's book fairs until after my children started school. During this hiatus I began ACT as a volunteer effort in my living room, and it grew and grew. . . . And now it's 30 years later, and my grandchildren have started school, and I'm still talking about children's television.

From my over 30 years' experience, what can I tell you about being an advocate? First of all, an advocate should be able to articulate a particular set of values, to encourage others to adopt those values, and to take action based on them. Of course, different advocates are motivated by different values.

So where did my values come from? First of all, they came from my mom and dad. The most important gift I received from my parents was a sense that one can go out and *fix* how the world works. They were Roosevelt Democrats who talked to me about the power of the ballot box. They also told me about prejudice, discrimination, and the rights of people of color—and this was before the civil rights movement. They sent me to camp where I didn't do too well at soccer but managed to learn just about every labor song. To this day I can recite the words to Pete Seeger's "Talking Union." Because of my parents' influence, I don't remember a time when I wasn't concerned about the rights of others. It started young for me, and it stuck.

In school I learned about constitutional values and rights, particularly the importance of free speech in a democracy, the right to speak and to be heard. This turned out to be a bedrock principle underlying my efforts to get more TV choices for children and to fight censorship as a solution to children's TV problems. In school I also learned to love books—for information and education, for delight and discovery. Through all the years of ACT, we had a librarian on our staff. Recently we donated the ACT library to the collection at Harvard University's Graduate School of Education so that students can benefit from the materials we accumulated over the years.

Advocates are leaders. But to lead, you need support, and I am lucky to have had the enthusiastic support of a husband who understood, even before Gloria Steinem, that women are people, too. And I had the somewhat less than enthusiastic support of my two children, who often wished that I would spend more time cooking and less time turning off the TV.

Most people think of me as a children's advocate. But, looking back over 30 years of speaking out about children's TV, I think I have spent an equal amount of time as an advocate for free speech. My opinions about how to influence communications policy are based on the importance of the right to speak, to be heard, and to hear the speech of others in our constitutional democracy.

Too often children are used as an excuse for banning speech—words and pictures in comic books, movies, textbooks, television, and new media. Sometimes groups try to censor valuable and significant speech that adults and even young audiences need to hear. And sometimes they turn to the government to turn off disturbing speech because they think the "off" button isn't used often enough by the general public.

But turning to government censorship is not the way to protect our children from television's violent content or language and lyrics not suitable for young audiences. Being subjected to what *some* consider offensive speech is the price we pay for freedom of speech for *everyone*, and we cannot afford to risk losing that freedom.

As we concerned parents, grandparents, teachers, and pediatricians learn to turn TV off more often, we can spend more time searching for what to turn on for our children, more time with public broadcasting's nifty commercial-free choices for young audiences, and more time evaluating whether the three hours per week of educational children's programs each TV station is now obligated to air fits the bill.

The most important result of the present focus on kids' TV issues may be that we parents will move TV sets out of our children's bedrooms so that we will have a better idea of what they are watching. And perhaps we will spend more time talking to our children, helping them to understand that violence is not the solution to problems, that just saying yes to teenage sex has fearsome consequences, and that dissing Grandma is unacceptable behavior. We might even think twice about the messages our own viewing habits send to our offspring. "Do as I say, not as I do" does not work any better for watching TV than it does for smoking cigarettes.

In running ACT I tried to exercise leadership through persuasion. With this in mind, through trial and error, I developed the following set of 12 strategies that helped ACT to make a difference and with which I would like to close:

One: Research your options.
Two: Set clearly defined goals.
Three: Get your facts straight.
Four: Analyze your competition.

These first four rules help you know what you need to know to present your case clearly.

Five: Build a coalition.

In a democracy, there is strength in numbers.

Six: Avoid conflicts of interest.
Seven: Be discreet.

I used to repeat often that memorable phrase of self-protection, "Never do or say anything you don't want to see on the front page of *The New York Times*."

Eight: Make the press a partner.

I believe that the press is one of the most important educational institutions in the country. Some people think my tombstone will read, "She was a sound bite!"

Nine: Keep a sense of humor.
Ten: Throw a terrific party.

Even if your cause is serious, sometimes you have to lighten up to get people to hear and to work with you.

Eleven: Stick with it.

Perseverance doesn't always mean that it will take the 30 years it has taken me to get more choices for kids on broadcast television. But making a difference usually requires patience and fortitude.

Twelve: Accept necessary compromise.

I agree with Voltaire, who said "the best is the enemy of the good." In other words, in our imperfect world of clashing interests, if one is not willing to compromise and settle for something less than "the best," nothing will be achieved. In politics and in parenting, you have to learn when to say OK, as well as when to stop giving in.

Using Soap Operas to Confront the World's Population Problem

Irwin Sonny Fox

In India, in a Doordarshan television network prime time serial, a fourteen-year-old girl is forced into an arranged marriage by her father. Angouri has a dream of becoming a barrister, and objects to being forced into consummating the marriage until she has had a chance to realize that dream. Her aspirations are destroyed by her mother-in-law who burns her books and beats her. Many months into the soap opera, the young girl dies in childbirth at the age of 15. The audience of 150 million viewers who watched this prime time series went into mourning, and a crucial point was made. Delaying the onset of childbearing is a good idea. Forcing children to start bearing children at 15 is not a good idea. For India, rapidly approaching a population of one billion, for the world, rapidly approaching six billion, and for all the Angouris of the world, this drama carried an impact no documentary or tract could possibly approach.

In Tanzania, the Philippines, St. Lucia, Brazil, and other countries where population and related health and social issues are of critical importance, other soap operas designed to change people's attitudes and behavior regarding family planning, health, women's empowerment, and other pro-social issues are being broadcast on radio and television. Behind this unique employment of the mass media is Population Communications International (PCI). Headquartered in New York, PCI has been developing this technique for 12 years.

The objective is to motivate individuals and communities to make choices in reproductive health and development that will contribute significantly to slowing world population growth. The work of PCI, based on the social learning theories of Professor Albert Bandura of Stanford University, is designed to complement the efforts of those involved in providing health services in these countries. With their emphasis on motivating audience members, these soap operas can break through the encrustation of many years of sexism and other anachronistic aspects of traditional culture that keep people from making sensible family planning decisions.

PCI works creatively with the media and other institutions to motivate individuals and communities to make choices resulting in population trends that will yield sustainable development and environmental protection. We at PCI operate in tandem with established groups who share our goals by forming relationships with government agencies as well as with nongovernmental organizations in host countries.

PCI values promotion of health and education and sensitivity to national and local cultures. Often we work with organizations that represent a variety of interests within a particular country, interacting, for example, with officials from the ministries of health, education, and population. In those nations with a national radio or television system, government cooperation is necessary to ensure that our programs are broadcast. Financial support for PCI's work comes in many forms. In general, PCI invests its money in training, research, and start-up costs associated with developing a soap opera. The production costs can come from foundations, corporate sponsors (such as in India), the United Nations (such as in Tanzania), or a combination of commercial and governmental sources (such as in China).

PCI has selected the soap opera format to communicate its messages for a number of important reasons. The longevity of a soap opera, in many cases several hundred episodes, allows characterizations and story lines to play out over a period of months or even years. The identification of the audience with characters they see regularly over a long period of time is substantially greater than it is for the less regular and less sustained presentations of other formats. Therefore, when a soap opera script models good or bad behavior, its impact can be exponentially greater than it is for other formats. The impact of the Angouri story was no doubt much more substantial than if it had played out as a two-hour movie.

Furthermore, the duration of soaps allows for the introduction of characters without immediately inserting social messages. This allows the audience to identify with the characters before they start their transition or journey through which they will deliver their message.

In all cases, the productions are country-specific. They are written, acted, and produced by talent in each country. PCI's role is in the training of the creative talent, in conducting research to help determine the issues, and in making the arrangements necessary for a program to be aired.

To create and produce a PCI serial drama, we cooperate with a wide range of groups that share a common goal to reduce family size and promote reproductive health. An example of such a collaboration is *Tinka Tinka Sukh,* a family planning radio soap opera first broadcast in India in February 1996. The program was broadcast by All Radio India, a national station, and made possible by a generous grant from the Indian government. In concert with the airing of the show, a comprehensive research project to evaluate the impact of the soap opera was conducted by Ohio University and the Centre for Media Studies of India.

In China, PCI has contracted with the China Population Information Service, a nongovernmental organization headquartered in Beijing. The goal of the program there, in keeping with China's national population policy, is to promote norms supporting small families and to reduce the strong preference for sons.

In Tanzania, where PCI has begun its third year presenting the radio soap *Twende na Wakati,* the collaboration involves Radio Tanzania, five Tanzanian ministries, representatives from PCI-Kenya and PCI-New York, and independent research teams from the University of New Mexico and the Population/Family Life Education Program in Tanzania. The Rockefeller Foundation provided financial support for the research.

Research is a critically important component of PCI's work. We facilitate the creation of independent research projects to measure the effects of its entertainment-education programs in various countries. In selected countries, these take the form of controlled field experiments that serve to isolate the effects of the programs.

Evaluative research includes nationwide surveys conducted before, during, and after a broadcast series; collection of clinic intake data; focus groups; in-depth interviews; analysis of letters from audience members; and analysis of other research findings such as those found in demographic and health surveys. In each case, the research is designed to measure changes in knowledge, attitudes, and behavior of audience members and within regions receiving the programs as opposed to those not receiving them.

In addition, similar research techniques are used to help form characters and story lines for programs in each country in order to ensure that all the elements of the programs are culturally accurate, relevant, appropriate, and acceptable.

Two recent reports on Tanzania and Kenya prepared by independent researchers have added substantial weight to the evidence that PCI's mass media entertainment-education programs are effective in changing behavior. The most recent study shows that 28% of the new adopters of family planning in Tanzania cited the PCI soap opera by name as a reason for seeking family planning services. In the areas of the broadcast, 52% of the population aged 15 through 45 indicated that they listened to the program, and 82% of the listeners said that the program had caused them to change their behavior in regard to AIDS prevention.

The Tanzanian program was designed under the guidance of Tom Kazungu, PCI's representative in East Africa, who applied his experience to produce *Ushikwapo Shikamana* (*When Assisted, Assist Yourself*) in Kenya in 1987-89. That serial was the top-rated program in the history of radio broadcasting in Kenya according to the advertising agencies of the time. A study of rural health centers by the University of Nairobi's School of Journalism pointed to the radio program as the most effective communications activity in the area of family planning in Kenya up until that time and credited it with convincing men that their wives should be allowed to seek family planning services.

The communications situation in the United States is different, so PCI's strategy here is different as well. There is a plethora of daytime dramas from which viewers can choose. Moreover, the competitive nature of the business makes it difficult for advocacy groups to promote their perspectives. Unlike many nonprofit organizations that try to encourage social consciousness through letter-writing campaigns or public relations efforts, PCI has developed a novel approach to gain the trust and cooperation of writers, producers, and executives in the soap opera industry and to foster their support.

PCI has organized three Soap Summits. The participants have included the head writers, executive producers, and network executives from the 11 daily American soap operas and the Fox shows "Beverly Hills 90210," "Melrose Place," and "Party of Five." We start each summit with a keynote address. In 1996 the keynote address was delivered by Secretary of Health and Human Services Donna Shalala. In 1998 the keynote speaker was Rob Reiner. We continue with a closed session the next day during which experts make 15-minute presentations on health and social issues that are not being adequately addressed in this country and ask the soap opera creators and network executives for help in addressing these problems. Attendees have been exposed to topics that include teen pregnancy, reproductive health, violence against women, and world population. Secretary Shalala emphasized the importance of soap operas in her opening speech: "Believe it or not you are part of the public health system in this country. . . . You increasingly fill the vacuums in this country once occupied by traditional institutions. From family to religion, from schools to communities, with light and with shadow, with words and with emotion, you reach over 40 million viewers a day and you reach them where they live."

Following the 1996 Soap Summit, PCI decided to conduct an evaluative research study to measure the effect of the conference. With a generous grant from the Ford Foundation we have been able to track the results of the meeting through extensive interviews with attendees. Participants reported that the summit reinforced their motivation to positively address social issues and generated awareness of the profound impact of their work. In addition, the summit fostered internal support for script and character changes by engaging a variety of decision makers—including executive producers, head writers, and breakdown writers. Said Lucy Johnson, CBS vice president for daytime programming, "The value of the summit . . . [was] to make us more aware of some of the consequences and the power of the message we put across."

Within a short period of time four of the ten programs that sent representatives to the summit made changes to specific scenes and plots to reflect some of the issues discussed at the conference. The writers of "All My Children," for example, abandoned a story line that would have given a single teen father custody of his baby. Instead, while the program cotinued to have the teen interested in his child, the baby was adopted by a married couple. At the end of episodes about domestic violence, "The Young and the Restless" broadcast information about 800-number help lines which were staffed and funded by the Department of Health and Human Services and the Kaiser Family Foundation.

Follow-up research demonstrated that the summits not only lead to changes in characterizations and story lines, but also contribute to an increased awareness of the topics presented, as well as of the important roles that writers and producers play in society.

Confident that there will be more Soap Summits in the future, PCI is now embarking on an ambitious new project. In partnership with the National Wildlife Federation, we are developing a new television soap designed to carry social messages and be commercially viable at the same time. We have contracted with a top writer and a respected producer, both of whose credits assure that we will have credibility when we take the project to market.

The success of our summits has also sparked the interest of several international organizations, which have identified our conferences as vehicles to promote programs supporting maternal and child health policies. PCI has been approached by the Pan American Health Organization to develop one or more summits for the telenovela community in Latin America. UNICEF has also indicated its interest in pursuing this project. Philippine television and government authorities have asked for our assistance in mounting a similar conference in that country and, subsequently, in the pan-Pacific region. Finally, PCI was asked to participate in a conference organized by the World Health Organization, which took place in Jakarta, Indonesia, to examine the role the media can play in developing and expanding partnerships for health in the 21st century.

The final document produced at a 1993 conference on population and development in Cairo, signed by 180 nations, urged countries to increase their communications efforts. Specifically the document mentioned soap operas as a format, a considerable tribute to what PCI has accomplished in its short history. But there is still much to be done. We are preparing to produce soaps in the future that deal with population control in Vietnam, Madagascar, Pakistan, India, and Kenya. These programs recognize that the problem in these countries is not just one of availability of contraceptives, but also of deeply held fears and superstitions, cultures that equate having children with virility, and the unequal social position of women.

Through our efforts in the area of population control, societies are being challenged to adopt new behavior patterns and to forgo maladaptive traditional ones. If we do nothing we will have consigned ourselves to those traditional methods of limiting population—war, starvation, disease, and maltreatment of women and children. PCI's efforts are meant to ensure that we choose a better way.

4

A Catholic Look at the Entertainment Industry

William A. Donohue

Beginning with the black civil rights movement, the 1960s and 1970s gave birth to many quests for equality. A politics of confrontation was quickly established that, along with a skepticism turned to cynicism, soon found its way into the dominant culture. Among reporters, this blend of politics and cynicism took expression in advocacy journalism. Among minorities, this stew overheated into exorbitant claims against private and public institutions. The attempt at redress of grievances, real and imagined, had become a full-court press.

Those involved in the civil rights movement of this period, especially African Americans and feminists, sought not only legal redress, but also to fundamentally alter the prevailing stereotypes of blacks and women. To do this they focused attention on the cultural images that the media, and Hollywood in particular, developed about them. This confrontational approach was soon mimicked by Asians, Hispanics, Native Americans, gays, and others.

The extent to which prejudicial attitudes are a function of media portrayals is debatable. More debatable is the effect that such attitudes have on promoting discrimination. What is not debatable is that this media portrayal-prejudice-discrimination link was, and still is, seen as valid by millions of Americans. It was from this social soil that an advocacy industry was founded to challenge the entertainment industry.

Entering very late into this advocacy circle are Catholics. Over the past generation, ethnicity has triumphed over religion as the master status for most Catholics. That explains why Hispanics, to take one example, have organized to change perceptions of their ethnic group, but not perceptions of their religion. It may be that, as Nathan Glazer and Daniel Patrick Moynihan have argued, ethnicity provides a bond of affection that other sources of identity cannot generate.[1]

There is another reason why Catholics have been slow to engage in the advocacy struggle. Perhaps owing to the sociological effects of the very hierarchical institution to which they are loyal, Catholics still tend to look to the clergy to respond to issues of anti-Catholicism. However, there is reason to believe that this submissiveness and acquiescence that have marked Catholic attitudes and behavior in the past are beginning to change. The result is a reawakening of interest in incidents of Catholic-bashing.

Leading the fight against anti-Catholicism has been the Catholic League for Religious and Civil Rights. Having grown from 11,000 members in 1993 to 350,000 members in 1998, the league is an independent lay organization that enjoys considerable support from the Catholic hierarchy; its headquarters is located in the Archdiocese of New York, with offices across the hall from Cardinal John O'Connor.

Unlike other advocacy groups, the Catholic League defends not only a group of people, but also an institution, that is, the Catholic Church. It has its work cut out for itself on both counts: a 1995 survey by the National Conference of Christians and Jews revealed that the number-one prejudice in the nation was that of non-Catholics against Catholics.[2] Add to this the rash of attacks against the Church by activist organizations and elements of the artistic community, the media, academia, and the government, and it is clear that the institutional basis of Catholicism is being challenged in a way not seen for some time.

Catholics are unlike members of other advocacy groups in another important way: they are much more likely to be thought of in a negative way by Hollywood executives. While Native Americans and gays, for example, must fight against the perceptions that the general public holds of them, Catholics must fight not only the public's perceptions, but those of Hollywood as well.

The principal reason Catholics are faced with this unique challenge is the religious and political orientation of the Hollywood elite. Study after study has confirmed what Robert Lichter and Stanley Rothman first concluded some years ago, namely, that the nation's cultural elites, including the elites in the film and television industries, are disproportionately likely to be agnostics or atheists. The cultural elites also sport a very liberal perspective on politics and culture.[3]

Catholicism can quite rightly be described as conservative in terms of sexual ethics and liberal in terms of issues affecting the poor. It is the former that puts it in disfavor with the entertainment industry. The vision of liberty that Hollywood trumpets (and this is seen most clearly in regard to sexuality) contrasts sharply with the perspective offered by the Catholic Church.

To put it differently, our cultural elites accept a notion of liberty that focuses on the right of individuals to do as they choose. The Catholic Church teaches that liberty involves the right to do what we ought to do. The tension between these two conceptions of freedom could not be more pronounced.

What is most astonishing is that many senior Hollywood executives are not comfortable disseminating to their own children the products of the vision of liberty that they themselves embrace. As evidence, consider that at the 1997 Conference on Advocacy Groups and the Entertainment Industry, three major figures in the industry found it necessary to confess to the audience that they would never allow their children to watch the kind of fare that they regularly produce. They said that as family men they make sure their kids watch only Nickelodeon. They did not say whose kids their sexually explicit programs were good for, but we do know that in their homes "just say no" is the rule.

It is not wrong for Hollywood executives to see Catholicism as an obstacle to its vision of liberty. The Church teaches restraint in a culture that teaches the abandonment of it. But understanding the etiology of a bias is quite different from providing justification for it, and that is why those in the entertainment industry must be held accountable for the flawed presentation of Catholicism that they too often present.

In this vein, it is not for nothing that Michael Medved, an orthodox Jewish movie critic, has argued that Hollywood shows more bigotry against Catholicism than any other religion. Indeed, the video *Hollywood v. Catholicism* gives many examples of just how deep this bias is.[4] Additional evidence is presented in the Medved book *Hollywood v. America* (as well as in the video of the same name)[5] and in all the work compiled by the Catholic League.[6] In light of all this information, Catholics indeed have much cause for concern.

No Catholic really expects that all movies about the Church will be like the *Bells of St. Mary's.* But they don't expect to see movies like *Priest* and *Primal Fear* dominate the screens either. And in this light it is notable that while today there are over two dozen gay characters on prime time network television, all of whom are portrayed positively, the priest or Catholic layperson who receives such treatment is rare indeed.

It will not do to say that the entertainment industry simply follows and reflects our culture. To be sure, it does to some extent. But it is also true that the entertainment industry generates changes in the culture, and it is on that score that advocacy groups want input. If what people think of others is important, to both the viewer and the viewed, then it is only right to expect that a pattern of negative stereotypes will be challenged; and this becomes even more critical given that many in our society think in terms of group characteristics, not individual ones.

There is no question that advocacy groups carry with them their own problems. In this light, if success is measured by the ruler of political correctness, then perhaps it is better to put up with occasional abuses than to be subject to the insufferable antics of today's ideological cops. But if the goal is simply to achieve equity, then there is plenty of room for reform in the entertainment industry, and this is especially true insofar as Catholics and the Catholic Church are concerned.

NOTES

1. Nathan Glazer and Daniel Patrick Moynihan, "Why Ethnicity," in *Commentary* (October 1974), pp. 33-39.

2. "Taking America's Pulse: The Full Report of The National Conference Survey on Inter-Group Relations," conducted by L H Research (Study No. 930019), The National Conference of Christians and Jews (1995), pp. 12-13 and Appendix.

3. Stanley Rothman and S. Robert Lichter, "Hollywood and America: The Odd Couple," in *Public Opinion* (January 1983), pp. 54-58.

Anecdotal evidence suggests that Hollywood has become more open to conservatives and conservative ideologies (Michael Medved, "Hollywood Makes Room for Religion," in Michael Suman, ed., *Religion and Prime Time Television* [Westport, CT: Praeger, 1997]), but the media elite still has roughly the same composition as catalogued by Rothman and Lichter in the early 1980s. For example, a 1995 poll found that members of the media elite are three to four times more likely to claim no religious affiliation and less than a third as likely to identify themselves as politically conservative than members of the general population. Media elite data from *U.S. News and World Report/* UCLA Center for Communication Policy *Values Survey* (unpublished, 1995). General population data from James A. Davis, *General Social Survey Codebook* (Chicago, IL: National Opinion Research Center, 1994).

4. *Hollywood vs. Catholicism*, video produced and distributed by Chatham Hill Foundation, Dallas, Texas, 1996.

5. Michael Medved, *Hollywood vs. America: Popular Culture and the War on Traditional Values* (New York, NY: HarperCollins, 1992).

6. The Catholic League's publications are available at www.catholicleague.org.

5

The Proactive Strategy of GLAAD

William Horn, as interviewed by Gabriel Rossman

What do you think about the state of portrayals of homosexuals in the mass media today, especially on television?

I think that portrayals of the lesbian and gay community are light years ahead of where they were even five or ten years ago. But there's still a lot of work to be done in terms of diversity of the characters that you see, especially regarding racial and ethnic diversity. But television specifically—because of the nature of the business—has done more concerning lesbian and gay issues than major motion pictures. And television has done it in an entertaining way that is very appealing to American audiences and in a way that helps them understand lesbian and gay Americans. Television has done this better than movies have and in a different and sometimes more powerful way than a newspaper story can.

How have portrayals of homosexuals in the media changed over time since the formation of GLAAD?

When GLAAD was formed 12 or 13 years ago, you could probably count on one hand the positive lesbian and gay characters that had been on television, recurring or otherwise. And you had your occasional police drama with a gay character who was portrayed in an extremely negative light. Last year we started our season with 30 recurring lesbian and gay characters on national television. That's leaps and bounds ahead of where we were ten, even five, years ago.

What depictions are still being presented that you would like to see changed?

You still have some negative stereotypes that keep popping up in movies that have LGBT (lesbian, gay, bisexual, or transgender) characters. Bisexuals are promiscuous. Gay men are all rich and white. Lesbians are unnecessarily aggressive and serial killers. These are stereotypes that to a certain extent still do exist, primarily in film—although sometimes on television, too. But I think that we're seeing fewer and fewer of these depictions.

Which depictions have especially pleased you?

"Ellen," of course. "Will and Grace," the new NBC show, is great. Both gay characters are fantastic because each represents a different type of gay male. One is sassy—what some people might term "flamboyant"—and the other is more "butch."

"The Object of My Affection" was wonderful because it dealt realistically with the strong relationships and love that exists between many gays and their straight friends. At the same time, it didn't whitewash anything. Paul Rudd's character was multifaceted; he was not portrayed solely on the basis of his sexual orientation.

In "Spin City," not only is the gay character a person of color, but he is also a respectable professional with many different interests and concerns who is a central member of the ensemble cast. His sexual orientation is dealt with as an essential part of his character, but it doesn't solely define him. It's refreshing to see this, and even more so since the character is a person of color.

What do you feel about ABC's use of advisories on "Ellen"?

I think a blatant double standard was evident in every single case that they used it. While they felt they were providing a service, they were actually doing a disservice to the nation. They were "informing" audience members around the country that what they were about to see was far more "dangerous" than depictions of heterosexuals kissing or holding hands on television. This is a dangerous precedent to set. I think ABC looked foolish in the long run, especially when they put this dramatic advisory on an episode in which two women do nothing more than hold hands.

At what stage in the production process do you aim your efforts?

Ideally we would like to aim our efforts at the development and preproduction phases for both television and movies, and we have been successful in doing that a few times. In the past GLAAD has had to deal with movies after they've been released. But now we're trying to work with the entertainment industry to make sure that the portrayals are fair and accurate before they make it on the screen.

What strategies or tactics do you use to influence the media?

One is to be a resource and to provide them with as much information as humanly possible. Often people in the media, especially in print, don't know how to handle or approach LGBT topics. This ignorance often breeds mistakes. So by offering ourselves as a resource, we can work to make sure that they don't make those mistakes in the first place. That's one way of influencing them. Another is to activate the lesbian and gay community to write, e-mail, or contact in any way possible media outlets when they do something good or bad.

Do you ever use more hostile tactics, such as boycotts?

We've moved away from boycotts and probably will never use them again.

Boycotts don't work because people don't like to be told what to do. I think the Southern Baptist Convention boycott of Disney is a perfect example of that. Boycotts just make the instigators look foolish.

Have you modeled your campaign on those of other groups?
I'm sure that other groups and their tactics were used as models during the formation of GLAAD. In terms of how we form our campaigns, certainly we looked at the successes and mistakes of other organizations. But, more often than not, we don't look to other groups because we are often doing things that are unprecedented, for instance the campaign behind "Ellen." That was completely new. This type of lesbian and gay content had not occurred before on television. So here we sort of had to invent the wheel.

How responsive do you think the media have been to the LGBT community, especially compared to other groups, and why?
There have been both good and bad. And it also depends on the media outlet. Some of them have been fantastic and have covered LGBT issues as part of covering the wider spectrum of communities that make up this country. An example of this is *The New York Times*. It often deals with lesbian and gay issues, especially in its "Living Arts" section. It reports on these issues just as part of reporting what's going on in New York and throughout the country.

I think that the struggle for civil rights in the sixties and a burgeoning awareness that the media should actively report on and reflect all different types of people have helped the lesbian and gay community in its struggle to be represented. I don't think that the media would be listening to lesbian and gay concerns as much—if at all—if it hadn't been for civil rights movements and this burgeoning notion in popular culture that media, including television and film, should represent all Americans. So cultural trends are fostering a shift in people's perceptions of all different types of people—and this is helping the lesbian and gay community in its struggle for equality.

To the extent the media have been responsive, has this been due to the presence of gay media professionals, the fact that gays constitute a valuable advertising demographic, or some other factor?
I think both of the factors you mention are important. A growing number of media professionals are lesbians and gay men. And there is the National Lesbian and Gay Journalists Association, which has been working for a number of years on such issues as coming out in the newsroom. The increased presence of lesbians and gay men can only lead to better media. The ad market also helps. Many corporations advertise in gay publications, and the entertainment media also realize that we constitute an important part of the market.

How has GLAAD's relationship with the media changed over time?
GLAAD was originally formed to organize a boycott of the *New York Post*. So, it certainly has changed. Originally GLAAD felt that the only way for it to be heard

was to scream, as with its boycotts and pickets of "Basic Instinct." Since then GLAAD has grown into an organization that entertainment and news media professionals turn to, listen to, and talk to. So we no longer have to scream at the front door; instead we are being invited in through the back door.

What effect do you think media representations of gays have on audience members, both homosexuals and heterosexuals?

For straight audiences, especially those who don't have—or think they don't have—gay friends or relatives, good representations can humanize lesbian and gay Americans. Good representations, which have been rare in the past, are extraordinarily useful for bringing about awareness of the issues of equality and discrimination.

For gay audiences, I don't think there's a uniform impact because there are different levels of being out and being gay. For people who are just coming to terms with their sexual orientation, these images can have an incredible impact on how they see themselves and on lessening their feelings of isolation. Consider the effect of "Ellen" on a young teenage girl living in Idaho who does not know any other lesbians, but knows that she has feelings for other women. Ellen can be a friend, somebody to look up to, and somebody to identify with. Role models like this are very important for anyone who's feeling isolated for any reason. And I think that for all gay people, no matter what stage of the coming out process that they're in, even if they're completely out, seeing themselves represented on the screen by such a role model can be a tool for reaffirming who they are.

Surveys such as *Sex in America* and the *General Social Survey* show that approximately 65% of Americans think that sexual relations between members of the same sex are always wrong. With this in mind, what responsibility, if any, do the media have to your opponents? Do the media have a responsibility for including your opponents' points of view within media portrayals? For example, within the "Ellen" show itself would the media have some responsibility to include a person who was opposed to homosexuality?

Television and the movies are simply trying to reflect the lives of lesbians and gay men. Television does not—and I think for good reasons—represent bigots in a positive light. I don't think that you have any racists on television on a week-to-week basis. If a character is a racist on a television show that is attempting to make some point about the evils of racism, then that is obviously appropriate. For example, Jack Nicholson's character in "As Good as It Gets" is a racist, homophobic, misogynistic pig, but one who realizes the errors of his ways by the end of the film. However, I don't think television or movies should ever be vehicles for hate.

If the radical right feels that to get the word of Christ across they need somebody who hates, then that's a shame. I don't think they need to. For example, consider "Touched by an Angel." This is a show that many Christians, both gay and straight, enjoy, as do people of other faiths. The values expressed in "Touched by an Angel" *should* be expressed through television—values such as love, compassion, faith, and respect. Those are the types of values that concerned religious people should be fighting to bring to the airwaves and movie screens. And GLAAD will join them in that fight. We certainly don't object to the sort of positive values seen in shows such as "Touched by an Angel."

The Harvard School of Public Health has advocated designated drivers, but no one is against designated drivers. How does the presence of an opposition affect your task? That is, some advocacy groups' efforts are opposed by no one, and all they have to do is convince the networks to give up some screen time. But there is an opposition in your case. Does that make your task more difficult?

Part of me wants to say that I don't know how it makes it more difficult, since we've never been without opposition. On the other hand, I don't think we would be here if there was not an opposition with the particular views it has. There wouldn't be a need for GLAAD if lesbian and gay characters on television and "Ellen" were not issues. So in an odd way the opposition created GLAAD and sustains the work that we do. On the other hand, they certainly make our mission difficult when they push a narrow-minded view of who Americans are. But I think that as society changes and as television and movie-goers change and understand the lesbian and gay community better, our opposition's job is going to become harder and ours is going to become easier. And it seems like that's happening on an ongoing basis.

Does GLAAD actively monitor the opposition? For instance, do you read Don Wildmon's newsletter, *The American Family Association Journal*?

We do, and there are other like-minded organizations that do as well. The National Gay and Lesbian Task Force and the Human Rights Campaign each pay more attention to these types of organizations than we do. We pay attention to the organizations if they get involved in our work. For example, we keep records on the American Family Association because they've taken such a prominent position in opposition to "Ellen." We keep records on Jerry Falwell because he has also been on his soapbox regarding "Ellen" and other gay characters on television. We also monitor how the news media cover those organizations.

There has been a general debate over whether advocacy groups are positive or negative forces for society. Some people have the perception that many advocacy groups are narrowly self-interested, hypercritical, and impractical and lack a broad world view. How would you respond to this perception?

I think that is an interesting perception. But many organizations, especially in the lesbian and gay community, are changing for the better. I think that GLAAD in the 1980s and early 1990s—when we had no model for dealing with LGBT issues in the media, when we were creating the rules as we went along—was reactionary. Moreover, our world view was inadequate because it lacked foresight. We didn't think about what we wanted movies and television to be like 10 or 20 years into the future. Fortunately, GLAAD has become a more proactive organization, as have many other lesbian and gay organizations.

To the extent that the criticism you mention was ever true in regard to lesbian and gay groups, it might reflect a particular moment in the lesbian and gay community's history. I think it reflects a time of fear, a time of death, in which the news media, when they did report on us, did a poor job. We reacted to that. Obviously with the pandemic of AIDS and many changes in attitudes, the media situation has changed—and so have we. You certainly still have reactionary groups, and you still have groups that fit the perception you mention, but, to the extent that these faults ever applied to GLAAD, I am confident that we have overcome them.

What do you see in GLAAD's future?

Air conditioning and cable.

Seriously, I see GLAAD becoming a much more highly visible resource organization for the entertainment community. Among entertainment media professionals there is already significant recognition of GLAAD and the work we do, and in time this will only increase. I see ourselves continuing to work proactively and as consultants on film and television shows. We will be there for anybody who needs us.

6

Strategies of the Media Action Network for Asian Americans

Guy Aoki

I remember spending hours on the phone talking with friends back in the 1980s complaining about the insulting ways Asian Americans were portrayed on television and in film. Growing up in Hawaii, where Asians make up the majority of the population, I knew all types of Asians. But for some reason, the media were only interested in our pretty women and the men were always depicted as asexual nerds or wimps. The men were never paired romantically with anyone and the Asian women were interested only in white men. The media seemed to be saying that Asian men are not attractive, even to women of their own race, and that Asian women, in order to be accepted and to get ahead, should get white boyfriends. Most irritating was the fact that the group that could potentially benefit from these portrayals was the one that, by and large, was perpetuating them—white men. (A 1998 study by the Writers Guild of America later revealed that white men wrote 70% of all prime time television shows and 80% of all feature films.)

Asian Americans were also depicted as if they were foreigners—more Asian than American. They were routinely portrayed as immigrants with accents. Fourth generation Americans like myself who speak perfectly good English were rarely seen. (There is nothing wrong with Asians who speak with accents, but on television and in films their accents were used to make fun of them and their race.)

On most television shows and films Asians were entirely absent, unless they were needed for comic relief or to provide a villain viewers could hate, such as the Hong Kong drug lord or the cold Japanese businessman out to take over America. There had to be some specific excuse for including us—we had to be waiters in Chinese restaurants, martial artists, or exchange students. We were not depicted as people in regular, mainstream jobs who just happen to be Asian.

Then in 1991 I took note of the stories that the media ran on the 50th anniversary of the bombing of Pearl Harbor. Rather than shedding new light on the subject, all too often the stories just revived old fears and prejudices. Readers and viewers were confronted with old false rumors about pro-Japanese espionage committed by some Japanese Americans and with exaggerated claims of a West Coast shelling by the Japanese navy. And these reports were having a harmful effect on the Japanese and Asian American communities. As one of my friends later said, "When people get mad at Japan, they don't hop on a plane and take it out on someone there; they find someone here who looks Japanese." A Japanese American man in Claremont, California had his porch defaced with human feces. The Norwalk Japanese Cultural Center was vandalized repeatedly with spray painted slogans and slurs such as "Nips Go Home" and "Japs."

All of this was more than I could take. I made calls trying to get people interested in forming a watchdog group that would finally respond to irresponsible coverage and depictions of Asian Americans, educate the image makers on what they were doing, and, if necessary, hurt those responsible where it counted if they wouldn't reform.

I began conversing with George Johnston who had been the media advocacy chair of both the Japanese American Citizens League (JACL) and the Asian American Journalists Association (AAJA). (We subsequently co-founded Media Action Network for Asian Americans [MANAA] in 1992.) In the meantime, during the week surrounding December 7, I helped the National Coalition for Redress and Reparations (NCRR) organize a press conference denouncing the irresponsible actions of the mainstream media and pointing out the positive contributions of Japanese Americans during World War II. Despite being interned in concentration camps, many Japanese Americans volunteered to fight in the 100th/442nd Regimental Combat Team which became one of the most decorated U.S. military outfits in U.S. history. Ironically, these people who were persecuted by people in their own country helped rescue another group of people who had been targeted in theirs—the Jewish survivors of the Dachau concentration camp in Germany.

Since the formation of the Media Action Network for Asian Americans in April of 1992, we have kept a careful watch over all facets of the media—television, film, radio, advertising, print, and news. We also monitor prominent public statements made about Asian Americans. Our 24-hour hotline has enabled the community to be our "eyes and ears" in reporting incidents they deem worthy of criticism or praise. We have no paid staff; all of us are volunteers. And not all of us work in the media; we have had architects, lawyers, insurance salespeople, artists, teachers, businessmen, and stock brokers as active members. All share a concern for how Asian Americans are portrayed in the mass media.

Within a few months of its founding, MANAA was already talking with 20th Century-Fox about its upcoming film "Rising Sun" based on the best-seller by Michael Crichton. Many in the community were concerned about how a book that was fiercely critical of Japan's business practices would play out as a sexy action picture pitting Americans against unethical Japanese businessmen intent on taking over the United States both financially and politically. Dennis Hayashi, then head of the JACL, and Ron Wakabayashi, then executive director of the Los Angeles City Human Relations Commission, had already begun talks with the studio. I was invited by Ron to join them at their next meeting.

However, the day before our meeting Fox President Strauss Zelnick left word that I was not invited because I had already written negative comments about the upcoming film in my *Rafu Shimpo* newspaper column. Dennis and Ron had to meet with Zelnick and company without me. Fox also cancelled two additional meetings with me. By the time I finally met with those involved with "Rising Sun," they were just two weeks away from finishing the shoot. One source at the studio later told a member of our board that they never expected us to take any serious action against the film and thought that the issue would go away if they just kept holding us up.

After the film was finished I wrote to Zelnick, requesting a prescreening of the movie. We felt this was a reasonable request given our expressed concern over how the film might impact the Asian American community. But the studio head told us that we would have to wait—like all other moviegoers—and see the film when it opened in theaters.

Not pleased with this situation, MANAA began collecting support—ultimately from 16 civil rights and community groups both inside and outside the Asian American community. (Our feeling has always been that our cause gains credibility when non-Asians join us in our fight.) With this support, we made three demands of Fox: (1) Include a statement at the beginning of the film acknowledging the very real problem of hate crimes directed against Asian Americans, clearly spelling out that the studio does not want "Rising Sun" to encourage such actions. (2) In the future, when producing films about Asians or Asian Americans, hire consultants sensitive to the effects such projects may have on those people. (3) Hire more Asian Americans in decision-making positions at Fox so that when racially charged films like "Rising Sun" are considered, potential problem areas can be identified.

We gave Zelnick two weeks to respond. At the end of the two weeks I called and talked to him for the first time. He rejected all of our points. He did say that he would consider showing us a cut of the film if we promised not to protest the picture; we declined. I told Zelnick that we felt that we had been more than reasonable, but had received no amount of good will from his studio. If "Rising Sun" was as bad as we feared, we would have to educate the public about it through protest. Zelnick replied that he did not think our protest would have any effect on the film's success at the box office.

We hit the ground running, getting stories in the *Los Angeles Times* and *Rafu Shimpo* and on CNN and the E! Channel. Equipped with a script we had obtained through our own sources who also kept us up to date on revisions, we had almost four months to do our work before the film was released. In that time we used the media to our advantage to point out the problems with the movie.

Our plan worked. By the time Fox started publicizing the film in July, it was already too late: "Rising Sun" was racist until proven otherwise. Fox spent a significant amount of money flying reporters to a press junket in New York to interview the stars. All of the interview clips that Los Angeles television stations aired of the conference were of the actors defending the film. We had set the agenda to which they had to respond.

Moreover, "Rising Sun" cost about $40 million to make and grossed only $62 million. Taking promotion expenses into account, the film did not break even until it was released overseas and on home video.

Working with JACL Chapters in Washington, D.C., San Francisco, and Chicago, the Committee Against Anti-Asian Violence in New York, and independent groups in Seattle and Minneapolis, we had successfully launched a nationwide protest—the first by Asian Americans against a film since 1985's "Year of the Dragon." Although most media stories labeled the issue a simple one of "Japan bashing," we were successful in presenting a more fundamental and important message: Asian Americans are sick and tired of the way Asians and Asian Americans have been portrayed and they are not going to take it anymore.

Although Fox attempted to brand us as censors who were trampling on their First Amendment rights, we did not interfere with their making of the movie and were now merely exercising *our* rights of expression to the fullest. We were merely presenting our concerns to the public, which was then free to see the movie and make up its own mind.

MANAA always tries to reason with its media adversaries to try to get them to do the right thing. But if this does not work, we will speak their own language by trying to affect them financially. Our breakthrough victory on that front occurred in 1995. For over a year and a half the "House Party" morning show of KKBT ("The Beat") radio in Los Angeles had imitated well-known Asian Americans, such as Los Angeles politician Mike Woo, news anchor Tritia Toyota, and Judge Lance Ito, using thick, exaggerated Asian accents. It is important to note that each of the Asian Americans imitated on the House Party speaks perfectly good English, yet the disc jockeys portrayed them all as bewildered immigrants.

In December of 1994, Daniel M. Mayeda, MANAA's founding legal counsel, and I met with station manager Craig Wilbraham to discuss the danger of always portraying Asian Americans as foreigners. We explained to him how this created racial divisions in society.

Wilbraham admitted that he did not really understand our concerns, especially since Asians were so respected and successful in American society. We pointed out that our perceived success only serves as a basis of resentment. Wilbraham did promise to relay our sentiments to the crew. But then in April of 1995 the House Party ran a skit on Dennis Fung, a principal in the first O.J. Simpson trial, featuring him making kung-fu kicks and screams. We decided that it was time to take action. We contacted four of the show's advertisers and sent them tapes of the House Party's shenanigans, including an on-air tirade by host John London in which he asserted that Asians had no right to complain because, compared to blacks, they "don't know what oppression is." Those were fighting words to people who had experienced or whose relatives had lived through the Japanese American internment camps, the targeting of Korean-owned businesses in the Los Angeles riots of 1992, the struggles of Vietnamese boat people, and the lynching of Chinese immigrant workers around the turn of the century.

Nike and Kaiser Permanente pulled their ads. AT&T refused to and McDonald's did not return our phone calls. In response, we staged a protest outside a McDonald's restaurant in Hollywood. Noted disc jockey Casey Kasem and members of the American-Arab Anti-Discrimination Committee joined us once again (as they had for "Rising Sun"), along with some UCLA college students and NCRR.

The following Monday morning London was livid and blasted all of us on the air, including Kasem. "The only way you're going to have a meeting with him now," Wilbraham told Mayeda, "is if you go on the air with him." We reluctantly agreed, but, a day before the much-hyped appearance, Wilbraham called it off.

Fans of London had been calling the station in support of the disc jockeys. Many of these fans were using racial slurs directed at us. Wilbraham did not want to have a race war on the radio.

Wilbraham agreed to a behind-the-scenes meeting. After two hours Wilbraham offered two alternatives: the House Party would continue with its accented skits, but also would invite Asian American guests on the show; or they would stop all humor focused on Asians, but would bar Asian guests.

Our board unanimously believed that the latter racially exclusionary policy was even worse than the status quo. Mayeda told Wilbraham to stop the humor *and* invite Asian American guests "or there will be pain." Finally, we offered a face-saving solution. We would end our pressure and issue a joint press statement with the Beat in which MANAA would praise the station for doing the right thing. After a couple of weeks of quibbling over the precise language that would be used, Wilbraham agreed. We had won a major victory: we changed the policy of one of the most highly rated radio stations in Los Angeles.

A short time later we used threats of advertiser boycotts to deal with another radio station. KFI-AM's Bill Handel commented on air that he was tired of seeing "slanted-eyed figure skaters winning all the time." The station manager refused to redress our grievances by submitting a written apology and making a promise never to use such slurs again. So we threatened to go after his advertisers. Two days later Handel went on the air to apologize. He also read a letter of apology he and the station manager had signed that had been sent to skaters Michelle Kwan and Kristi Yamaguchi the day before.

In the spring and summer of 1997 we found ourselves dealing with yet another Los Angeles radio station. In March and April, Power 106 ran skits featuring imitations of the "parents" of rival Beat disc jockey Theo Mizuhara. Mizuhara is a Japanese American whose speech is filled with urban slang. The "Bakka Boys" morning show on Power 106 tried to "out" Theo by contrasting his voice with the voices of his parents who were heard speaking with an exaggerated Chinese accent. Since Theo is a third generation American it is extremely doubtful that his parents would have any foreign accent at all, and even if they did, it certainly would not be Chinese! More importantly, once again Asian Americans were unfairly being portrayed as foreign and as a source of humor.

We met with the station manager, program director, and producer in late June and asked them to make basically the same agreement that the Beat made with us—and we implicitly threatened to use the same tactics that worked so well against KKBT. Station manager Marie Kordus tried to avoid meeting our terms by offering us the chance to go on the air with the Bakka Boys. Then, if one or two Asians called in and agreed with us, "that would be enough for us," she said—and they would stop the accents.

We were insulted that they felt that they needed callers to confirm the validity of our claims. Finding her solution unacceptable, we threatened advertiser pressure. With this she yielded and agreed to write a letter. After we rejected the initial one she had written—she denied that the skits had been aimed at anyone in particular—Kordus asked us to draft a letter that would be acceptable. We did so, specifying that the station would not use racially based humor in the future, and our letter was used almost verbatim. Moreover, the disc jockeys made an on-air apology within a week.

It is ironic that we went to such lengths to defend a disc jockey at our former adversary, KKBT, but we did so to remain true to our principles and be consistent in applying them to everyone. It is also notable that whereas it took us over a year and a half to resolve our problems with KKBT, the Power 106 case was closed within a month.

In another important campaign, in the spring of 1996 MANAA helped Jesse Jackson and his Rainbow Coalition organize a protest during the Oscars regarding the exclusion of people of color from significant acting roles that could get them *considered* for Academy Awards. The press misreported our demonstration as a "boycott" by blacks. The demonstration did, however, get us a meeting with the president of CBS, Leslie Moonves.

Along with Jackson, 18 civil rights and media advocate groups representing a wide range of constituencies met with executives at CBS. Jackson asserted that the entertainment business is racist, sexist, and ageist. Moonves countered the last two points by pointing out that many CBS programs feature female actors in leading roles and that many of their shows appeal to the older demographic groups. I suggested that CBS extend this vision by offering more roles to racial and ethnic minority group members. If it did so, members of these groups would tune in and watch because they are so hungry to see positive images of themselves on television. I added that studies show that Asian Americans are loyal consumers of products aimed at their community. In addition to watching television shows featuring Asians, they would be loyal to the products advertised.

Moonves smiled and said that he would accept the challenge. I also praised him for taking a step in the right direction with "Nash Bridges." This show featured Asian American actor Cary Tagawa and Latino actors Cheech Marin and Jaime Gomez, all portraying SFPD detectives, as the heroes of the show. For once, the diversity of San Francisco—where the show is based—was being shown.

Subsequently we had a follow-up meeting with Maddie Horne, CBS's vice president of current programs, and Sonya Augustyne, the manager of current programs. They told us of an Asian American student who was going to be seen in the Rhea Perlman sitcom, "Pearl," then in development. At first, they conceived of her as a straight-A student without much of a personality. They believed that this portrayal was a basically positive one until an Asian American staffer pointed out how stereotypical it was. With this in mind, the CBS executives assured us that the character was going to be changed. But when the program finally aired, to our shock the character had not been changed. The Amy Li character, played by Lucy Alexis Liu, ran as originally conceived.

This was a harbinger of other unfortunate turns at CBS. Six episodes into the second season of "Nash Bridges," Tagawa was written out of the script. "The only Asian American character in any of your series," I later wrote Horne, "is Amy Li. And she is an embarrassment." Subsequently, showing the validity of our concerns, CBS spent the rest of the season trying to develop her character from an overachieving robot into a three-dimensional person.

Then in late February of 1997 sources told me that CBS was reviving "Hawaii Five-O" with all new characters. Three of the four leads were going to be white men and the other was going to be a token Eurasian female. I left messages with

CBS's vice president of drama development, Anita Addison, who left word that I should call Kim LeMasters, president of Stephen J. Cannell Productions.

In the original series two of the four lead characters were Asians/Pacific Islanders. Why was this number being reduced to one? LeMasters said he could not consider Asians for the "white" parts without changing the characters themselves and their backgrounds. He wanted to shoot the pilot in two weeks and was unwilling to change anything. I obtained a script and found that there was no reason why any of the three characters had to be white. I wrote to Moonves that the only thing stopping these characters from being Asian was the ignorance of the writers and producers as to what Asian Americans can and cannot be. I also sent CBS information from the 1990 Census stating that 62% of the state of Hawaii was Asian/Pacific. Whites made up only 33%. Moreover, the police chief of Honolulu was Michael Nakamura, a Japanese American. Ben Cayetano, a Filipino-American, was governor. Yet in the script they are both portrayed as white men. This was Moonves' commitment to diversity? We demanded that one of the costars be Asian American. In response the casting in Hawaii and Los Angeles was delayed for weeks. The controversy made the front page of the *Honolulu Advertiser*. "For us to be second bananas in our own state," I asserted, "is patronizing and insulting. I think it reflects the patronizing haole [white] attitude . . . it's more business-as-usual, defending the status quo."

The issue was discussed thoroughly in the *Honolulu Advertiser* letters to the editor section. To my surprise many in my home state agreed with me. Meanwhile I continued terrorizing the VPs at CBS. In a fax sent to me Moonves denied that there was going to be only one Asian in "Five-O" (although he was referring to the entire cast which included guest stars) and reaffirmed his commitment to diversity. He asked that I wait until the casting was completed.

In the meantime another Honolulu paper, the *Star Bulletin*, ran excerpts of the pilot script's attempt to capture the Hawaiian pidgin, a major dialect of the islands. The "language" was so inaccurate and embarrassing that one local actor refused to work on the pilot. Then, reportedly, all of the pidgin was thrown out and the dialogue was rewritten.

In late March the final cast was announced. Not only would Russell Wong be a costar, he would be *the* star, Nick Irons. Asian American Elsie Sniffen would play the female lead, Rellica Sun.

It was one of the biggest victories we had ever had—affecting the casting of a potential series in a proactive way. Unfortunately, "Five-O" was not picked up as a series in 1997, and the pilot has not been broadcast to date. But most importantly we did not let CBS get away with ignoring Asian Americans. We held them to their "commitment" to diversity.

The lesson I have learned from all of this is that diversity has to be enforced through constant outside pressure. If the studios, networks, and news stations really believed having people of color in positions of power would help them garner bigger revenues, they would find qualified people and put them there. But they do not believe it, even with our society's changing demographics. The white powers-that-be arrogantly believe they can continue to conduct business as usual and make use of only white talent. Minorities—who are quickly becoming the majority—are still treated like second-class citizens. So until the media realize that it is in their own best financial interest to include minority members within the industry, pressure must be applied from without.

And just as most of white America would love to believe that prejudice and discrimination no longer exist, the powers-that-be in the media would love to believe they are sensitive in depicting people of color. And they are constantly insulted when we tell them otherwise. They seem to have a serious blind spot. It seems that the only way things will really change is if minority group members get into the industry and begin calling the shots themselves. Unfortunately institutionalized racism at most of these media companies is preventing this. Very few minority group members get in, and, when they do, they soon hit their head on a glass ceiling.

In the meantime, we have no choice but to continue to use the strategies we have devised in combating various media entities, including use of the news media to get our point out to the average American and slowly but surely win them over to our cause. As the multiethnic coalitions we have built over the years have always tried to say through their support of our issues, this is not about being Asian. It is about being sensitive, fair-minded people who cannot let these insults and injustices continue. Realize what is going on, and join us in calling for an end to them.

7

How Church Advocacy Groups Fostered the Golden Age of Hollywood

Ted Baehr

Millions of people long for the golden age of movies—50 years ago when the studios released one classic after another, like "Gone with the Wind," "Mr. Smith Goes to Washington," and "It's a Wonderful Life." They often contact me to ask, "Why don't the studios produce any great family films or great biblical epics any more, such as 'Ben Hur,' 'The Ten Commandments,' 'The Robe,' and 'The Greatest Story Ever Told'?"

One reason for the dearth of "good" movies today is the fact that the various denominations abandoned their entertainment advocacy offices in the 1960s. Many people have forgotten that churches instituted the first advocacy offices in Hollywood as a result of America's widespread dissatisfaction with the values of the entertainment industry in the 1920s.

Many people forget that during the 1920s and early 1930s the moral caliber of many Hollywood movies was extremely coarse. The documentary video "Hollywood Uncensored"[1] illustrates some of the more salacious and immoral movies of the 1920s and early 1930s, including the notorious 1933 film "Ecstasy" in which Hedy Lamarr appeared nude on screen for several minutes and the infamous "Babyface" which depicted a father who prostituted his young daughter to pay his gambling debts. Of course, the film and storytelling techniques of these movies were not as sophisticated as those used in current movies so they did not quite have the same emotional intensity. However, the immoral content of these early films enraged the American people, who reacted by taking legal action against Hollywood. To avoid constant legal harassment, the movie studios asked representatives of the churches to advise them. Consequently, between 1933 and 1966, representatives of the church offices read scripts from every major studio to help them make sure that the industry's films attracted the broadest possible audience. As a result of this process, the movies and television programs were better. The Roman Catholic, Protestant, and Jewish entertainment offices helped the major studios avoid senseless violence, sexual immorality, and antireligious bigotry by helping the Motion Picture Association of America and the television network standards and practices offices understand the Judeo-Christian values held dear by 88% of the American people.

These values were set forth in the Motion Picture Code and the National Association of Broadcasters' Code. The short form of the Motion Picture Code provided, in part, that:

"The basic dignity and value of human life shall be respected and upheld. Restraint shall be exercised in portraying the taking of life."

"Evil, sin, crime, and wrong-doing shall not be justified."

"Detailed and protracted acts of brutality, cruelty, physical violence, torture, and abuse shall not be presented."

"Words or symbols contemptuous of racial, religious, or national groups shall not be used so as to incite bigotry or hatred."

"Excessive cruelty to animals shall not be portrayed and animals shall not be treated inhumanely."

During this halcyon period there was no excessive violence in movies made for television. Also, films did not mock a minister of religion or a person's faith (the religious persecution in Nazi Germany in the 1930s and 1940s prompted this wisely followed path). For the most part, movies and television programs communicated the good.

But then the churches voluntarily withdrew from the entertainment industry in 1966, and the Motion Picture Association of America instituted the rating system to take the place of the Code. With the fox guarding the hen house, the results were predictable. Suddenly, everyone was taking the easy way out: producers were producing movies with objectionable sex and violence, claiming that the ratings protected children; children were tempted to sneak into movies with more mature ratings; parents were lulled into believing that the ratings protected their children; and box office admissions fell by more than 50% and never recovered as people abandoned the tarnished silver screen.

The consequence of the churches' retreat from Hollywood has been a hideous outpouring of filth and obscenity posing as entertainment. Within a few months after the Protestant Film Commission was shut down, Anton Le Vey opened up a Church of Satan Film Office. Soon thereafter a plethora of political groups opened up film offices to lobby the entertainment media for their points of view. Within three years movies came out featuring excessive violence and sex, and even Satanism.

Even the film critic of the liberal *New York Times*, Vincent Canby, became repulsed by the escalating levels of violence in Hollywood movies. Just before he retired from film reviewing, he wrote of his dissatisfaction with the product of Hollywood. He found that the 1990 box-office smash "Die Hard 2" depicted approximately 264 deaths, which was significantly higher than 1988's bloody "Rambo III" and the ground-breaking violence in 1969 of "The Wild Bunch" which, by comparison, contained a paltry 89 killings. Canby recognized several factors that contributed to this increase in graphic violence in Hollywood, including the replacement of the industry's Motion Picture Code in 1968 by the MPAA ratings.

With all this in mind, the Christian Film and Television Commission (CFTVC) was established in the mid-1980s to help the entertainment industry recover its credibility with the large number of film and television audience members around the world who still believe in traditional morality. The CFTVC employs the same strategy originally developed by the leaders who wrote and monitored the Motion Picture Code, a strategy now used by many groups that lobby Hollywood.

One prong of this strategy involves educating Americans concerned about moral issues through *Movieguide: A Family Guide to Movies and Entertainment* so that they can make discerning choices at the box office and thereby influence the entertainment industry financially and through their correspondence.[2]

The other prong involves helping media leaders understand the concerns of Americans who believe in traditional morality. Like the church offices which inspired the Golden Age of Hollywood, the CFTVC reviews scripts and helps those in the media to work out creative solutions to moral questions so as to improve the dramatic and the moral quality of the movies and programs they produce. The CFTVC also helps them portray religious people in a realistic and wholesome light.

Over the last several years, as a result of the growing concern of Americans, the aging of America, and the work of the Christian Film and Television Commission and others, there has been a significant increase in the number of good family films produced, such as "Toy Story" and "Babe," movies for more mature audiences such as "Shadowlands" and "Sense and Sensibility," and even movies with a strong Christian witness such as "Dead Man Walking." We will work diligently to ensure that this trend continues.

NOTES

1. "Hollywood Uncensored," Baker & Taylor Video, 1987.
2. *Movieguide* is available as a magazine and also on the Web (movieguide.crosswalk.com) and is featured on radio and television programs.

II

Articles by Lawyers

8

Influencing Media Content Through the Legal System: A Less Than Perfect Solution for Advocacy Groups

Rex S. Heinke and Michelle H. Tremain[1]

INTRODUCTION

Criticism of the contents of newspapers, movies, television broadcasts, and other media appears with increasing frequency. Discontent has been expressed both with regard to the media's portrayal of groups and individuals and with their treatment of a broad range of issues. As evidenced by the recent boycott of the Walt Disney Company by the Southern Baptists, those who are unhappy with the media's content do have means to make their displeasure known. Attempts to influence the media's content through the legal system, however, which is the subject of this paper, are currently unlikely to be successful for several reasons. First, although the Federal Communications Commission (FCC) has in the past provided means for influencing the content of broadcasts, this traditional method of content control is falling by the wayside. Second, courts have not been receptive to attempts to control newspaper content through methods similar to those used by the FCC. Third, courts have refused to compel government broadcasters to air particular programming. Fourth, the Supreme Court has imposed severe limitations on the government's ability to censor films. Finally, attempts to thwart derogatory portrayals of groups through suits for defamation are not likely to be successful because constitutional, common law, and statutory restrictions have been imposed on such suits. As a result, those dissatisfied with the media's content are increasingly unlikely to influence that content through lawsuits or other legal proceedings.

CONTROL OF TELEVISION

One traditional method of gaining access for alternative viewpoints has been through the regulations imposed on broadcasters by the FCC. The Communications Act of 1934 gave the FCC authority to regulate broadcasting through renewable licenses issued to those serving the "public convenience, interest, or necessity."[2] In short order, the FCC concluded that "in light of the limited availability of broadcast frequencies and the resultant need for government licensing, . . . the licensee is a public fiduciary, obligated to present diverse viewpoints representative of the community at large."[3] The FCC therefore promulgated five main rules designed to provide a balanced presentation of issues of importance to the community: (1) the equal time/opportunities rule, (2) the reasonable access rule, (3) the political editorializing rule, (4) the Fairness Doctrine, and (5) the personal attack rule. Although these rules do not provide a basis for suing a broadcaster for their infraction, parties have been able to file complaints with the FCC for violation of the rules.[4]

The first three rules deal with the access afforded to political candidates. Broadly stated, the "equal time" or "equal opportunities" rule provides that if a broadcaster furnishes air time to a legally qualified candidate for any public office, the broadcaster must afford an equal opportunity to obtain air time to all other such candidates.[5] Under the reasonable access rule, broadcasters must provide candidates for federal office reasonable access to, or permit the purchase of reasonable amounts of time on, their station.[6] The political editorializing rule requires stations to provide candidates an opportunity to respond to an editorial endorsement or opposition.[7] Because these rules apply only to political candidates, they have had a limited impact on attempts to influence how the media portray particular issues or groups.

The Fairness Doctrine and Personal Attack Rule

The Fairness Doctrine imposed two duties on broadcasters: (1) the broadcaster had to seek out and devote an adequate amount of time to controversial issues of public importance, and (2) the coverage had to be fair in the sense that it accurately reflected opposing views.[8] Members of the public could file complaints with the FCC against any station that they believed was not fulfilling either duty. However, the Fairness Doctrine did not provide the public with a means of getting a particular message on the air. In *CBS v. Democratic National Committee*,[9] the Democratic National Committee and the Business Executives' Move for Vietnam Peace complained that the widespread broadcaster policy not to accept advertisements on public issues violated the First Amendment and the Fairness Doctrine. The Supreme Court found that, in promulgating the Communications Act, "Congress intended to permit private broadcasting to develop with the widest journalistic freedom consistent with its public obligations."[10] The Court also observed that the responsibilities imposed on broadcasters under the Fairness Doctrine were intended to further " 'the right of the public to be informed, rather than any right on the part of the Government, any broadcast licensee or any individual member of the public to broadcast his own particular views on any matter.' "[11] Therefore, the Court concluded, the Fairness Doctrine did not require broadcasters to accept paid editorial advertisements.[12]

The personal attack rule is a corollary of the Fairness Doctrine and requires licensees to provide notice and an opportunity to reply whenever an attack is made upon the honesty, character, or integrity of an identified person or group during presentation of views on a controversial issue of public importance.[13] As with the

Fairness Doctrine, the broadcaster is given discretion in determining whether a violation of the rule has taken place; the personal attack rule, however, imposes more specific obligations than the Fairness Doctrine, and the broadcaster lacks control over the spokesperson and format of the reply that it maintains under the Fairness Doctrine.

The Supreme Court upheld the validity of the Fairness Doctrine and the personal attack rule in *Red Lion Broadcasting Co. v. Federal Communications Commission.*[14] *Red Lion* arose out of a series of broadcasts by fundamentalist preacher Billy James Hargis. In these broadcasts Hargis discussed a book written by Fred J. Cook, which was critical of Barry Goldwater, and made a number of disparaging comments about Cook and his political affiliations. When Cook learned of the broadcast, he demanded free reply time, which the radio station refused to grant. After the FCC determined that the refusal violated the station's obligations under the Fairness Doctrine, the station appealed, arguing that the regulations violated its First Amendment rights. The Supreme Court upheld the FCC's rulings, finding that the Fairness Doctrine and the regulations promulgated under the doctrine, that is, the political editorializing rule and the personal attack rule, did not violate the First Amendment rights of broadcasters.[15] While concluding that broadcasting is clearly a medium affected by a First Amendment interest, the Court observed that the inherent characteristics of the broadcast spectrum, in particular the scarcity of frequencies, distinguished the broadcast medium from more traditional forms of communication.[16] In addition, the Court rejected the argument that the Fairness Doctrine might lead to self-censorship on the part of the broadcasters, concluding that historical evidence did not support such a view.[17]

The Fairness Doctrine and the regulations promulgated under it therefore provided a means for people to compel broadcasters to address issues of public importance in a balanced manner, although the selection and method of addressing such issues were generally left to the broadcaster. As technology changed, however, the rationale for the Fairness Doctrine and therefore the Fairness Doctrine itself were undermined.

The Demise of the Fairness Doctrine

In 1985 the FCC reexamined the Fairness Doctrine and concluded that it no longer "serves the public interest."[18] In particular, the FCC determined that the Fairness Doctrine: lessened the amount of diverse views available to the public, inhibited the expression of unorthodox opinions, placed government into the intrusive role of scrutinizing program content, created the opportunity for intimidation of broadcasters by government officials, imposed unnecessary economic costs upon broadcasters and the FCC, and did not protect either broadcasters or the public from undue influence.[19] The FCC also concluded that "the growth of traditional broadcast facilities, as well as the development of new electronic information technologies, provides the public with suitable access to the marketplace of ideas so as to render the fairness doctrine unnecessary."[20] After a court ruled that the FCC had the power to do so,[21] the FCC in 1987 unanimously adopted a memorandum opinion and order that repealed the Fairness Doctrine.[22]

Repeated attempts by Congress to revive the Fairness Doctrine have failed.

Like the Fairness Doctrine, the four other main content regulations imposed by the FCC, including the personal attack rule, were originally promulgated pursuant to the scarcity rationale. As a result, their viability was seriously called into question by the FCC's decision to repeal the Fairness Doctrine. All four rules nevertheless remain in effect today due to both inaction on the part of the FCC and the Supreme Court's unwillingness to reexamine the scarcity rationale.[23] However, unlike the Fairness Doctrine, the personal attack rule ultimately leaves the content of broadcasts to the broadcasters because only the activity of the broadcaster can trigger its obligation to provide access. And, as mentioned before, the other three rules apply only to political candidates and thus have very limited impact on attempts to influence how the media portray particular issues or groups. Through the repeal of the Fairness Doctrine, therefore, those hoping to control the content of broadcasts lost the most potent legal weapon in their arsenal.

CONTROL OF NEWSPAPER CONTENT

Newspapers have historically enjoyed a much broader right than television broadcasts have to control their content. As a result, advocacy groups hoping to influence the content of newspapers will be hard pressed to find a way to do so through the courts unless the actions of a newspaper violate a law of general application.

Government Imposed Access

Unlike television, newspapers are not subject to governmental content control pursuant to a theory that they are public fiduciaries. Rather, the Supreme Court has established that newspapers have a general right to control their own content. *Miami Herald Publishing Co. v. Tornillo*[24] grew out of an editorial critical of a candidate for the Florida House of Representatives. A Florida "right of reply" statute provided that if a candidate's personal character or official record is attacked by a newspaper, "the candidate has the right to demand that the newspaper print, free of cost to the candidate, any reply."[25] Failure to comply with the statute was a misdemeanor. In the *Tornillo* case the candidate demanded that the newspaper print a reply, but the newspaper refused.

The Supreme Court recognized in *Tornillo* that the establishment of national news organizations and the increased concentration of newspaper ownership "[have placed] in a few hands the power to inform the American people and shape public opinion."[26] However, after reviewing its past opinions, the Court concluded that any government-imposed "compulsion to publish that which 'reason tells them should not be published' is unconstitutional. A responsible press is an undoubtedly desirable goal, but press responsibility is not mandated by the Constitution and like many other virtues it cannot be legislated."[27] The Court also found that such a right of access would chill speech and intrude upon the function of editors.[28] The Court therefore unanimously concluded that the Florida statute was unconstitutional,[29] without once mentioning its decision in *Red Lion* that an access requirement imposed on broadcasters was constitutional. According to the Court, economic scarcity, for example, the limited number of newspapers in most cities, is not the same as technological scarcity, for example, the limited number of broadcast frequencies that exist.[30]

Newspaper Advertisements

The broad right of editorial discretion recognized in *Tornillo* extends to all contents of the print media, including advertising. However, the First Amendment does not shield newspapers from the operation of generally applicable laws, including the antitrust laws, laws concerning the enforceability of contracts, and, perhaps most important for those who feel they are underrepresented in the media, antidiscrimination law. As a result, private publishers' editorial discretion may be limited where their refusal to publish ads violates an antidiscrimination law.

Since the publishing of a privately owned newspaper does not involve state action,[31] the Equal Protection Clause,[32] which affords relief for deprivation of constitutional rights under the cover of state law, does not apply where a newspaper allegedly discriminates in its refusal to publish an advertisement. Since the Equal Protection Clause does not apply, private print media legally may discriminate against a class of persons unless a local antidiscrimination law prohibits them from doing so. Thus, absent specific statutory authority, for example, federal or state antidiscrimination laws, claims of discrimination have failed to prevail over the First Amendment's guarantee of freedom of the press.

Decisions that involve such claims against the print media under the Ku Klux Klan Act of 1871[33] consistently have failed because the courts did not find the necessary "class based invidiously discriminatory animus" to constitute a violation of the Act.[34] For example, courts have found no showing of such class-based discrimination where defendant newspapers adopted a policy rejecting all advertising from movie houses that habitually showed only adult films[35] or where a newspaper refused to print an advertisement that was "not in accordance with the newspaper's standards."[36] Therefore, groups whose ads have been rejected by newspapers will face considerable difficulty in establishing violation of antidiscrimination statutes. As a result, this avenue is unlikely to provide advocacy groups who wish to control media content with a satisfactory means of doing so.

CONTROL OF GOVERNMENT BROADCASTS

In general, courts will not grant individuals any more control over the programming of public television stations than they will over that of private commercial broadcasting stations. The most extensive discussion of this issue arose when two public television stations decided not to broadcast a program entitled "Death of a Princess." The program dramatized an investigation into the July 1977 execution of a Saudi Arabian princess and her lover for adultery. One Alabama station elected not to air the program after protests by members of the community who feared retribution against Alabama citizens working in the Middle East. Another station, affiliated with the University of Houston, decided against airing the program based in part on concerns that the program was in poor taste and would adversely affect contributions from oil companies. Both stations were subsequently sued by members of the communities that they served who sought to compel the stations to broadcast the film and/or to enjoin the stations from making political decisions on programming based on their own First Amendment rights.[37]

In *Muir v. Alabama Educational Television Commission ("Muir II")*, a plurality of the Fifth Circuit held that viewers did not have a right to compel the stations to air "Death of a Princess" and refused to accept the argument that government-funded public broadcasters lost their editorial discretion.[38] In a concurring opinion, which is now considered to be the holding of *Muir II*, Judge Rubin stated that "[t]he function [or mission] of a state agency operating an informational medium is significant in determining first amendment restrictions on its actions."[39] Examining the television stations in this light, Judge Rubin concluded that, while they "are operated by state agencies, neither station is designed to function as a marketplace of ideas, a medium open to all who have a message, whatever its nature."[40] He also held that "the state may regulate content in order to prevent hampering the primary function of the activity."[41] In Judge Rubin's view, judicial intervention is appropriate only where the public licensee "adopt[s] or follow[s] *policies or practices* that transgress constitutional rights."[42] Accordingly, Judge Rubin agreed with the plurality that judicial intervention was neither required nor warranted for that *single* programming decision.[43]

As with their precursors,[44] *Muir II*'s progeny support the proposition that government funding does not enhance access rights to public broadcast outlets.[45] Groups seeking to control programming of public television stations are therefore unlikely to gain such control through this avenue.

CONTROL OF MOTION PICTURES

Movies have historically been a leading target of interest groups. In the early days of film those concerned about the content of movies were quite successful in persuading governmental authorities to censor them. Censorship boards in cities and states, including Chicago, Maryland, New York, Pennsylvania, Detroit, and Memphis, deleted material or refused licenses based on political, religious, racial, and moral prejudices.[46] Exhibitors were reluctant to challenge the process because this would involve "assum[ing] the burden of instituting judicial proceedings and of persuading the courts that the film is protected expression."[47]

This all began to change in 1952 with the Supreme Court's holding in *Joseph Burstyn, Inc. v. Wilson*[48] that movies are entitled to First Amendment protection. After this ruling, the decisions of censorship boards were often challenged and overturned by the courts, and the number of active censorship boards markedly decreased.[49] In 1961, the Supreme Court seemed to take a step backward in the recognition of free speech rights for movie producers and exhibitors when it determined that requiring prior review by a censorship board is not a *per se* violation of First Amendment rights.[50] However, just a few years later, the Supreme Court held in *Freedman v. Maryland* that movie censorship systems are constitutional "only if [they] take place under procedural safeguards designed to obviate the dangers of a censorship system."[51] These safeguards include: placing the burden of proving that the film is unprotected expression on the censor; setting up a procedure whereby, within a brief period of time, the censor must either issue a license or seek to enjoin the exhibition of the film; and requiring prompt and final judicial review.[52] Although falling short of an outright ban, *Freedman*'s "carefully circumscribed requirements" dealt the fatal blow to state censorship of movies.[53] As a result, attempts by advocacy groups to persuade state and local governments to establish movie review boards are likely to fail.

DEFAMATION ACTIONS

Much of the concern regarding media content revolves around the manner in which newspaper articles and television programs depict groups. It is not unusual for an individual to feel that people of his ethnicity or national origin, or even with his hobbies, have been presented in a derogatory manner by the media. Many have tried to seek recourse for such portrayals by suing the media for defamation. At first blush, this may seem like a fitting solution: defamation suits are generally designed to compensate those whose reputations have been damaged by false statements. This method has proven unsuccessful for numerous plaintiffs, however, because defamatory statements must be "of and concerning" a particular plaintiff. In addition, plaintiffs have encountered procedural difficulties in bringing this type of suit as a class action.

As a matter of common and now constitutional law, a defamatory statement must be of and concerning a plaintiff to be actionable, that is, the statement must be about the plaintiff.[54] The plaintiff need not be mentioned by name—it is sufficient if the plaintiff can be identified by other statements in the broadcast or article or by extrinsic facts known to viewers or readers.[55]

Courts generally have refused, however, to allow any member of a group to sue for defamation that refers to an entire group if the group consists of more than 25 people.[56] There are two rationales for this rule. First, defamatory statements do little damage to the reputation of any member of a group larger than 25 if the defamation refers to all members of the group. For example, a statement that all police officers in Los Angeles are corrupt is extremely unlikely to have any effect on the reputation of any given officer. Second, the price to be paid by making such statements actionable is simply too high. The discussion of many matters of great importance would be stifled if every teacher in Chicago could sue for defamation over a statement that all Chicago teachers are incompetent, or if all doctors could sue because a television news magazine reported that doctors "cheat" their clients by agreeing to fix their fees.

Numerous cases illustrate this point. For example, the broadcast of "Death of a Princess," discussed above, spurred a class action lawsuit alleging that all Muslims, which at that time included over 600 million people, were defamed by the program.[57] The plaintiffs asserted that the program was "insulting and defamatory" to the Islamic religion.[58] The court dismissed the suit, reasoning that "[i]f the court were to permit an action to lie for the defamation of such a multitudinous group we would render meaningless the rights guaranteed by the First Amendment to explore issues of public import."[59] Similar results were obtained in suits brought on behalf of "all sport game hunters in the State of Michigan" regarding two hunting documentaries,[60] and "all Nigerians engaged in international business with United States citizens" regarding a "60 Minutes" segment that included a statement that

"Nigerians engaged in international business with United States citizens are fraudulent and deceitful."[61]

In addition, class actions for defamation are inappropriate. Suits may be brought as class actions only where common issues of law and fact outweigh individual issues. Individual issues in a class action for defamation, however, including the reputation of each plaintiff, each plaintiff's damages, and malice by the defendant as to each plaintiff, would outweigh the common issues of law and fact.[62] As a result, defamation actions are not useful vehicles for advocacy groups to use to try to influence media content.

CONCLUSION

Advocacy groups hoping to influence media content are unlikely to find success by attempting to use the legal system to do so. Because of the demise of the FCC's rules regarding balanced presentation of issues, the total absence of similar rules regarding newspapers, the lack of control over government broadcasts, the restrictions imposed on movie licensing schemes, and the particular requirements of defamation suits, the courts are an increasingly inhospitable place to address the concerns of those wishing to change the way the world views them.

NOTES

1. Mr. Heinke and Ms. Tremain are with the Los Angeles law firm of Gibson, Dunn & Crutcher LLP. Copyright 1997. All rights reserved. The discussion below is based on Heinke, *Media Law* (1994 BNA).

2. 47 U.S.C. ' 307(a).

3. Fairness Doctrine Obligations of Broadcast Licensees, 50 Fed. Reg. 35,418, & 4 (FCC 1985) ("1985 Fairness Report").

4. See, e.g., CBS v. Democratic Nat'l Comm., 412 U.S. 94 (1973), discussed *infra* pp. 3-4.

5. 47 U.S.C. ' 315(a).

6. Federal Campaign Election Act of 1971, 47 U.S.C. ' 312(a)(7) (1971).

7. 47 C.F.R. ' 73.1930 (1990).

8. Red Lion Broadcasting Co. v. Federal Communications Commission, 395 U.S. 367, 377 (1969). The doctrine is described in 47 C.F.R. ' 73.1910 (1990).

9. 412 U.S. 94 (1973).

10. *Id.* at 110.

11. *Id.* at 112-13 (quoting Report on Editorializing by Broadcast Licensees, 13 F.C.C. 1246, 1249 [1949]).

12. *Id.*

13. 47 C.F.R. ' 73.1920 (1990).

14. 395 U.S. 367 (1969).

15. *Id.* at 390.

16. *Id.* at 386-90.

17. *Id.* at 392-95.

18. 1985 Fairness Report at & 5.

19. *Id.*

20. *Id.* at & 82.

21. See Telecommunications Research & Action Center v. Federal Communications

Commission, 801 F.2d 501 (D.C. Cir. 1986), *cert. denied*, 482 U.S. 919 (1987).

22. In re Syracuse Peace Council, 2 F.C.C.R. 5043 (1987), *cert. denied*, 493 U.S. 1019 (1990).

23. See, e.g., Federal Communications Commission v. League of Women Voters, 468 U.S. 364 (1984); Metro Broad. v. Federal Communications Commission, 497 U.S. 547, *reh'g denied,* 497 U.S. 1050 (1990).

24. 418 U.S. 241 (1974).

25. *Id.* at 244.

26. *Id.* at 249-250.

27. *Id.* at 256.

28. *Id.* at 257-58.

29. *Id.* at 258.

30. *Id.* at 257.

31. Sinn v. Daily Nebraskan, 638 F. Supp. 143, 148 (D. Neb. 1986), *aff'd,* 829 F.2d 662 (8th Cir. 1987).

32. U.S. Const. amend. XIV, ' 1.

33. 42 U.S.C. ' 1985 (1981 & Supp. 1983). This law provides for civil penalties where a defendant is proven to have conspired to deprive a party of a constitutional or other federal right with racial or other class-based "invidiously di animus." Bray v. Alexandria Women's Health Clinic, 506 U.S. 263 (1993).

34. See, e.g., Kops v. New York Tel. Co., 456 F. Supp. 1090, 1095 (S.D.N.Y. 1978), *aff'd,* 803 F.2d 213 (2d Cir. 1979).

35. America's Best Cinema Corp. v. Fort Wayne Newspapers, 347 F. Supp. 328, 335 (N.D. Ind. 1972).

36. Cyntje v. Daily News Publ'g Co., 551 F. Supp. 403, 405 (D.V.I. 1982).

37. Muir v. Alabama Educ. Television Commission, 688 F.2d 1033, 1037 (5th Cir. 1982) ("Muir II").

38. *Id.* at 1040-41. *Muir II* was an en banc decision by 23 judges. The lead opinion was adopted by a total of 11 judges (one of whom wrote separately but concurred in the opinion). Two other judges authored concurrences, one of which was joined by three judges. Seven judges dissented.

39. *Id.* at 1050 (Rubin, J., concurring).

40. *Id.* at 1052 (Rubin, J., concurring).

41. *Id.* at 1050 (Rubin, J., concurring).

42. *Id.* (Rubin, J., concurring) (emphasis added).

43. *Id.* at 1053 (Rubin, J., concurring).

44. See, e.g., Gottfried v. Federal Communications Commission, 655 F.2d 297, 311-12 n.54 (D.C. Cir. 1981), *rev'd in part on other grounds,* 459 U.S. 498 (1983); Community Serv. Broad. of Mid-Am. v. Federal Communications Comm'n, 593 F.2d 1102, 1104 (D.C. Cir. 1978) (en banc); Accuracy in Media v. Federal Communications Comm'n, 521 F.2d 288, 297 (D.C. Cir. 1975), *cert. denied,* 425 U.S. 934 (1976).

45. See, *e.g.,* Chandler v. Georgia Pub. Telecommunications Commission, 917 F.2d 486, 488 (11th Cir. 1990), *cert. denied,* 502 U.S. 816 (1991); Schneider v. Indian River Community College Found., 875 F.2d 1537, 1540-42 (11th Cir. 1989). However, the Supreme Court has recently decided to review a decision by the Eighth Circuit that "a governmentally owned and controlled television station may not exclude a [legally qualified] candidate . . . from a debate organized by it" on the ground that he is not a viable candidate. Forbes v. Arkansas Educ. Television Comm'n, 93 F.3d 497, 500 (8th Cir. 1996), *cert. granted,* __ U.S. __, 117 S. Ct. 1243 (1997).

46. Jesse H. Choper, *Consequences of Supreme Court Decisions Upholding Individual Constitutional Rights,* 83 Mich. L. Rev. 1, 58 & n.371 (1984).

47. Freedman v. Maryland, 380 U.S. 51, 59-60 (1965).

48. 343 U.S. 495 (1952).

49. *Id.* at 61.

50. Times Film Corp. v. City of Chicago, 365 U.S. 43 (1961).

51. 380 U.S. at 58.

52. *Id.* 58-59.

53. Choper, *supra* note 46, at 62.

54. New York Times Co. v. Sullivan, 376 U.S. 254 (1964); Geisler v. Petrocelli, 616 F.2d 636, 637 (2d Cir. 1980); Farber v. Cornils, 487 P.2d 689, 691 (Idaho 1971).

55. Cosgrove Studio & Camera Shop v. Pane, 182 A.2d 751, 753 (Pa. 1962); Harwood Pharmacal Co. v. National Broadcasting Co., 174 N.E.2d 602, 603 (N.Y. 1961).

56. *Cases Articulating "25-Person" Rule:* Barger v. Playboy Enters., 564 F. Supp. 1151, 1153 (N.D. Cal. 1983), *aff'd*, 732 F.2d 163 (9th Cir.), *cert. denied*, 469 U.S. 853 (1984); Schuster v. U.S. News & World Report, 459 F. Supp. 973, 977 (D. Minn. 1978), *aff'd*, 602 F.2d 850 (8th Cir. 1979).

57. Khalid Abdullah Tariq Al Mansour Faissal Fahd Al Talal v. Fanning, 506 F. Supp. 186 (N.D. Cal. 1980).

58. *Id.*

59. *Id.* at 187.

60. Michigan United Conservation Clubs v. CBS News, 485 F. Supp. 893 (W.D. Mich. 1980), *aff'd*, 665 F.2d 110 (6th Cir. 1981).

61. Anyanwu v. Columbia Broad. Sys., 887 F. Supp. 690, 692 (S.D.N.Y. 1995).

62. Los Angeles Fire & Police Protective League v. Rodgers, 86 Cal. Rptr. 623 (Cal. Ct. App. 1970).

9

Public Policy Advocacy: Truant Independent Producers in a Federal City Fixated on a "Values Agenda"

Mickey R. Gardner

INTRODUCTION

The independent producer community in the United States has flourished over the years because of the creative flexibility appropriately afforded it by the First Amendment. Whether it was programming produced for television or theatrical release, the content of that creative programming was largely immune to federal regulators who could not overcome the constitutional hurdle of the First Amendment. As a result, Hollywood has exploded economically as the ever-expanding domestic and international delivery systems for U.S.-produced television programming created expanded markets around the globe—markets clamoring for the diverse, uncensored, quality programming that is distinctly "Hollywood."

Based on the dynamic make-up of the current U.S. television programming marketplace, Hollywood producers, large and small, have generally been relaxed about public policy changes in Washington as long as there was a Democrat in the White House or a Democrat-controlled Congress. Ironically, when the 104th Congress turned Republican with the fearsome Speaker Newt Gingrich at the helm, Hollywood remained relatively sanguine because Bill Clinton and Al Gore firmly held the reins of the White House's massive public policy apparatus. Not to worry!

Well, program producers—particularly independent TV producers—were wrong, and the consequences of their indifference to First Amendment-hostile policy initiatives from Washington may haunt the creative community for years to come.

The basis for this gloomy prognosis is simple. On the one hand, many current leaders of the federal government, particularly those in the White House, have adopted a "values agenda" that seriously erodes First Amendment protections—protections that the creative community has taken for granted. The philosophical foundation of this "values agenda" is the belief that society's ills can be greatly reduced, if not eliminated, by various forms of content regulation of television programming. This trend toward content regulation can be seen in the Clinton Administration's successful attempts at social engineering, for example, the adoption of rules requiring three hours per week of children's television and the V-chip ratings system. Importantly, while this re-regulatory trend intrudes into the First Amendment rights of Hollywood's creative community, the U.S. television marketplace also is undergoing considerable consolidation due in large part to the elimination of the FinSyn Rules and the structural deregulation of the Telecommunications Act of 1996. This consolidation is limiting creative outlets and necessarily homogenizing television programming as an ever-smaller group of executives dictates the content of programming of prime time television in the United States.

Taken collectively, recent trends in Washington have resulted in an unprecedented level of intrusive "values"-based regulation affecting an increasingly concentrated media industry. In this context, will there be efficiencies of scale? Possibly. But what about diversity—both of content and of distribution sources? In this emerging consolidated and content-regulated electronic media environment, diversity of programming, one of the most important results of free speech the First Amendment is designed to protect, is at risk—big time.

THE "VALUES AGENDA" AND STRUCTURAL DEREGULATION OF THE BROADCAST INDUSTRY

For those who might question this gloomy prognosis about content regulation and excessive consolidation in the U.S. media marketplace, one merely has to look at recent regulatory by-products of Washington's "values agenda" and structural deregulation:

1. Broadcasters must now air three hours of "core educational and informational children's television per week" or jeopardize their TV license renewal from FCC bureaucrats who will tell them what children's programming is acceptable.

2. With the elimination of the FinSyn Rules, television networks can now produce their entire prime time schedule, and when they decide to use an "outside producer," they can now legally extract ownership rights from those independent producers.

3. Networks can now buy studios and vice-versa, which means fewer outlets for independently produced programming.

4. With the elimination of the 12-station ownership limit for television groups, the networks' market power and ability to limit diverse programming will grow larger as their O&Os (owned and operated stations) approach the new limit of 35% of the national market.

5. The V-chip-inspired TV ratings system will label television programs, and the subjective label given to an independent producer's program could mean no advertiser support, that is, it won't air.

6. The President has publicly supported the position of former FCC Chairman Reed Hundt to keep "hard liquor ads" off TV, ignoring beer and wine for the time being (despite federal equivalency data suggesting beer is the major source of alcohol-related accidents). And what happens to commercial broadcasting and independent producers' access if the FCC adopts new rules restricting responsible alcohol beverage advertising on

television—advertising which currently totals over $700 million a year?

This cursory look at the "values agenda" currently being advanced in Washington should be terribly troublesome to broadcasters and programmers alike. Yet, to date, these groups have generally focused their lobbying clout on other priorities—such as securing free spectrum space for digital television or global copyright protection. Ironically, while there was no obvious Hollywood pressure in opposition to the troublesome First Amendment-intrusive content regulation trend, the Hollywood community provided enormous financial support for the President's reelection effort in 1996. The independent producer community has been largely absent as an effective advocacy group in Washington during the past few years. In fact, independent producers have not even appeared on the federal public policy radar screen for most of the '90s.

While independent producers largely ignored events and trends in Washington, federal policy wonks and regulators were having a public policy picnic with a First Amendment-intrusive menu, particularly during the last presidential election campaign year. In fact, in 1996 politicians at the White House, Congress, and the FCC aggressively pursued the politically attractive but First Amendment-insensitive "values agenda"—an agenda that has resulted in two recent big victories for the federal social engineers: adoption of the new "children's television regulations" and enactment of the V-chip-inspired ratings system legislation.

TROUBLESOME NEW CHILDREN'S TELEVISION RULES

In examining the new children's television rules and the prolonged public debate that preceded their adoption by the FCC in August of 1996, it is helpful to stipulate that everyone in Hollywood and in Washington is in favor of quality children's television. The critical issue then is: who determines what is good and adequate children's television? That question ignited a public policy debate in Washington when Vice President Gore arrived at the Old Executive Office Building and his friend Reed Hundt was appointed Chairman of the FCC. The debate finally concluded on August 8, 1996, with the FCC's adoption of an unprecedented set of quantitative and qualitative children's television rules that require all television broadcasters in the United States to air three hours per week of regularly scheduled "core programming."[1]

Ironically, just two years before Vice President Gore and Chairman Hundt assumed control over the federal communications public policy agenda after the 1992 presidential elections, a group of bipartisan leaders in the Senate and the House enacted the Children's Television Act of 1990 (CTA) that explicitly *rejected* quantitative requirements for broadcasters. Specifically, Senator Daniel Inouye (D-HI), in his Senate floor remarks, stated that "the Committee does not intend that the FCC interpret this legislation as requiring or mandating *quantification* standards governing the amount or placement of children's educational and informational programming."[2] Senator Tim Wirth (D-CO), in his remarks, stated that "the FCC *will defer to the licensee's judgement* to determine how to serve the educational and informational needs of children."[3] Even Congressman Ed Markey (D-MA) indicated upon passage of the bill in the House that "the legislation does not require the FCC to set quantitative guidelines to educational programming, but instead requires the Commission to base its decision upon an evaluation of a station's overall service to children."[4]

Despite this clear expression of bipartisan congressional intent in 1990 *not* to impose specific, quantifiable programming requirements under the 1990 CTA, FCC Chairman Hundt, working in tandem with Vice President Gore and Congressman Markey, dramatically expanded the scope of this Act in 1996 to include a new requirement that broadcasters air three hours of "core educational and informational programming" for children under the age of 16. Since September 1, 1997, broadcasters that "certify" to having aired three hours of "core" children's educational and informational programming per week between the hours of 7 A.M. and 10 P.M. have been "assured" of Commission staff-level approval of their license renewal applications. Efforts that fall short of these benchmarks, however, automatically result in the very troublesome prospect of a full Commission review of the broadcaster's renewal application.

While seemingly reasonable on their face, the FCC's expanded children's television requirements for broadcasters effectively empower FCC bureaucrats to determine what programming complies with the broad and subjective definition of "core educational and informational television programming for children." And if that presumably well-intended FCC bureaucrat, or committee of bureaucrats, concludes that a certain station's three hours of programming is inadequate—for example, deciding that such programming was entertaining but "too weak" from an educational standpoint—then the Commission can take away a broadcaster's most valuable asset, his or her FCC license. Although it is too early to assess how the broadcasters' certifications will be handled by FCC bureaucrats, the fact remains that those bureaucrats are now mandated to make this subjective form of determination about the content of children's programming on television.[5] In effect, federal regulators will be determining our children's television choices.

Incredibly, despite the clear intent of Congress in enacting the CTA in 1990, this nebulous three-hour "core educational and informational programming" requirement went unchallenged by the broadcast industry and television programmers alike. Their silence is all the more confounding in view of the unequivocal 1994 admonition by the Supreme Court in *Turner Broadcasting* that "the FCC's oversight responsibilities do not grant it the power to ordain any particular type of programming that must be offered by broadcast stations."[6] The leadership of the broadcast industry, which includes some major TV programmers, apparently was reluctant to offend the White House and other federal officials, who simultaneously were deciding the fate of free spectrum space for digital broadcasting. Concerns about their basic First Amendment protections and the creative flexibility that flows from the First Amendment became secondary to the prospects of the multibillion-dollar windfall that free spectrum space represented.

Despite the obvious and First Amendment-intrusive implications of these new qualitative and quantitative children's television rules, independent producers remained on the lobbying sidelines, as the White House, in a frenzy of election-year activities, announced its latest "victory for children." It was a classic lesson in "advocacy retreat," and in the case of independent programmers, it was a case of total "advocacy truancy."

Now, with the new three hours a week children's television rules in place, a First Amendment-intrusive minefield awaits programmers and broadcasters who will soon see what children's programming FCC bureaucrats decide is "OK"—and based on that determination, which TV stations' licenses are worthy of renewal.

In view of the vagaries of Washington politics, the troubling question is: What happens if an FCC bureaucrat, down the road, has a political axe to grind against a broadcaster or programmer—for whatever reason? In the regulatory environment that now exists, the FCC is empowered to revoke that license if it, *not the public*, determines that the station's three hours of core children's television programming per week is not informative or educational enough. Talk about a leveraged situation where the FCC can ultimately dictate the content of children's programming in the years to come!

THE TELECOM ACT OF 1996

Just six months before the Commission's August 8, 1996 adoption of new "tough" children's television rules, Congress passed the Telecommunications Act of 1996 which, among other things, mandated a new high-tech form of government censorship through the V-chip and its attendant television ratings system. Although the concept of requiring a V-chip for every television may be constitutionally sound, since the V-chip is "content neutral," basing the use of this technology on a government-sanctioned ratings system is constitutionally infirm. The Telecom Act empowered the FCC, "in consultation with appropriate public interest groups and interested individuals," to make its own determination as to whether or not the industry has established an "acceptable" ratings system.

While the V-chip is designed to provide parents with the final say on which programs their children should watch, a content-based ratings system approved or devised by the federal government raises serious First Amendment questions that should be sending shrill alarm signals to independent producers of television programming. Importantly, a content-based ratings system will have the effect of chilling speech, particularly in an advertiser-supported venue such as broadcast television, where programming decisions are regularly made on the basis of advertiser demand. As product image is an integral part of a company's marketing campaign, advertisers are understandably sensitive to the programming in which their ads are aired. Many advertisers can be expected to shy away from promoting their products in a program labeled as "violent" or "sexual," despite any artistic importance that program may have. Lacking sufficient advertiser demand, such programming could virtually disappear from broadcast television, resulting in less diversity for the U.S. television viewer.

Obviously, since the era of the television ratings system is in its nascent stages, it is unclear what adverse impact this new form of content regulation will have on the creative community's flexibility and success in producing diverse programming for American consumers. Yet one thing is clear at this point: while the networks and cable executives acceded to White House wishes for a "values agenda," the creative community failed to effectively advocate its interests with members of Congress and within the Clinton Administration. As a result, few in Congress, with the exception of Representative Billy Tauzin (R-LA), have expressed any appreciation of the vital nexus between First Amendment-based creative flexibility and continued robust diversity in the television programming produced in the United States. To the degree that ignorance persists in the halls of Congress on this key point, more content-based, First Amendment-intrusive rules are likely to be enacted by Congress and/or adopted by the FCC, which, even without Chairman Hundt at the helm, will continue to be influenced by a White House that has an expansive "values agenda."

MORE FIRST AMENDMENT PROBLEMS ON THE HORIZON

The current political environment in the Federal City continues to provide fertile ground for additional legislative and regulatory proposals that represent more "industrial policy-making" at the expense of the First Amendment. For example, a policy battle is currently brewing between the FCC and the liquor industry—threatening both the ability of the alcohol industry to responsibly advertise its lawful products and the rights of broadcasters to accept much-needed revenues generated from responsible alcohol beverage advertisements. For program producers, restrictions on television advertising of various lawful products may seem a remote threat. But what happens to the programming industry if broadcasters lose the $700 million a year in ad revenues they currently enjoy from the beer industry, and, because of that shortfall, broadcasters necessarily cut their budgets for movies of the week or first-run syndication programming produced by independent producers?

Furthermore, in Congress, more than 100 members are sponsoring legislation to reinvigorate the concept of a "family viewing hour" which would require broadcasters to set aside the first hour of prime time for "family-oriented" programming. Finally, another potential breeding ground for future First Amendment-intrusive regulations has originated from the White House with the formal appointment of the "Gore Commission," a group of private-sector and public-sector representatives charged with codifying broadcasters' public interest obligations in a new digital world.

MEDIA CONSOLIDATION: BREEDING PROGRAMMING HOMOGENIZATION

While the Washington "values agenda" continues to usher in content re-regulation of television programming, additional federal initiatives in the 1990s have simultaneously fostered structural deregulation and consolidation of the U.S. television marketplace. Credible arguments are routinely made that the efficiencies of scale brought about by media consolidation are good for the broadcasting industry, particularly as commercially supported broadcast television faces increasing competition from alternative outlets, including cable, direct broadcast satellite (DBS), local multipoint distribution service (LMDS), and other video providers. However, the media consolidation and increased vertical integration that have reshaped the industry in the '90s raise the serious prospect of diminished program diversity for American consumers.

Consolidation of the U.S. media marketplace was set in motion in 1993, when the Federal Communications Commission eliminated the Financial Interest and Syndication (FinSyn) Rules, which prohibited the networks from owning or retaining a financial interest in the programs they aired. Importantly, the FinSyn Rules also prohibited networks from acquiring any financial interest in the sale of these properties for syndication. The purpose of the FinSyn Rules was to "promote a diversity of programming sources and distributors by curbing the excessive power of the three major broadcast networks in the financing, development and syndication of television programming."[7] The FinSyn Rules effectively provided the nurturing regulatory environment in which great independent producers like Marcy Carsey, Marian Rees, and Stephen J. Cannell developed diverse, quality programming like the made-for-television movie "Decoration Day," "The Cosby Show," and action/adventure programs like "Hunter" that became beloved programming fare for television viewers in the United States and around the globe.

Following the contentious FinSyn battle, the Commission in 1995 also eliminated the Prime Time Access Rule (PTAR) which prohibited a network affiliate from airing network programming from 7 to 8 P.M. In eliminating both the FinSyn and PTAR rules, the FCC determined that market conditions had grown sufficiently competitive that programming diversity was assured without the need for further regulation of the three, four, or even six national networks.

As predicted by some fearless independent producers who lobbied in the '80s and early '90s to retain the FinSyn Rules, the elimination of these rules cleared away the regulatory hurdles that prevented the major studios and networks from merging. In this regard, recent developments in the syndication television marketplace are proving that the FCC was wrong in its decision to totally eliminate the rules designed to promote program diversity. Based on the Commission's elimination of FinSyn and PTAR, the industry is now experiencing a level of vertical integration never before seen. With the mergers of ABC and Disney, Westinghouse and CBS, Time Warner and Turner, and most recently, Rupert Murdoch's Fox Kids Worldwide and Pat Robertson's International Family Entertainment, unaffiliated independent programming producers are finding it harder than ever to find a window for their programming on any network's prime time television schedule. The result of this massive multibillion-dollar consolidation is simple: a steadily increasing amount of network prime time programming is produced in-house, diminishing the need for independent producers. Equally important from a diversity standpoint, a smaller group of people now determine what programming will be shown to the television viewing public in the United States.

Moreover, freed of the regulatory constraints of the FinSyn Rules, networks are exercising enormous and increased influence over programmers at the expense of programming diversity. For example, the trade press reported on an apparent dispute between NBC and DreamWorks that highlighted the newfound unilateral power of the networks. In this case, as a condition precedent to confirming a series order, NBC reportedly sought an ownership stake in a pilot produced by DreamWorks. According to press reports, NBC, which owns a majority of its comedy pilots, routinely seeks an ownership stake in any program produced by the occasional outside production house from which it seeks to acquire programming.[8]

This is the very type of market abuse that the FinSyn and PTAR rules were meant to preclude. Network influence over both the ownership and the content of programming not produced in-house is likely to increase in the deregulated post-FinSyn marketplace. Moreover, since it is no longer illegal to extract back-end rights from producers, why shouldn't the networks work to increase their shareholders' profits by maximizing their financial stake in programming that is produced by the few truly independent producers who remain viable after the elimination of the FinSyn Rules?

An unrelated and enormously significant event occurred after the Commission's elimination of the FinSyn and PTAR rules, when Congress enacted the Telecom Act of 1996, which was signed into law on February 8, 1996. Among other things, the Telecom Act of 1996 eliminated the 12-station ownership cap for broadcast television and increased the permissible national market reach of networks to 35%. Congress also directed the Commission to apply its presumptive waiver of the one-to-a-market rule (prohibiting common ownership of a radio and television station in the same market) to the top 50 broadcast markets. In addition, the Act required the FCC to reexamine its local ownership rules, including the duopoly restriction which currently limits dual television station ownership in the same market.[9]

The massive structural deregulation resulting from the Telecom Act of 1996 has led to an unprecedented level of ownership consolidation—beyond even Congress's wildest expectations. In 1996 alone, $25 billion changed hands in mergers within the television and radio industries, representing an astonishing 204.8% increase over the previous year. The average number of stations owned by each of the ten largest television groups doubled to 14 while their average national audience reach grew from 15.85% to 22.28%.[10] Amazingly, 1997 nearly matched the frenetic megaconsolidation of 1996, with the year's top ten deals reaping between $500 million and $2.6 billion at all-time-high cash-flow multiples.[11] As a result of this massive consolidation, it will be increasingly difficult for independent producers to successfully air (and own) their programming.

INDEPENDENT PROGRAMMERS MUST "GET REAL"—AND GET ACTIVE IN WASHINGTON

Based on the federal public policy scoreboard during the past several years, independent producers are more at risk than ever of becoming an endangered species, relics of the "good old days" of diverse, commercially supported free television. This is due in large part to the fact that the Clinton Administration has successfully advanced a "values agenda" that has resulted in a plethora of content regulations that seriously erodes programmers' First Amendment freedoms. These are the very freedoms that in the past have provided the solid basis for the U.S. creative community's enormous success in producing diverse television programming. Coincidental with the adoption of First Amendment-intrusive regulations, the opportunities are narrowing for truly independent producers to license their programming in a consolidated broadcast marketplace where an ever-shrinking number of mega-media executives are deciding whose programming is aired on television. Furthermore, in this greatly deregulated, consolidated media marketplace where network and studio heads are often one and the same, it is both logical and legal that these executives will favor their own in-house programming or, if they resort to an independently produced program, insist on owning part of that programming.

This is the real world today, and if independent producers and others who value program diversity don't wake up and advocate effectively, they could find themselves entering the twenty-first century bereft of the next generation of Marcy Carseys, Marian Reeses, Thomas Carters, Stephen J. Cannells, and Dick Wolfs.

Advocacy does not happen on its own. Moreover, as is evident from both the current political environment in Washington and the consolidated U.S. broadcast marketplace, without effective and enlightened advocacy by the creative community, even a well-intended federal government can erode the First Amendment rights of broadcasters and programmers. Unless the ongoing erosion of the First Amendment is addressed and effectively checked, diverse television programming and the independent producers who create much of it are at serious risk and could become the next endangered species to disappear from the scene.

NOTES

1. "Policies and Rules Concerning Children's Television Programming," MM Docket No. 93–48, in 11 *FCC Rcd.* 10660 (1996).

2. *136 Congressional Record.* S10122 (July 19, 1990).

3. *136 Congressional Record.* S10127 (July 19, 1990).

4. Remarks of Congressman Markey (D-MA), *136 Congressional Record.* H8536 (October 1, 1990).

5. Dennis Wharton and Joe Flint, "The Battle Rages On: The Old Educate/Regulate War Flares; FCC Vote Looms," in *Variety*, January 1, 1996, p. 67.

6. *Turner Broadcasting v. FCC*, 114 S.Ct. 2445 (1994) (noting further that "the Commission may not impose upon [broadcasters] its private notions of what the public ought to hear").

7. "In the Matter of Evaluation of the Syndication and Financial Interest Rules," MM Docket No. 90–162, in 6 *FCC Record* 3094, 3096 (1991).

8. Lynette Rice, "NBC Pushes for Piece of Prime Time," in *Broadcast and Cable*, April 7, 1997, p.14.

9. "Review of the Commission's Regulations Governing Television Broadcasting, Second Further Notice of Proposed Rulemaking," MM Docket No. 91–221, released November 7, 1996.

10. Donna Petrozzello, "Trading Market Explodes," in *Broadcast and Cable*, February 3, 1997, p. 18.

11. Sarah Brown, "Living Large in 1997," in *Broadcast and Cable*, February 3, 1998, p. 32.

III

Articles by Academics

Gatekeeping in the Neo-Network Era

Michael Curtin

Access to prime time television historically has been one of the key concerns of advocacy groups in the United States. Consequently, many advocates and others have perceived network gatekeepers as playing especially powerful roles because they ultimately determine what is produced and broadcast nationwide. Although advocacy groups and public policy makers periodically attempt to influence the decision-making process, corporate officials shape the contours of popular culture and information on a daily basis. To many critics, this means that television content is driven by commercial considerations that result in a bland homogeneity. Quality programming that does exist is, in their eyes, merely an unintended by-product of the system. These critics conclude that advocacy groups should challenge the concentration of media ownership and struggle for control over prime time television.

This essay argues, on the other hand, that television has changed dramatically over the past two decades and that a diverse menu of programming is more readily available than ever before. Moreover, corporate executives today exercise far less control over media content than their counterparts did during television's classical network era of the 1960s. Instead, the average consumer is confronted by a blizzard of options, creating both uncertainty for corporate executives and opportunities for public advocacy groups. Given the current conditions, the challenge for advocacy groups is less a matter of struggling over access to a few hours of prime time than it is to help citizens make sense of the options available to them. Yet these new opportunities can be realized only if advocates understand the logic of the neo-network era, a logic that is best revealed by examining the changing nature of gatekeeping practices in the media industries. This essay begins with an anecdote about reputedly the most powerful media mogul of our time and then moves backward to compare the recent actions of News Corporation executives with the actions of an earlier era. Such historical comparisons will help to reveal the institutional conditions that frame the work of contemporary advocacy groups.

In February 1998 Stuart Proffit, a senior editor at HarperCollins, received a draft of the first chapters of *East and West: China, Power, and the Future of Asia*, a memoir of Chris Patten's experiences as the last British governor of Hong Kong. Proffit was enthusiastic about the project from the very beginning, both because it offered a definitive account of the protracted wrangling between the Chinese and British governments concerning the handover of the former colony and because Patten has a reputation as a dynamic speaker and writer. When Proffit perused the first installment of the manuscript in early February, he said he was delighted with both the content and the prose.

Executives higher up in the management structure at HarperCollins, though, expressed misgivings shortly after the chapters arrived at the office and, in a surprising turn of events, they derailed the project, citing "quality" problems with the first submission. Proffit disagreed so strongly with this reversal that he tendered his resignation, claiming that external pressures clouded the judgment of his superiors. When the story became public, critics were quick to point out that HarperCollins is owned by Rupert Murdoch's News Corporation, which in turn owns STAR TV, a satellite service that transmits five channels to audiences in mainland China. While investing more than two billion dollars in the development of STAR, Murdoch has personally shown a remarkable willingness to be influenced by the sensitivities of the Beijing leadership, and this seemed to be one more example of that inclination.

Murdoch's concern stems in part from the chilly reception he received when, shortly after he purchased STAR, he was quoted as saying that satellite television would spell the end of authoritarian regimes around the globe. Seeing themselves as one of the targets of this remark, Chinese officials quickly responded by outlawing satellite dishes throughout the country and forcing cable systems to relinquish the STAR signal. Although not completely enforceable, these actions alerted Murdoch to the fact that STAR could not make money without the cooperation of the Chinese government. Consequently, News Corp. conspicuously began to cultivate good relations with party leaders. In 1993 STAR canceled its contract with BBC News because it ran a documentary about Mao Zedong that displeased Chinese officials. In 1996 Murdoch launched a Chinese-language satellite channel with mainland partners reputed to have an extensive network of contacts in Beijing. And in 1997 News Corp. developed an Internet service that is a joint venture with the official paper of the Communist Party, the *People's Daily*. As part of this ongoing effort to curry favor with Beijing elites, Rupert Murdoch furthermore showed a personal interest in Deng Rong's biography of her father, the late Deng Xiaoping—so much so that Murdoch threw a lavish book-signing party for her when the book was first released by HarperCollins. Speaking to Asian broadcasters at a conference in Tokyo in May 1997, Murdoch enthused, "We recognize that China is a distinctive market with distinctive social and moral values that Western companies like News Corporation must learn to abide by."[1]

If Murdoch has maneuvered his way close to the inner circle in Beijing, Chris Patten has done the opposite. While governor of Hong Kong, he pushed relentlessly to institutionalize democratic processes during the last decade of British rule, earning the wrath not only of Chinese officials but also of the British foreign service, which Patten claimed had betrayed the people of Hong Kong while negotiating the handover. Known for his outspokenness, Patten went even further, criticizing "the most seedy of betrayals" by those who reap profits from free speech in one country while censoring it in another, a thinly veiled reference to media executives like Murdoch. Patten is notable, quotable, and unpredictable, which is perhaps why executives at HarperCollins were concerned about the manuscript.[2]

The decision to pull the plug on *East and West* suggests the most naked form of "gatekeeping," the process by which media firms select, acquire, and promote materials for sale to audiences. Over the past several decades, journalism and mass communication researchers have explored the complex filtering processes at work in gatekeeping and concluded that the operational structure and prevailing values of media organizations impose a set of constraints that shape editorial decisions on a daily, commonsense basis. Typically, some stories, books, movies, or programs are deemed acceptable according to the shared beliefs of the gatekeepers, not according to an explicit set of standards for quality. Usually gatekeeping is not a result of mandates from above, but is instead a product of unspoken agreements among a set of professionals who, based on their shared experience, understand the objectives of the organization.[3] The controversy over the Patten manuscript was exceptional because it explicitly revealed some of the pressures that implicitly shape the gatekeeping process.

Many scholars contend that the most influential force at work in this process is ownership. Media reflect the interests of owners more than they reflect the tastes of audiences or the judgments of media professionals. According to these critics, media activism therefore should concentrate on the struggle over ownership. This is especially important in the current era because we are witnessing an unprecedented trend toward conglomeration and concentration of media ownership engineered by a few moguls, such as Rupert Murdoch. These researchers contend that, as a result, we are getting less information and less socially conscious entertainment. Some voices are suppressed, while others are filtered excessively, so that the end product is bland infotainment that perpetuates social, economic, and political inequities.[4]

Although this approach seems to explain why Chris Patten's memoirs were suppressed, it does not easily explain why, in the preceding fall, adjacent to Chinese President Jiang Zemin's visit to the United States, three major Hollywood studios released films that are explicitly critical of mainland human rights violations. Sony's "Seven Years in Tibet" and Disney's "Kundun" both provide accounts of China's invasion and occupation of Tibet from the perspective of the Dalai Lama. Meanwhile, MGM ponied up a thriller, "Red Corner," about the misadventures of a Hollywood entertainment lawyer who is working for a global media magnate and hoping to land an agreement with Chinese officials to sanction a new satellite television service aimed at mainland audiences. Without any trace of irony, Richard Gere, playing the lead character, finds himself mired in a web of intrigue among influence peddlers within the Chinese bureaucracy, ultimately leading to his arrest on trumped-up murder charges. As might be imagined, the real Beijing bureaucracy expressed its displeasure with all three films and reportedly tried to pressure the studios to think twice before releasing them. None of them succumbed, despite the fact that each is trying to expand into the rapidly growing mainland China film market, a market that would grow even faster if government officials would relax existing import quotas. In other words, each studio chose to go ahead with its film in spite of pressures that are similar to those experienced by News Corp.

One could argue, however, that events in the fall of 1997 were an aberration. Just as the derailment of Patten's memoirs stood out as an exceptional instance of blatant censorship, so too did these films stand out as exceptional examples of critical and creative freedom. And yet the examples of creative freedom do not stop there. Only a few months after the Patten imbroglio, Rupert Murdoch's Twentieth Century-Fox film studio released one of the most searing satires of American political corruption and racial prejudice in recent memory, Warren Beatty's "Bulworth." This was shortly after Time-Warner weighed in on Clinton's sexual infidelities with a similarly edgy film entitled "Wag the Dog." And it was shortly before Paramount countered the Godzillian summer blockbusters of 1998 with "The Truman Show," a self-reflexive comedy that raises questions about the authenticity of media imagery in everyday life. In fact, several critics contend that "The Truman Show" may be one of the most thoughtful films ever produced by a major studio.

But Hollywood cinema is not the only hotbed of critical thinking in the commercial media. Chris Patten's manuscript no doubt *increased* in value as a result of the HarperCollins brawl, and he received numerous offers from other publishers, including Times Books, which is currently publishing *East and West*. Some might argue that differences of opinion can be tolerated only within the realm of "elite" media, such as publishing and film, but in a shrewd commentary essay, John Leonard notes that television also displays a remarkable range of perspectives. "The surprise is that if you actually watch the stuff, it's not as bad as it ought to be," he writes. "And I'm not just talking about the remedial seriousness of public TV series like 'Frontline' and 'P.O.V.,' Bill Moyers on Iran/Contra, Frederick Wiseman on public housing, Ofra Bikel on the satanic-ritual-abuse hysteria, 'Eyes on the Prize' and 'Tongues Untied.' "[5] After rattling off a list of more than a dozen documentaries that feature analysis of everything from breast cancer to homophobia to the rape of the Ecuadorian rainforest by U.S. oil companies, Leonard then turns his attention to entertainment programming and concludes:

> Commercial television, in its movies, dramatic series and even its sitcoms, has more to tell us about common decency, civil discourse and social justice than big-screen Hollywood, big-time magazine journalism and most New York book publishers. Seeking to please or distract as many people as possible . . . it is famously inclusive, with a huge stake in consensus. Of course, brokering social and political gridlock, it softens lines and edges to make a prettier picture. But it's also weirdly democratic, multicultural, utopian, quixotic and more welcoming of difference and diversity than much of the audience that sits down to watch it with a surly agnosticism about reality itself. It has been overwhelmingly pro-gun control and anti-death penalty; sympathetic to the homeless and the ecosystem; alert to child abuse, spouse-battering, alcoholism, sexual discrimination and/or harassment, date-rape and medical malpractice. . . . And television may be the only American institution outside public school to still believe in and celebrate the integration of the races, at least on camera.

How then can we explain this seemingly paradoxical behavior by the commercial media industries, especially television? Television has always been reviled as the great repository of Masscult drivel. In their attempt to draw the largest possible audience for their advertisers, television's gatekeepers have been accused of seeing the medium as little more than blocks of commercial advertising separated by black holes that need to be filled up with eye candy. Advocacy groups base their very existence on the presumption that such attitudes should be counterbalanced by campaigns to restore a semblance of public interest to the airwaves. If John Leonard is right, they would argue, it is only because of the earnest efforts of advocacy groups. And to some extent this is true. Advocacy groups no doubt help people in the television industry expand their frames of reference. Such groups draw public attention to needs that cannot be expressed through ratings data or advertiser preferences. Other structural and institutional forces, however, are transforming the nature of television from a medium that once controlled audiences to one that is forever anxious about its ability to attract viewers. This transformation, more than anything else, has changed the role of gatekeepers in the industry and may well suggest a need to alter the strategies of advocacy groups as well. To understand these changes, we need to look back at the development of network television.

FROM NETWORK TO NEO-NETWORK TELEVISION

In many ways television, more than any other popular form of communication, seems to embody the defining features of a mass medium. During its first three decades, the medium stood at the intersection of entertainment and information, of imagination and consumption, of private leisure and public life. Huge audiences were engaged by it on a daily, simultaneous basis, making it the most central cultural institution in U.S. history.[6] Even though the television audience has been splintering for close to 20 years, the heyday of network television continues to shape much of our thinking about the role media play in contemporary society. Television is assumed to have powerful effects, which is why advocates, lobbyists, and policy makers struggle to influence the medium's standards of conduct and ultimately the nature of its content.

The "classical" or "high network" era of television began in the early 1950s and lasted roughly until the early 1980s when cable and satellite television began to siphon off significant portions of the audience. The classical era existed because the government established a system of television licensing that provided for the development of only three national services. In the 1950s many other media companies, such as Time-Life and Paramount, wanted to start networks of their own, and indeed the technology was available. But during this early licensing phase government regulators favored the existing radio networks and their lobbyists, thereby setting in place an officially sanctioned oligopoly. No major objections were raised at the time because of the widespread presumption that given the heavy cost of developing the new technology, large broadcast corporations could best serve the needs of vast national and even international audiences.

As with most monopoly or oligopoly corporations that are sanctioned by the government, the new television networks tried to legitimize their special status by promoting their services as offering something for everyone. This also had practical economic benefits since most television advertisers manufactured products for mass consumer markets. Thus, even though TV audiences of this period were fragmented along numerous axes, network executives aspired to represent them as a unified entity in ratings, marketing reports, and promotions. Moreover, they characterized the overarching mission of the networks as integrative: pulling people together, uniting various regions, forging ever larger markets. Television was conceived as a mass, national medium. Of course, niche markets existed then as now, but they were not celebrated in trade discourse among the major corporate players who controlled the medium.

The operative principles of the classical network era still exercise a powerful hold on our imaginations, suggesting that power and control over national consciousness reside primarily in the boardrooms of a few major networks. And over the past decade, as we have witnessed the merging of gigantic media firms into huge conglomerates, many critics seem to assume that this concentration of ownership means even greater control at the top of the corporate pyramid and an increasing standardization of cultural products.

Yet the principles that guide the television industry have undergone significant change over the past 20 years. Transformations in national and global economies have fragmented the marketplace, pressuring the culture industries to reorganize and restrategize. Television advertising is no longer dominated by firms that manufacture products or provide services exclusively for mass markets. Niche products have led companies to target their advertising at particular demographic groups and to disperse their messages throughout a variety of media. Furthermore, transnational marketing has become increasingly popular as both advertisers and their ad agencies have sought out new customers around the globe.

As opposed to nationally based television corporations that prevailed during the classical network era, the current period is paradoxically characterized by both transnationalization and fragmentation. New technologies, deregulation, and relentless competition have undermined national frameworks that once shaped the industry. Although mass markets continue to attract corporate attention and blockbuster media products are still a priority, industry discourse about the mass audience no longer refers to one simultaneous exposure to a particular program, artist, or event, so much as a shared, asynchronous cultural milieu. That is, we less frequently experience something like the 1964 pop-rock "British invasion" by collectively gathering around the television set at eight o'clock on Sunday night to watch the Beatles' first television performance in North America. Instead, trends and ideas now achieve prominence in often circuitous and unanticipated ways. Ed Sullivan, who was the consummate 1960s gatekeeper of popular entertainment, has no counterpart in television today.

In part this is because the culture industries exercise less control over the daily scheduling of popular entertainment; audiences time-shift and channel surf or they pursue a myriad of other entertainment options. As a result, media executives strive instead for broad exposure of their products through multiple circuits of information and expression. They also seek less to homogenize popular culture than to organize and exploit diverse forms of creativity toward profitable ends.[7] Besides their heavily promoted blockbusters, media corporations also cultivate a broad range of products intended for more specific audiences. Flexible corporate frameworks connect mass market operations with more localized initiatives.

Two strategies are now at work in the culture industries. One focuses on mass cultural forms aimed at broad national or global markets that demand low involvement and are relatively apolitical, such as blockbuster Hollywood films or broadcast television. Media operations that deal in this arena are cautious about the prospect of intense audience responses either for or against the product they are marketing. By comparison, the other strategy focuses on niche audiences, fashioning products that actively pursue intensity. This strategy seeks out audiences that are more likely to be highly invested in particular forms of cultural expression. Among industry executives these are referred to as products with "edge." Thirty years ago they received little attention, but today product development meetings are peppered with references to attitude and edge, that is, references to products that sharply define the boundaries of their intended audience. Programs with edge can be marketed on cable, satellite, videocassette, or via the new television networks started by Warner and Paramount. They have even found their way onto broadcast television as the major networks attempt to respond to the new competitive environment. For example, NBC picked up Michael Moore's politically provocative "TV Nation" after an initial run on Fox, and ABC ran "Ellen," which in time explicitly revolved around issues of sexual orientation. Both series eventually succumbed to the residual pressures of classical network reasoning, but the fact that they were aired by national broadcasters and survived as long as they did highlights the changes currently taking place.

In response to this rapidly changing cultural environment, we are witnessing the organization of huge media conglomerates around these two movements toward mass and niche marketing respectively, as well as the so-called synergies that exist between them. This is what I refer to as the neo-network era, an era characterized by the multiple and asynchronous distribution of cultural forms, an era that operates according to the logic of what David Harvey refers to as a "flexible regime of accumulation." Rather than a network structure anchored by a three-network economy, the neo-network era features elaborate circuits of cultural production, distribution, and reception.[8]

This transformation is not a radical break with the past; rather, it is a transitional phase with both traditional network and niche network tendencies existing side by side. Blockbuster films that appeal to a transnational audience are still the desideratum of major Hollywood studios, but the same conglomerate that may own a studio may also own a boutique film distribution company, a specialty music label, and a collection of magazines that target very specific market niches.[9] "As you get narrower in interest," one media executive observed, "you tend to have more intensity of interest [and] the person is more likely to pay the extra money."[10] The key to success is no longer the ownership and control of a centralized and highly integrated medium-specific empire but the management of a conglomerate structured around a variety of firms with different audiences and different objectives.

Although the mass market is still attractive, micro markets can be extremely lucrative, a realization that has engendered an intense search for narrowly defined and under-served audiences. Race, ethnicity, gender, and age have now joined socioeconomic status as potentially marketable boundaries of difference. Despite the intensity of interest that these media companies may find among a micro audience, their participation in the market is not based on a commitment to the material interests or political principles of any particular group. Rather these firms simply are following a marketing strategy that they characterize as strictly capitalistic and generally disinterested in content issues.[11]

Ideally, this neo-network strategy will present opportunities whereby a micro market phenomenon crosses over and becomes a mainstream phenomenon, making it potentially exploitable through a greater number of circuits within the media conglomerate. Some rap artists' careers obviously followed this trajectory, perhaps best illustrated by the success of Will Smith, whose rap music career was leveraged into the hit television series "Fresh Prince of Bel Air" and then into a leading role in "Men in Black," one of the highest-grossing films in Hollywood history. But the converse is also true. A product that was originally a mass product can be spun out through a myriad of niche venues, which has been Viacom's strategy behind "Star Trek," one of its most profitable brands.[12]

GATEKEEPING IN AN AGE OF OVERPRODUCTION

One of the most useful explanations for advancing our understanding of how gatekeeping works in the neo-network era of television was written by sociologist Paul Hirsch in 1972, at the height of the classical network era.[13] Interestingly, Hirsch was writing about the publishing and music industries rather than the television industry. Yet his explanation of how the publishing industry "processes fads and fashions" can be fruitfully applied to neo-network television. To begin, Hirsch identifies several prominent features of the book publishing industry: relatively low cost production (when compared to potential market return), demand uncertainty, and overproduction as a rational response to market uncertainty. Book and music publishers have for a long time wrestled with the fact that they cannot anticipate shifting tastes with any confidence. As a result, they work hard to acquire key products that they will in turn heavily promote in an attempt to spark consumer interest. But they know that most products, including some of the most heavily promoted ones, will fail and that a few marginal products will succeed beyond expectation. Thus it makes sense to release a large and diverse menu of offerings each year.

In this environment, gatekeepers play an important role, especially those who manage the acquisition and promotion of products. "Due to widespread uncertainty over the precise ingredients of a best-seller formula," writes Hirsch, "administrators are forced to trust the professional judgment of their employees. Close supervision in the production sector is impeded by ignorance of relations between cause and effect."[14] Those who operate as gatekeepers—editors, producers, and agents—achieve notoriety for their "discoveries" and become very mobile within the industry. Their reputation provides a level of autonomy that insulates them from the particular cultural tastes and political preferences of their superiors.

Critics are another important group of gatekeepers because their work often guides the purchasing behaviors of readers. Acting as surrogate audiences, critics have autonomy largely because this independence encourages audiences to trust the critics' judgments, since these judgements appear to be untainted by commercial considerations. Even though critics may be influenced by a variety of promotional strategies, their claim to legitimacy is based on their reputed autonomy. According to Hirsch, both editors and critics play important roles in managing the uncertainties of a cultural market that is flooded with products.

By comparison, during the classical network era most television executives knew that the industry's success was based primarily on the control of technology via government regulation of television licenses. Networks stood between audiences and performers, controlling interactions between the two via the only medium that could truly be described as a national, mass culture phenomenon. Almost regardless of what the networks put on, audiences would continue to watch, in many cases due to sheer inertia. The threshold of failure for a particular program was higher at that time than the threshold of success is today. In 1962, the average network documentary—the least commercial genre in the history of prime time television—drew higher ratings than most of the top ten shows do today. Another way to characterize this difference is to note that the final episode of "Seinfeld," which many see as a major television event of the 1990s, drew lower ratings than the average weekly broadcast of "The Beverly Hillbillies" during the early 1960s.[15]

During the classical network era, television's gatekeepers operated according to a logic that is very different from the one that guides gatekeepers today. Yet advocacy groups and media critics sometimes act as if the rules have not changed. They sometimes suggest that the logic of the classical network television era still applies, and even more so because of conglomeration. Murdoch's ownership of Fox, the Fox Family Channel, FX, several sports stations, STAR TV, newspapers, and book publishing firms leads many to assume that he controls global media flows the same way that William Paley used to control national television. Yet Murdoch's direct intervention in the case of the Patten memoirs was a rare event, and it was prompted by his anticipation of how Chinese officials might react. Rather than wielding power capriciously, he was instead kowtowing before the Beijing leadership. Furthermore, Murdoch ultimately could not suppress the publication of the memoirs or control audience access to them.

Most commonly, media moguls today find themselves chasing after audiences by offering a plethora of information and entertainment alternatives, resulting in a flood of material crying for attention. Consequently, promotion has become ever more important within the media marketplace, where consumers confront a blizzard of options. One of the key strategies to address such confusion in the marketplace is the concept of "branding." Companies like Disney and Time-Warner try to develop a collection of products that are linked across media platforms and beyond. Disney's films, cartoons, toys, and theme parks are the most obvious example. The look, feel, and packaging of Disney products give consumers a fairly good idea of what to anticipate from each item. Pursuing the same strategy, Time-Life magazines—the purveyors of *Time*, *Fortune*, and *Entertainment Weekly*—have recently developed special television news magazines on CNN, providing a classic example of synergistic relations between components of the Time-Warner-Turner empire. Likewise, MTV (owned by Viacom/Paramount) is moving into feature film production, where it will target the same audiences that watch the cable channel. In an environment characterized by overproduction rather than artificially imposed restriction, media conglomerates are trying—via the concept of branding—to help audiences make sense of the informational and cultural options available to them.

Advocacy groups and activists may need to consider a similar approach. It seems that two strategies should receive most prominent attention. One strategy is to continue to work for the promotion of alternative cultural resources and venues. As many critics have noted, public broadcasting in the United States is a pale imitation of the much more robust services available in other countries around the globe.[16] Instead of struggling over what gets on network TV (or does not), it might be better to work toward developing more alternative resources. A second strategy would be to build alliances under the rubric of particular "brands." The Whole Earth Catalogue and its allied publications and products are one enormously successful example of this and REI (the outdoor products cooperative) is another. One may not agree with the politics of either of these organizations, but their strategy is one that works well in the current environment. Audiences want information, enlightenment, and entertainment, but they also want to associate themselves with particular political agendas. They will do this through voting, petitioning, and protesting, but ironically, they will also do it through the consumption of particular products. What I am suggesting is a strategy of branding that is based on social and political principles rather than the marketing logic of a media conglomerate. Such a form of branding would produce political synergies by helping citizens make connections between products and ideas emanating from a variety of sources. Some feminist and environmentalist Web sites now help Internet users make precisely these sorts of connections.

Activists need to attend to the important work of building linkages that are flexible and far-reaching. The linkages also need to be intelligible to broad audiences. Struggling over access to a few hours of prime time television may be less important than building a "brand" identity for politically progressive products, projects, and cultural resources. Some of these resources might be produced by progressive organizations while others might be available from the very conglomerates that seem willing to cater to the interests of niche consumers. By helping citizens make connections between offerings in the cultural marketplace we can enhance the availability and visibility of media texts such as "Ellen," "Bulworth," and "TV Nation."

Unlike critics who express concern about the political implications of current trends toward media conglomeration, I am not convinced that ownership of a media conglomerate provides centralized control over the diverse range of material produced by such a firm. Nor am I convinced that current social problems are significantly enhanced by artificial constraints on citizen access to alternative forms of information and expression. In an era of cultural overproduction and diverse distribution channels, we therefore should be cautious about how much energy we expend on questions of ownership and access. Rather, a more important focus may be the daunting challenge of building alliances that will help citizens make sense of the flood of information now available in the neo-network era.

NOTES

1. John Ridding and John Gapper, "A Media Giant Treads Very Lightly in China," in

Financial Times, February 28, 1998, p. 7.

2. Ridding and Gapper, "A Media Giant," p. 7. Other details of the flap can be found in Philip Johnston and Ben Potter, "A Small Sacrifice in a Much Bigger Game," in *Financial Times,* February 28, 1998, p. 4 and "Of Moguls and Mice," in *Financial Times,* March 2, 1998, p. 20.

3. The concept of gatekeeping has been the subject of extensive research in journalism studies. See, for example, W. Gieber, "News Is What Newspapermen Make It," in L. A. Dexter and D. Manning White, *People, Society and Mass Communications* (New York: Free Press, 1964); M. Janowitz, "Professional Models in Journalism: The Gatekeeper and the Advocate," in *Journalism Quarterly* 57 (1975): 618-626, 662; and P. J. Shoemaker, *Gatekeeping* (Newbury Park: Sage Publications, 1991). Sociologists have also taken an interest in related phenomena, but the approach is more ethnographic. Well-known studies include Edward J. Epstein, *News from Nowhere: Television and the News* (New York: Vintage Books, 1973); Herbert J. Gans, *Deciding What's News: A Study of CBS Evening News, NBC Nightly News, Newsweek and Time* (New York: Vintage Books, 1980); Todd Gitlin, *Inside Prime Time* (New York: Pantheon, 1983); and Gaye Tuchman, *Making News: A Study in the Construction of Reality* (New York: Free Press, 1978).

4. See, for example, Ben H. Bagdikian, *The Media Monopoly* (Boston: Beacon Press, 1992); Edward S. Herman and Robert W. McChesney, *The Global Media: The New Missionaries of Corporate Capitalism* (Washington, DC: Cassell, 1997); Masao Miyoshi, "Borderless World? From Colonialism to Transnationalism and the Decline of the Nation-State," in Rob Wilson and Wimal Dissanayake, eds., *Global/Local: Cultural Production and the Transnational Imaginary* (Durham, NC: Duke University Press, 1996); and Herbert I. Schiller, *Mass Communication and American Empire,* 2d ed. (Boulder, CO: Westview, 1992).

5. John Leonard, "Of Love and Bile," in *The Nation,* June 8, 1998, p. 6.

6. By comparison, the film studios dealt only with entertainment and, even though their movies were widely popular, they were not enjoyed as a simultaneous mass experience. Radio in many ways anticipated the television era by generating huge national audiences, yet most stations remained independent, and programming was primarily in the hands of sponsors and ad agencies, not the networks. Neither the newspaper nor music industry has ever been as centralized as television, and their audiences have been subdivided by geography and/or taste. As for the general circulation magazine, it was national in scope, but its audience skewed more toward the educated and affluent.

7. The suggestion that television ever attempted to "homogenize" culture is dubious. See Michael Curtin, "Connections and Differences: The Spatial Dimension of Television History," in *Film and History,* in press.

8. Michael Curtin, "On Edge: Culture Industries in the Neo-Network Era," in Richard Ohmann, Gage Averill, Michael Curtin, David Shumway, and Elizabeth G. Traube, eds., *Making and Selling Culture* (Hanover, NH: University Press of New England, 1997); David Harvey, *The Condition of Postmodernity: An Inquiry into the Origins of Cultural Change* (Cambridge, MA: Basil Blackwell, 1989).

9. For example, Interscope, an "independent" music company formerly owned by Time-Warner, became very controversial because it distributed the niche label, Death Row Records, which prominently featured gangsta rap artists like Snoop Doggy Dogg and the late Tupac Shakur. After intense public pressure, Time-Warner put Interscope up for sale, which quickly attracted the attention of Sony and MCA/Universal, with the latter taking control after a high-stakes bidding war. So rather than actually going independent, the label is now associated with MCA/Universal and is racking up record-breaking sales in new niche markets that include ska-punk and Gospel music. Interestingly, these recent shifts were reported in a niche insert of *Time* magazine called "Time Select, Show Business," see David E. Thigpen, "A Sound Rebound," in *Time,* November 10, 1997, p. B2 and A. Sandler,

"MCA Finishes Interscope Odyssey," in *Variety*, February 26, 1996, p. 62.

10. This quote comes from the transcript of a roundtable discussion with publishing executive Mark Edmiston in Richard Ohmann et al., *Making and Selling Culture*, p. 137.

11. I have found this to be true in most of my conversations with media executives, but the pattern is rendered rather explicitly in transcripts of roundtable discussions with media executives published in Richard Ohmann et al., *Making and Selling Culture*. It should be noted, however, that while this pattern holds true for subsidiaries of large corporations, many independent producers are very much concerned with content issues. For instance, although they are both independent punk rock labels based in Southern California, the ardently secular Epitaph and the fundamentalist Christian Tooth and Nail distribute artists with extremely dissimilar ideologies, as reflective of their owners' respective beliefs.

12. It should be pointed out that the trajectory of Smith's career is what fascinates media executives who are building synergistically integrated conglomerates. They aspire to provide multiple venues for a star like Smith or a product like "Star Trek." Yet these hopes have not yet been fully realized because brands still jump from one company to another in many cases. Smith, for example, landed a popular television series with GE/NBC in the prime time series "Fresh Prince of Bel Air," but then scored a film success with Sony/Columbia in "Men in Black," which earned over $500 million in global box office revenues four months after its premier, making it the tenth highest grossing film in Hollywood history. See "Box Office," in *Variety*, October 27, 1997, p. 16 and Leonard Klady, "Sony Sent Soaring by 'Summer,'" in *Variety*, October 27, 1997, p. 16. Regarding Viacom's strategy for the exploitation of product brands like Star Trek, see John Batelle, "Viacom Doesn't Suck," in *Wired*, April 1995, pp. 110-115.

13. Paul Hirsch, "Processing Fads and Fashions: An Organization-Set Analysis of the Cultural Industry Systems," in *American Journal of Sociology* 77 (1972): 639-659.

14. Hirsch, "Processing Fads," p. 643.

15. James Collins, "Goodbye Already," in *Time*, May 18, 1998, pp. 82-86.

16. See, for example, Thomas Streeter's essay in this volume.

11

What Is an Advocacy Group, Anyway?

Thomas Streeter

The phenomenon of "advocacy groups" means different things to different people. To activists, advocacy groups are a part of political organizing, useful and perhaps necessary for protecting the rights of a minority group or marginalized interest against the entrenched powers of giant media corporations. To executives, the groups are perhaps annoying, but in any case an inevitable part of the complex terrain of the media business. To lawyers and policy experts, the groups raise all kinds of interesting procedural and technical issues about the appropriate boundaries between rights and responsibilities of stakeholders in this complicated area.

This chapter looks not at the differences among these perspectives, but at what they all share: the set of underlying assumptions from which the existence of such groups makes sense in the first place. What do we mean when we say "advocacy group"? How has it come to be the case that advocacy groups seem "practical," "inevitable," a part of the legal landscape? The answer is in part historical: collectively advocacy groups compose an institution that is peculiar to our time and can be explained in terms of the history of the relationship between business and government in the twentieth century. And the answer is also in part theoretical: advocacy groups, this chapter will argue, embody a particular theory or vision of politics and democracy. The chapter concludes that they are an important but circumscribed vehicle for democratic political action in the media field.

HOW SHOULD WE ORGANIZE CREATIVITY? THE STRUGGLE OVER GOVERNMENT/BUSINESS RELATIONS IN THE 20TH CENTURY

The romantic tale of the isolated artist writing the Great American Novel in a freezing garret, as popular as it is, has little to do with creativity in mass media today. Individual variations in experience, talent, and effort are of course crucial, but they do not occur in a vacuum. Mass mediated culture is generally created in structured collectivities or institutions and always in social contexts that profoundly condition its character. TV and film production is a matter of vast budgets, elaborate technologies, and highly coordinated efforts of large numbers of people. One of the enduring questions of artistic creativity in the modern world—*especially* if one wants to maximize individual freedoms to create—is, "How do we best organize the production of media content? Who should have control over what and in what institutional contexts?"

In the United States, the short answer to that question has almost always been "free enterprise" or "the market." But that short answer conceals more than it reveals. Markets are made, not born, and they can be made in many different ways with different implications and outcomes. So the key issue is not really whether or not to have markets, but how to organize and structure whatever markets we nurture into existence. The "market approach," in other words, is less a solution to the problem of organization than a series of questions: What is it exactly that will be bought and sold in the marketplace? What will be the character of ownership? What institutional structures will cultivate and regulate that ownership?

In answer to *these* questions, American mass media have generally turned to the institutional structure of the large, multi-unit, bureaucratic, for-profit corporation—a rather less politically popular entity than "free enterprise." For most of this century, the bulk of the control over radio, television, film, and, increasingly, newspaper and book publishing has been in the hands of a handful of oligopolistic corporations: networks, studios, and electronics manufacturing conglomerates, often in combination with one another. The corporations, to be sure, rarely control everything. They are typically surrounded by a periphery of smaller, nimbler, and less enduring businesses and individuals that supply much of the actual creativity: independent production houses, agents, free-lance writers, and the like. But (with a few interesting exceptions) the large corporations are the dominant gatekeepers: as a general rule, no screenplay will go anywhere without the approval of one or another corporate vice president at some point in the process.[1]

One of the key features of large corporations is that they have gotten into the habit of relying on government to coordinate and legitimate their activities. Corporations long ago discovered that good "public relations" were helpful for garnering favorable actions (or at least avoiding negative ones) on the part of legislatures and other public bodies. Government- and public relations departments are a standard feature of any large corporate bureaucracy. Public institutions and structures, with varying degrees of explicitness, thus are routinely called on to support private profit-making endeavors. In a country that calls itself a democracy, this raises an issue of legitimacy: any effort on the part of government to extend a helping hand to private interests requires some kind of consent or at least acquiescence from the polity at large. This fact is one of the sources of what Jurgen Habermas called "the legitimation crisis" of Western democracies.[2]

Advocacy groups basically have inserted themselves into the opening created by this "crisis" or condition. As long as the regulations, procedures, and venues are in place to allow the Time-Warners, RCAs, and Microsofts of the world to solicit positive press coverage, file petitions with the FCC, and lobby congressional subcommittees, the Action for Children's Televisions of the world will get in line alongside the rest of the lawyers and lobbyists, produce their own press releases, and file their own petitions. Advocacy groups have essentially jumped into the terrain created by corporate public- and government-relations departments, trying to nudge corporate activities in directions that reflect a group's agenda using the same or similar tactics.

The obvious example of how this relationship has developed is found in the realm of broadcast frequency regulation. The FCC exists basically because in the 1920s the then-fledgling broadcast radio industry faced a "chaos in the airwaves," in which stations were interfering with one another's frequencies. Here free enterprise had created a mess, not a market. The industry insisted that an agency be created by Congress in order to limit access to and stabilize behavior in the spectrum so as to allow for the spectrum's commercial exploitation.[3] The Radio Act of 1927 established such an agency and stipulated that stations must be licensed and operate in the "public interest, convenience, and necessity." At least a large part of the impulse behind the notoriously vague "public interest" clause of the Radio Act came from the fact that it was less politically awkward to throw small broadcasters off the air in the name of the "public interest" than it was to do so in the name of Westinghouse and RCA. But from the point of view of advocacy groups, once the public interest principle was enshrined in law to serve corporate interests, this created both legal and political opportunities: if large corporations can invoke government powers in the name of the public interest, then what is to stop advocates from using the same mechanism to address other popular nonmarket concerns, such as moral values or the well-being of children?

It is fashionable these days to argue that FCC broadcast regulation has become outmoded by a media diversity made possible by new technologies. Even if this is so, it remains the case that all of the major players in the industry continue to involve themselves with the government constantly. Whether the issue is export regulation, intellectual property laws, technological standards, or antitrust matters, the large corporations in the media business can not ignore the political arena. Nobody is closing their government relations office in Washington, and in some sectors (e.g., computers) the office staffs have been expanding dramatically of late.[4] It is safe to say that cultivating good relations with government has been standard business practice for most of this century and will continue to be well into the next.

Of course, given the fundamental ambivalence of the culture toward this system, intricate questions of legal standing, free speech, and proper procedure will continue to be posed; the law and policy experts will always have something to analyze. But there is really no question of *removing* government from business (libertarian assertions to the contrary notwithstanding); the only question is what the specifics of the interdependent relations between government and business will be. And as long as those interdependent relations exist, opportunities to bring nonbusiness concerns into the workings of the system will exist and undoubtedly be exploited.

LIMITS TO ADVOCACY GROUPS

One former activist (who has done some important and valuable work) once told me: "Revolution is just another interest group." The implicit assumption he was making is a common one: that the entire universe of political activity can be understood as a series of organized "interests," each using legal and procedural processes to get its way. The fact that advocacy groups are a pragmatic reality of our time, however, should not be taken as an inevitability; they are an accident of history, not a fact of nature. They should also not be mistaken for the whole of the political process. Yet in both some formal theory (often called "interest group theory") and in much commonsense wisdom, they are often taken to be the *only* "real" kind of political actors, taken as the *only* way in which interests and concerns are and could be expressed and acted upon. FCC officials regularly portray themselves as embattled arbiters struggling to find a moderate position between the extremes of various interest groups—as if they themselves were completely devoid of any political persuasion. Similarly, producers and network executives are fond of telling anecdotes about steering a middle course between conflicting criticisms from groups on the left and the right—thereby implying that their own position is the neutral or democratic one. In each case, they speak and act as if this *specific* set of interests and procedures was in fact the *totality* of possible concerns and forms of democratic action. Even advocates themselves at times speak as if they are the only ones doing anything "practical" to serve their cause, as if their like-minded friends who choose other less focused or long-term approaches are not doing anything at all.

The danger here is that description becomes prescription. Many people in positions of decision-making power seem to feel that if they grant an organized advocacy group a hearing and perhaps make minor adjustments to a policy now and then, they have then fully addressed "minority" issues. Send a few guidelines to the standards and practices department, add a V-chip here and a children's programming guideline there: all are heard, the argument goes, but nobody dominates, so democracy has been served. This line of thinking reifies a peculiar historical circumstance into a model of politics as a whole; the resulting impoverished idea of democracy then serves as an apology for existing relations of power.

But, of course, in this system not everyone is heard from, not all arguments are heard, and, even among those who do get a hearing, the power to influence the process is not evenly distributed. On the one hand, structural issues are not on the table. It is fairly obvious, for example, that a primary cause of gratuitous sex and violence in television is exclusive reliance on advertising support; compelling narratives can generate enthusiasm and sometimes large audiences, but they are high risk and less reliable at generating sizable ratings and advertising income than formulaic sex and violence. American TV is so often what Aaron Spelling called "cotton candy for the eyes" not because that is the *only* thing that audience members want, but because supplying this "candy" is a reliable way to draw enough audience attention to satisfy advertisers; it is a tried-and-true advertising package. There is considerable evidence that Americans are not entirely pleased with this arrangement: an industry-funded study showed that two thirds of Americans disapproved of funding Internet content with advertising, for example.[5] And one need only turn to European broadcast systems to see examples of the way that structural differences can generate differences in content (think of the regulated commercial programming of Britain's ITV or Channel 4, much less the BBC). Yet as a general rule questions of fundamental industry structure are not considered (or are shunted off into antitrust and technological discussions, where the content concerns of advocacy groups are considered secondary, if not irrelevant). Corporate structure itself—and thus the long-term imbalance of power that provides much of the motivation for the advocacy groups in the first place—is thus taken as a given. The discussion is limited in this way not because ordinary Americans are not interested in broader questions, but because the peculiar arena in which advocacy groups operate has been circumscribed by the broader goal of corporate organization for which the arena was originally created.[6]

A related limitation to advocacy group action is more subtle: the filtering process associated with administrative procedure. To advocates themselves, the process often seems like an obvious, practical way to enact one's ideals: instead of simply complaining about the content of the media, you organize a board of directors, rent an office, put on some nice shoes, and get to work. But the full-time advocate presenting a petition to a hearing examiner or holding a press conference is certainly not a direct or mechanical link to the complex concerns and dissatisfactions of the perhaps millions of scattered individuals he or she represents. The advocacy process is not direct democracy. Advocates are often selfless, dedicated idealists, but are also often skilled professionals, backed not so much by throngs of directly involved citizens as by mailing lists, subscriptions, and compelling arguments. They work not by simply relaying a fully formed message from the grass roots, but by translating perceived concerns and interests into a language and context that works inside the Beltway, the courts, and executive suites. That process of translation is subtle, complex, and very often immensely useful, but it is not neutral or transparent; it filters out some possibilities for expression and action at the same time that it enables others.

A classic and historically central example of this filtering process has recently been explored by Steven Classen in his forthcoming book, *Watching Jim Crow*, a study of events surrounding the successful campaign against the broadcast license renewal of racist WLBT-TV in Jackson, Mississippi in the 1960s. Classen's study departs from typical discussions of the case in that it grounds its analysis not in legal proceedings based in places like Washington, D.C., but in oral histories of African Americans in Jackson—the people the case was ostensibly about. Classen shows that, even though the case resulted in a substantial victory for the civil rights movement, the court documents and the activities of the lawyers and judges involved can hardly be understood as directly expressing the interests of the citizens of Jackson. Instead, social and political struggles involving race relations were translated and shoehorned into categories that fit the legal machinery of the time.

For example, to justify granting "standing" in license proceedings to an advocacy group representing African Americans (the United Church of Christ's Media Bureau), one could not argue directly on behalf of African Americans or discuss in detail the legacy of oppression under which they have suffered. Instead, the case had to be made on behalf of an abstraction called "consumer welfare," not citizens living in communities with a particular ethnicity and past, but a neutral, passive, statistical aggregate that was badly serviced in this particular market.

Similarly, the advocacy process involved disaggregating the campaign against WLBT's license renewal from the many other nonlegal cultural and political struggles of the time. The actual struggles in Jackson were multileveled, involving everything from boycotts to various forms of what Umberto Eco has called "semiotic guerrilla warfare." In the advocacy process, those struggles were distorted and reduced to a single, narrow plane. Government intervention was called for, the legal argument went, not because racism justified a redistribution of power over the media in Jackson, but because racism was *distorting* an imagined "normal" market relation between the station and its "consumers"; the "normal" market needed to be restored. This act of legal translation and reduction was key to legal success, but also had the effect of eclipsing the lived reality of the situation.[7]

Knowing how to frame one's arguments is a difficult task; it is part of the art of advocacy. Exactly which legal translation works varies from time to time and situation to situation. Classen suggests that the United Church of Christ's argument in the WLBT case, for example, gained some of its efficacy from the Ralph Nader-influenced consumer movement of the 1960s. But over the decades, certain general patterns emerge: most broadly, any advocacy group's argument has to be presented as consistent with the basic organizing principles and goals of for-profit corporate media. This does not preclude calls for government intervention in the name of the public interest, because the corporate world itself regularly relies on government intervention and justifies that intervention in the name of the public interest. But it does mean that, with the possible exception of urgent matters of public health (e.g., cigarette advertisements), one cannot explicitly call for, say, a reduction of corporate profit margins or for actions that would substantially reduce capital investments.[8]

The easiest tactic, then, is to try to argue that the desired policy is somehow congruent with one or another corporate goal. Appeals to "economic competition" are particularly powerful, in part because such an appeal can lead to alliances between advocacy groups and nondominant firms seeking to hobble their larger rivals. Restrictions on network power, such as the Prime Time Access Rule, were typically defended in this way, and even actions such as minority preferences for broadcast licenses gained some weight from the argument that they were congruent with economic competition. Similarly, since corporations regularly claim that they are desperately interested in "serving the consumer," it is often effective for advocacy groups to argue that their proposals further this purpose, as in the WLBT case, the (now defunct) Fairness Doctrine, and calls for more or better treatment of minorities.

The more difficult case to argue is when, as with quality children's television programming requirements, a proposed policy is likely to directly impinge, however slightly, on the corporate freedom to extract maximum profits. Describing the problem as a medical one (as is implied by the numerous studies of the negative effects of television on children and the even more numerous references to those studies in policy debates) seems to carry some rhetorical force here. But even this is a hard case to make. The principal remaining tactic is to argue that some form of market failure is present. In broadcasting, since the Supreme Court eliminated justifications of regulatory intervention based on economic concentration per se in *Miami Herald Publishing Co. v. Tornillo*, spectrum scarcity historically has been the principal form of market failure in the advocate's rhetorical arsenal.[9] The interesting thing about contemporary spectrum scarcity arguments is not that they are called into question by today's diversity of electronic media outlets, but that they remain in circulation at all. And if the previous analysis is correct, they remain in circulation because the corporate world, particularly over-the-air broadcasters, need a justification for regulatory intervention on their behalf, such as the assignment of digital television frequencies.

CONCLUSION

It is not wildly idealistic to envision a society in which the organization of the media is a matter subject to full, open, public debate. If sports fans can debate the fine points of team financing and understand the intricate relations between, say, players' salaries and stadium tax write-offs, television watchers can understand and debate the complexities of media organization, such as the common carrier model or the effect of redefining fair use in copyright. In the former case, however, citizens are given a chance: sports management issues are heavily reported in the sports pages and on the local evening news. Media management issues rarely make it out of the trade magazines (with the occasional exception of easily sensationalized issues such as pornography and censorship). When given the opportunity, ordinary citizens can care about more than the cost of their cable service. Public service systems in Europe (and to some extent in the United States) continue to weather the promarket onslaught against them to a large degree because of broad public support. And Classen's book shows how, in the context of the civil rights struggles of the 1960s, both the white and the black citizens of Jackson, Mississippi came to care deeply about the control and regulation of their local commercial television stations.

The simple persistence of advocacy groups through the deregulatory 1980s and the market-fanatic 1990s is ample evidence that many people in our society want to be more than mere consumers of the media, that there is genuine popular enthusiasm for democratic control of media organization. But the constraints that limit those same groups' actions are symptoms of the ways that our society tends to shy away from the open-endedness and uncertainty of real democratic politics and robust open debate. We have kept democracy hemmed in behind barriers of unequal wealth and professionalization, forcing it to run gauntlets of complex legal procedure and inside-the-beltway abstruseness.

Advocacy groups, in sum, need to be understood as a peculiar and attenuated variation on representative democracy characteristic of our corporate-centered age. This need not imply that advocacy groups are invariably engaged in a pact with the devil. Certainly, at least until other, more direct forms of citizen input into the organization of our media can develop, the advocacy process is absolutely necessary. But those of us with an interest in a more fully democratic media need to simultaneously keep in mind both what is and is not possible within the given framework. In the short term, advocacy groups are capable of having important, substantial impact. But because of conditions not of their own making, on their own they are not likely to generate serious public debate about structural alternatives to the current corporate-dominated, advertising-supported system.

NOTES

1. This and subsequent analysis of the role of the corporation in contemporary media is elaborated in Thomas Streeter, *Selling the Air: A Critique of the Policy of Commercial Broadcasting in the United States* (Chicago: University of Chicago Press, 1996).

2. Jürgen Habermas, *Legitimation Crisis* (Boston: Beacon Press, 1975).

3. The classic telling of this tale remains Erik Barnouw, *A Tower in Babel: A History of Broadcasting in the United States to 1933* (New York: Oxford, 1966). Also see Chapter 3 of Streeter, *Selling the Air*.

4. Most of the newer, microcomputer-related companies (including Microsoft) have opened government relations offices in Washington in the last three or four years. See Dan Carney, "Tech firm lobbyists scrape by sans limo; Dragged into D.C., industry," in *Austin American-Statesman*, August 17, 1997, p. H1. Relatedly, Jack Valenti recently objected to the *National Journal*'s methodology when it dropped him to No. 2 on its list of the highest-paid leaders of trade associations, which necessarily have interests in Washington. W. John Moore, "From The K Street Corridor," in *The National Journal* 29:40, October 4, 1997, p. 1976.

5. Addrienne Ward Fawcett, "Interactive Awareness Growing," in *Advertising Age*, October 16, 1996, p. 20, cited in Robert W. McChesney, *Corporate Media and the Threat to Democracy* (New York: Seven Stories Press, 1997), p. 46.

6. For a detailed discussion of the range of policy debate and the means by which it is circumscribed, see Streeter, *Selling the Air*, pp. 113-162.

7. Steven Douglas Classen, *Watching Jim Crow: The Struggles Over Mississippi Television, 1955-1969* (Duke University Press, forthcoming). See also "Southern Discomforts: The Racial Struggle Over Popular Television" in *The Revolution Wasn't Televised: Sixties Television and Social Conflict*, edited by Lynn Spigel and Michael Curtin (New York: Routledge, 1997); and "Standing on Unstable Grounds: A Reexamination of the WLBT-TV Case" in *Critical Studies in Mass Communication*, 11 (1), 73-91 (Spring 1994).

8. For an example of the former, see the "Blue Book" released by the FCC in the 1940s (FCC, "Public Service Responsibility of Broadcast Licensees") which frankly argued that broadcasters should forgo some profit and broadcast "sustained" programming; the Blue Book's proposals generated vociferous opposition and were thoroughly rejected. For an example of the latter, see John Kittross's proposal to completely redesign the American broadcast system in a way that would separate transmission from production and thereby effectively remove much of both the networks' and local broadcasters' power. Nowhere in legislation does it say that existing broadcasters have a right to government protection of their economic interests in the existing system of spectrum allocations, yet the proposal is known today in the policy arena only as an archetype of madcap impracticality. See John Kittross, "A Fair and Equitable Service Or, A Modest Proposal to Restructure American Television to Have All the Advantages of Cable and UHF Without Using Either," in *Federal Communications Bar Journal* 29: 1 (1976) pp. 91-116.

9. Miami Herald Publishing Co. v. Tornillo, 418 U.S. 241, 254 (1974).

12

Hostile and Cooperative Advocacy[1]

Gabriel Rossman

Sociology grounded in the Weberian school constructs ideal types of social phenomena and then assesses deviance of real cases from these ideal types as a means of analysis.[2] A Weberian ideal type need not represent the average of the empirical aggregate of a phenomenon, but rather it should exemplify that phenomenon and distinguish the traits that define it and grant it uniqueness. Once an ideal type is established, empirical examples can be contrasted with it, both showing the variety within a single phenomenon and testing the validity of the type.

Television advocacy groups are clearly a social phenomenon and thus are suitable for Weberian analysis. Much like Weber defined Western Europeans by two ideal types, the Roman Catholic and the Protestant, it is appropriate to define television advocacy groups by two ideal types, the hostile and the cooperative. Hostile groups are the dominant form, both historically and currently, though cooperative groups, a relatively recent innovation, have garnered some impressive successes.

In this essay I offer ideal types of offensive media portrayals, advocacy groups, and advocate tactics. I then attempt to explain whether the hostile or cooperative strategy is most effective, what the prerequisites are for using a strategy, and how groups come to choose a strategy. Finally, I examine how closely real groups adhere to the dichotomous ideal types.

Throughout this essay I will apply ethnographic data and content analyses gathered from a diverse set of advocacy groups. I gathered most of the ethnographic data during a six-month participant-observation study at the Los Angeles offices of the Gay and Lesbian Alliance Against Defamation (GLAAD).[3] I also have participant-observation data from considerably less extensive involvement with a conservative Christian group, and I interviewed representatives of several other groups by telephone.

The material for my content analysis is drawn from two sources. The first source of content is this book. The second source is composed of the publications—mostly Web sites, but also magazines, books, and newsletters—of the advocates themselves.

OFFENSIVE MEDIA CONTENT

Historically advocacy groups have arisen in reaction to media depictions that offend a certain identity group or element thereof. Advocates not only declare their offense at a portrayal, but also tend to explain why they take offense. Through the advocates' explanations it is possible to determine the ideal type of offensive portrayal a particular portrayal approximates. Note that this reliance on perception makes the nature and degree of offensiveness of any given media portrayal subjective. The offensive media portrayals can take three forms: the stigmatizing, the diminishing, and the poor role model.

The most obvious form of offensive portrayal is the stigmatizing. Advocates imagine that these media depictions will cause the balance of society to view the depicted identity group negatively. Examples of stigmatizing portrayals include depictions of an identity group's members as shiftless, incompetent, dangerous, immoral, or excessively alien to mainstream society. Advocates despise these portrayals because they fear that members of mainstream society will incorporate them into their social expectations of the depicted group.

GLAAD perceived portrayals of certain stereotypically gay characters and behaviors to be stigmatizing. For instance, GLAAD refused to include in its annual list of gay television characters a character in "Fantasy Island" that a public relations person at the network described as "not explicitly called gay, but you just know he is because of the way he acts." Members of GLAAD expressed to me that the public relations person's description probably meant the character was a stereotypical, limp-wristed, effeminate queen, which is a negative, or at least limiting, stereotype, and thus did not deserve to be endorsed. GLAAD singled out another, and even more obviously offensive, media portrayal in the film "There's Something About Mary." In the offending scene the protagonist literally stumbles upon several gay men having anonymous casual sex on the lawn of a highway rest stop. GLAAD recognizes that mainstream society is disgusted by promiscuity and so decried this portrayal, which associates homosexuality with casual public sex. However, it is notable that certain fairly innocuous stereotypes, such as the flamboyant queen, which in isolation would be considered offensive, are inoffensive or even laudable when shown alongside less stereotypical images. This is the case for "Will and Grace," a sitcom about a straight woman and two gay men, one "butch" and the other "flamboyant." This program is consistently praised by GLAAD for showing the diversity of American gay men.

The second type of offensive portrayal is the diminishing. A lack of portrayals can be offensive because advocates think this absence will diminish their respective identity groups' perceived presence in society.[4] Just as negative portrayals are imagined to stigmatize a group, positive or value-neutral portrayals are assumed to legitimate a group and make it seem less alien to other elements of society. Reference group theory posits that we see our personal experiences as a microcosm of society.[5] In a folk version of this theory advocacy groups believe that the public perceives television as depicting a microcosm of American society. Thus the perceived presence in American society of any identity group not depicted in television will be diminished, and the group will seem foreign, alien, or un-American to the mainstream.

In an instance where this seemingly amorphous complaint is directed at a tangible target, the Media Action Network for Asian Americans (MANAA) opposed a proposed remake of the television police drama "Hawaii FIVE-O" because the cast had disproportionately fewer Asians and Pacific Islanders than the state does in reality.[6] More often offense taken at a lack of media portrayals is broadly directed at the industry as a whole. For example, the Reverend Donald Wildmon, the head of the American Family Association (AFA), complained that the minimal attention given to religion in prime time television is not commensurate with religion's prominent place in American society.[7] Likewise, when I asked William Horn of GLAAD how television portrayals of homosexuals have changed over time, he focused on the general increase in frequency of portrayals, implying that for his constituency a lack of depictions was once, but is no longer, a serious problem.[8] Mr. Horn also said that the main effects of media portrayals of homosexuals are to "humanize" homosexuals to mainstream society and affirm the identities of homosexuals themselves, implying that a lack of media portrayals would do the opposite.

A third type of portrayal is composed of those media images that an advocate sees as promoting undesirable behaviors, ideas, or mental states among members of his or her group's constituency. This type can include portrayals that would fall within the previous two categories. Portrayals that are offensive as stigmatizing or diminishing will almost always also be considered negative role models by virtue of generating alienation and poor self-esteem for members of the identity group, if nothing else. However, portrayals deemed to be poor role models can include depictions not criticized on either of the previous two lines. There are two main forms of this, the child-corrupting and the assimilating. In the first case advocates believe a media depiction will model for children undesirable behaviors such as smoking, drug use, violence, cursing, or sexual conduct. The second case comes into play when a group is undergoing transition—usually assimilation into mainstream society—and the more conservative portion of the group is opposed to those depictions that would legitimate the transition. This last class is clearly distinct from stigmatizing portrayals since assimilationist content rarely stigmatizes a group to the mainstream, but rather makes it seem less alien.

The category of portrayals that advocates think provide poor role models for children is to a large extent a catchall. Whatever an advocate's pet peeve—especially if it is not directly related to identity—his or her opposition to the objectionable content can be justified on the basis that it will adversely affect children. This is especially true for opposition to sex, violence, and cursing on television. For example, Ted Baehr, a conservative Christian film critic who is opposed to seeing all three of these things in the mass media, entitled one of his books *The Media-Wise Family*.[9] Likewise, the American Family Association, a conservative Christian group with concerns similar to Mr. Baehr's, includes the word "family" in its very name, implying that it is opposed to loose morals on television for the sake of children. This does not mean that all children-based arguments take this form; for example, some advocates, like Action for Children's Television, focus their efforts on the educational content of children's programming and actively oppose attempts to sanitize television on behalf of children.[10]

Anti-assimilationist concerns are difficult to pin down because the advocates sometimes argue that portrayals that promote assimilation are stigmatizing portrayals. The Catholic League for Civil and Religious Rights is notable for this conceptual sleight-of-hand. The League often asserts that the programming it reacts to stigmatizes Catholics and Catholicism, but much of this programming is favored by liberal Catholics.[11] Indeed a priest created the now-cancelled drama "Nothing Sacred"—one of the programs most despised by the League. This suggests that the League's goal here is not to keep non-Catholics from thinking that the Church is overly strict on sexuality, but rather to keep Catholics from entertaining this notion and thus potentially attempting to change the Church or leaving it altogether—either of which would constitute assimilation into secular society. However, not all anti-assimilationist concerns are so ambiguous. Probably the most unabashed reaction to assimilationist content was when several rabbis organized against "Bridget Loves Bernie" because of its sympathetic portrayal of miscegenation.[12] Likewise, MANAA formed, in part, because its founders thought the media were conveying the message that "Asian women, in order to be accepted and to get ahead, should get white boyfriends."[13]

THE ADVOCATES THEMSELVES

Who are the advocates that are offended by these portrayals? Although it is not a logical necessity that the advocates be members of the identity groups they represent, they usually are. The exceptions are usually advocates who represent those who are not able to represent themselves, especially children. The prevalence of self-representation is explained by incentive. An individual has an interest in protecting his/her own group from defamation because by extension this protects that individual as well as his or her kin and probably many of his or her personal friends.

The notion of protecting one's own suggests not only that advocates will belong to the group they represent, but also that they will be those group members who identify most strongly with the group. As such, the membership of an advocacy group is by no means a representative sample of its constituent population. By virtue of their strong identification, members of advocacy groups are also more likely to cherish the distinctiveness of their group and therefore be more opposed to assimilation than other members of the identity group. By definition anti-assimilationist groups like the Catholic League differ from their constituency because they exclude that portion of their constituency that wants change, in this case socially liberal Catholics. Other groups can differ from their constituencies as well. MANAA was insulted when a radio station offered to ask its Asian American listeners if they were offended by broadcasts that MANAA didn't like.[14] The radio station seemed to assume—rightly or wrongly—that its Asian American listeners were less sensitive than members of MANAA. If the radio station was correct, it would show a discrepancy between MANAA and elements of its constituency.

Another difference between advocates and their constituencies stems from the fact that advocates often form coalitions with other advocacy groups representing other constituencies. Coalition building can either address immediately shared interests or function as a form of "reciprocal altruism."[15] The latter occurs when a group aids another group in whose cause it has no direct interest because it expects the latter group will reciprocate at a later time, and on balance each group will gain. The very act of coalition building can further distance an advocacy group from its constituency. Contrary to the rhetoric of academics and politicians interested in building multicultural coalitions, the world is not a dichotomy of mainstream insiders versus marginalized and dissenting voices. Reality is more accurately described as an infinite array of identity groups, many of which are suspicious of one another.[16] But advocates are very different from other members of their identity group, and as such they will routinely work with advocates representing constituencies for which much of their own constituency may hold antipathy. Thus members of an advocacy group, while drawn from the identity group they represent, will differ from that group in systematic and important ways.

STRATEGIES AND TACTICS

In military terminology there is a distinction between strategies and tactics. Strategies are broad and over-arching goals. Tactics are the specific and focused means to implement strategies. For example, consider General Tecumseh Sherman's famous march to the sea during the Civil War. General Sherman's strategy was to destroy the Confederacy's economy and infrastructure. His tactics included such means as freeing slaves, burning warehouses, and warping railroad lines.

Like armies, advocacy groups use strategies and tactics. However, it is in their strategies and tactics that hostile and cooperative groups differ dramatically. The hostile strategy is to express dismay with offensive media depictions and try to eliminate them. In contrast, the cooperative strategy is to proactively seek to reward desirable media portrayals with the intent that this will stimulate better portrayals in the future.

The hostile advocacy groups' strategy involves criticizing offensive media portrayals and punishing those responsible for them. Their strategy is to pressure for the withdrawal of ongoing media content from the market by embarrassing and financially harming the content's producer. Potentially they may use several antagonistic means to eliminate or mitigate offensive portrayals and skew the media toward their ideal. To implement their broad strategy of attacking offensive media portrayals, hostile groups use a variety of tactical moves, all of which reflect the group's negative orientation, including letter-writing campaigns, boycotts, meetings with advertisers and the media elite, legal action, and legislation.

The classic action of a hostile advocacy group is orchestrating a letter-writing or petition-gathering campaign. Writing letters and gathering signatures require very few resources and can be accomplished by groups of any size; indeed, disorganized individuals can spontaneously write letters. However, the low initial costs of letter writing and petition gathering do not preclude more sophisticated groups from using the tactic. Indeed, large organized groups may be more effective in orchestrating letter-writing campaigns than smaller groups and individuals because they can mobilize more people to write similar letters through such means as soliciting the letters in widely circulated publications, or even providing constituents with preprinted postcards. In this respect advocacy groups affiliated with larger groups have an advantage, for they can draw upon the whole group's membership to write letters or sign petitions. Note that this reflects the advocate's presupposition that sheer mass of correspondence contributes to the campaign's effectiveness. The Catholic League is an especially good example of an organization that uses petitioning and believes tonnage to be effective, as it collected a million signatures against "Nothing Sacred," 350,000 of them before the series' premiere.[17] Letter writing need not be aimed at the direct producer or distributor of media content, but can instead be aimed at the sponsors of objectionable programming, as is the case with the AFA's "Dirty Dozen" list of corporations that heavily advertise on objectionable programs.[18] Hostile letter writing and petitions can also occur on a local scale, and according to the national office of the Christian group with which I worked, can serve as a useful way of recruiting membership.

Another hostile tactic that relies on mass action is the boycott. In mass societies, where a typical product is purchased by millions of consumers, a boycott must have significant numbers of potential supporters to make an appreciable dent in a company's profits. This suggests two points. First, boycotts will often be coupled with letter-writing campaigns so that the subject corporation will reckon that activism, rather than mundane market forces, is the cause of diminished business. Second, only groups with massive membership and/or support can launch successful boycotts. For this reason, advocacy groups affiliated with broader groups may be more successful because they can tap into those groups' larger memberships. For media that the consumer pays to use, such as theatrically released movies, the boycott will usually be aimed at the offensive content itself. For free media, such as television and radio, the boycott includes the offensive content, but it usually encompasses some or all of the sponsors of the programming as well. Advertiser boycotts often produce exhaustive lists of products which the conscientious consumer is expected to avoid. Yet objectionable content may have dozens of corporate sponsors, each with hundreds of products, so the list of products to be boycotted can be quite large, making advertiser boycotts unwieldy. But actual diminution of profit can be secondary to embarrassment that the sponsor will suffer through being portrayed publicly as a purveyor of smut, racism, or some other unpleasantry.[19] An advertiser's desire to avoid this embarrassment may provide the real rationale for meeting an advocate's demands.

The most prominent current media boycott is the widespread conservative Christian boycott of Disney. The Catholic League started this boycott, which by way of the AFA subsequently spread to other Christian groups, including the Southern Baptist Convention. This boycott is attracting much more publicity and may well have an appreciably greater economic impact with the potential participation of 16,000,000 Southern Baptists rather than just the 500,000 subscribers to the *AFA Journal*. This shows the value of coalition building for mass-based tactics.

Boycotts and letters are private sector action, but hostile advocates also seek intercession of the state through both legal action and legislation. Legal action is used in a broad sense here and encompasses a variety of actions, including petitions to bureaucracies, civil suits, and criminal prosecution. One form of legal action used by hostile advocacy groups is filing a complaint with the Federal Communications Commission (FCC). Some of these complaints take the form of a petition to deny the renewal of a television station's broadcasting license on the grounds that it is not serving the "public interest."[20] The Catholic League filed a complaint with the FCC over the educational cartoon "Histeria's" portrayal of the Spanish Inquisition.[21] To express its offense at an allegedly sexually indecent commercial aired during the Super Bowl, the AFA filed a complaint against its local Fox affiliate with the FCC and urged subscribers to its e-mail list to do the same.[22]

Advocates also bring affirmative action suits against television stations before conventional courts or, until recently, the FCC.[23] Affirmative action suits do not directly impact media content, but they can potentially change the composition of media-producing entities to include advocacy group constituents, who presumably are more sensitive to the needs of their own in-group than are the white males who currently dominate the industry. Another advocacy group tactic is encouraging local officials to prosecute on obscenity charges those responsible for producing or distributing certain offensive content. Although network television is typically too subdued to approach the legal definition of obscenity, this tactic has been used against cable stations and is sometimes used to prosecute and intimidate the producers and distributors of music and movies.[24]

In addition to using lawsuits and petitions, many hostile advocates also lobby the state to enact legislation that will further the advocate's goals or facilitate the advocate's other tactics. The simplest actions a legislator or legislature can take on behalf of advocates are passing nonbinding resolutions condemning offensive content, using the bully pulpit, and conducting report-generating "investigations." Although these official actions have no direct coercive effect, they can lend tremendous moral support to advocates and, more ominously, deliver an implied threat of direct state intervention. One group that uses this lobbying tactic is the Parents' Television Council which works with Senator Joseph Lieberman to decry television sex and violence.[25] In another example, a coalition of black activists was able to convince the Los Angeles City Council to denounce the short-lived sit-com "The Secret Diary of Desmond Pfeiffer" on the grounds that its portrayal of the Civil War and slavery was insensitive.

Government content guidelines, although they are usually technically "voluntary," carry a great deal of weight and are usually followed by most broadcasters. Thus hostile advocates lobby both the FCC and Congress for the establishment of guidelines that will discourage offensive content. Broadcast requirements resemble content guidelines, but carry actual legal weight. Because they are arguably prior restraints, requirements are legally problematic, but their potential for legal enforcement makes them a desirable prize for hostile advocates.

Beyond using rhetoric to shape television, Senator Lieberman has pushed for legislation to create content guidelines. The senator was an enthusiastic supporter of the "V-chip" legislation, which encourages television networks to rate their programming so that parents who own the V-chip can block content they find objectionable. Likewise, Action for Children's Television successfully lobbied Congress for the creation of standards that mandate television stations to broadcast three hours of educational children's programming per week.[26]

The use of such vicious tactics as boycotts and lawsuits does not preclude hostile groups from actually meeting with representatives of the media elite to discuss their concerns. However, those meetings that do occur are typically antagonistic. When meeting with the media, hostile advocates tend to deliver concession-seeking ultimatums. Although an advocate may make arguments from morality, his or her speech typically contains many arguments from force. This stems largely from advocates' belief that the media elite are unsympathetic, immoral, and guided only by their own self-interests—especially financial interests.

Guy Aoki of MANAA has described his organization's meetings with several Los Angeles radio stations. At one meeting, Aoki's colleague, Daniel Mayeda, told the station to meet his demands or "there will be pain." At another meeting, MANAA distributed news clippings detailing its past tactics, implicitly threatening to use them again should they be unhappy with the meeting's results. It is likely that meetings between media representatives and hostile groups are not only less amicable than those with cooperative groups, but also less frequent. In several issues of the *American Family Association Journal* that I examined there was not a single mention of a meeting with the media. In contrast, GLAAD's Web site and print publications abound with accounts of such meetings.

The hostile strategy is not the only one available to advocates. Instead, they may use the cooperative strategy, which requires tactics based on rewarding the good and building relationships with the media rather than delivering threats and applying coercion. Cooperative tactics include letter-writing campaigns, awards, friendly meetings, free consulting, and promotion.

Letter writing requires few resources, and, like hostile letters, letters of praise can be written spontaneously by unaffiliated individuals. As with the letter-writing campaigns of hostile groups, mass of correspondence can help. But for cooperative groups a single letter may suffice, for the object is to appeal to the elite's sensibilities through flattering prose rather than to crush their resistance under a tide of signatures.

The GLAAD Monitoring & Response Committee, a group of unpaid volunteers, devotes itself almost entirely to writing appreciative letters to the media, thanking them for providing content that positively portrays homosexuals. Likewise, the staff at GLAAD routinely writes such letters, and every article in *GLAADAlert* ends with information on how to contact the media and express appreciation (or disdain).[27]

Awards are another form of praise available to advocates. [28] They award those specific media portrayals that are exemplary in reflecting the world in a way that is in sync with an advocacy group's ideology. This brings publicity to both the advocacy group and the desirable portrayal. Furthermore, awards may enhance the careers of those sympathetic members of the media who created the portrayals, creating an incentive for more of the same.[29] Ideally some media producers will create desirable content with the express purpose of receiving an award. Many groups give awards, including GLAAD, the NAACP, MANAA, and the Christian Film and Television Commission (through its subsidiary *Movieguide*).

A key tactic for cooperative advocates is the use of meetings. Cooperative groups will never use arguments from force in these meetings, but rather will rely on arguments appealing to morality and self-interest. In using moral arguments cooperative advocates attempt to get the media elite to sympathize with the advocates' constituencies. Arguments from self-interest are not threats, but rather an attempt to convince the media elite that, by creating desirable media portrayals, they will actually enhance their market position, usually by attracting the advocate's constituency as an audience. Neither of the two prongs in a cooperative advocate's spiel is hostile, and thus the media elite will not be placed on the defensive and view the meeting as a confrontation.

GLAAD fairly regularly meets with the media elite to discuss its concerns. Other groups meet with the media elite only rarely, if ever. It is notable that the production company for the film "Prince of Egypt," DreamWorks, actively sought the input of many religious advocacy groups, most of which rarely meet with the media on friendly terms.[30] That no group turned down DreamWorks' invitation suggests that the hostile/cooperative distinction is a function not only of the advocates' behavior but of the media's behavior as well.

The most proactive tactic a cooperative advocacy group can use is offering free consulting. The ideal for a cooperative advocacy group is to be the media elite's source for expert information concerning their constituency. Cooperative advocates want to ingratiate themselves with the media producers so that the producers will contact the advocates any time media content deals with issues that concern their constituency. In this way the advocates can take a proactive role in shaping all content issued from connected sources, thus eliminating all offensive portrayals and bolstering the number and quality of desirable portrayals.

GLAAD regularly distributes a guide to the media on how to handle lesbian, gay, bisexual, and transgender issues. This guide outlines and explains preferred language, stereotypes that GLAAD feels are inaccurate, and, of course, how to contact GLAAD for further information. Members of GLAAD believe that this approach is effective because ignorance rather than contempt is the source of most offensive content in the mainstream mass media. Beyond the printed guide, members of GLAAD make it a very high priority to speak with members of the media who seek their advice. For instance, several members of GLAAD leave pager numbers on their voice mailboxes with the express purpose of being instantly accessible to members of the media.

Another tactic cooperative advocates use is collaborating with the media elite to advertise, endorse, or promote a desirable portrayal. Usually this takes the form of a brief article in the advocacy group's publication, but it can also take the form of special screenings and local viewing parties. Because an advocacy group can only effectively promote something to its constituency, advocacy group promotion has a limited effect on the size of a media portrayal's exposure to the balance of society. There are two more important effects of promotion. First, promotion provides an incentive for the media to cooperate with advocates as the advocates deliver large portions of their constituencies as audiences. Second, promoting desirable content creates support for the advocacy group among its constituency, which takes promoted portrayals as evidence that the group is accomplishing something. Through promotion a constituency can also come to rely on its advocacy group as a resource for information about where to find affirming media.

An especially elaborate instance of promotion was GLAAD's "Coming Out With Ellen" campaign. At viewing parties constituents watched the "coming out" episode of "Ellen" together. Most groups, including GLAAD, MANAA, the AFA, and the Catholic League,[31] provide reviews of desirable media on their Web sites and/or in their print publications.[32] Ted Baehr, head of the Christian Film and Television Commission, takes promotion of desirable content to the limit by being a combination advocate and movie reviewer with his publication *Movieguide*, which ranks films not only by their entertainment value, but according to their "moral acceptability" as well. Although Baehr tends to see most of Hollywood as a sort of Babylon,[33] he is so serious about promoting desirable content that he publicly opposes the Disney boycott and continues to recommend Disney's children's films to his readers.[34] Although Baehr agrees with Disney's critics that much of the content produced by Miramax, Touchstone, and other subsidiaries of Disney is "evil," he argues that the media content carrying the brand name Disney is quite congruent with fundamentalist Christian morality. Therefore, he concludes that fundamentalists do themselves no favors by abstaining from one of the few acceptable sources of content that does exist.

CAUSES AND CONSEQUENCES OF THE DISTINCTION BETWEEN HOSTILE AND COOPERATIVE GROUPS

For a variety of empirical and conceptual reasons I will not evaluate how successful advocates have been in using each of these tactics. An empirical problem is that almost all of my data regarding hostile advocates are self-reported, coming either from articles in this book or from the advocates' publications. It is reasonable to assume that in self-selected and self-reported accounts advocates will focus on their successes and gloss over their failures. Moreover, a major conceptual quandary is inherent in determining whether a media campaign was a "success" or "failure." That is, one cannot be sure whether media advocacy was the cause of shifts in media content or the correlation between advocate activity and content change was merely coincidental. For example, the Catholic League claimed ABC's decision to not renew the drama "Nothing Sacred" as a success, but it is very doubtful that the League was responsible for the show's demise. The League did actively seek the cancellation of "Nothing Sacred," and the show was cancelled, thus creating prima facie evidence for successful advocacy. "Nothing Sacred" had abysmal ratings, however, and undoubtedly would have been cancelled without any action from the League. One could even argue that ABC kept the struggling program on the air as long as it did only to prove that they could not be bullied and thus that the League's protest actually *sustained* an offensive portrayal. Likewise, "Ellen" was cancelled when it had very low ratings, but also faced tremendous opposition from the American Family Association and other conservative groups. For "Ellen" and "Nothing Sacred" one cannot reasonably determine whether media advocacy was effective, useless, or even counterproductive. For these reasons I am not comfortable assessing the success of tactics or advocates.

Although I cannot accurately measure a group's success, it seems that, on the whole, cooperative groups tend to be more successful than hostile ones. This might be largely due to the fact that cooperative advocates provide the media with resources and demand little sacrifice in either financial cost or social honor. There seem to be two main reasons for the hostile advocates' poor results. The first is financial and the second is cultural.

Television content is extremely expensive to develop and produce. The media elite, like all rational actors, are reluctant to declare an investment a sunk cost and cut their losses. Because hostile advocates are often reactive, by the time they hear of and begin to attack a specific program, the media elite have usually invested substantial resources into developing, if not actually producing, the offensive product. For this reason the media elite are very reluctant to discard their investments by ceasing development of projects or, even worse, shelving finished products or lucrative franchises.

Aside from financial considerations, there are ideological and cultural reasons why the media elite are unresponsive to the demands of hostile advocates. Although detractors describe commercial television as the selling of eyeballs to advertisers, the media elite consider themselves to be creative individuals—if not artists—and place tremendous value on their freedom of expression. In their perception this freedom is compromised whenever anyone tells them what to do, be it the state or advocates. Thus the media elite, in defending their asserted right to creative freedom, are, on the basis of principle, skeptical of any demand relating to content. Moreover, like anyone else, they do not like being told what to do, especially by outsiders. The value placed on autonomy and creative freedom is so strong than any member of the media elite who does cede to advocate demands also may be viewed as spineless by his or her peers. Because of these financial and cultural factors, there will always be some conflict between hostile groups and the media elite.

In contrast to hostile groups, the overarching strategy of cooperative groups is to promote desired portrayals through amicable contact with the media elite. A corollary of this is that protests over offensive portrayals will be secondary, and, when they do occur, they will be subtle, civil, and nonthreatening so as to avoid alienating the media elite. At first glance there seems to be no conflict between praising the good and decrying the bad. But, in fact, hostile and cooperative strategies are largely mutually exclusive. One cannot simultaneously antagonize and cooperate with someone, for the recipient of antagonism will seldom be in a mood to cooperate. Because of this, groups tend to approximate one ideal type or the other.

If there actually is a discrepancy of success between cooperative and hostile advocacy groups, the question arises as to why the less successful form still exists. Why don't hostile groups adopt a cooperative strategy? Of course actors are not always rational, but this does not adequately account for the preserved discrepancy. Many groups are hostile because the media will not cooperate with them.

The cooperative advocate's relationship with the media elite requires a tremendous amount of trust and good will. This sort of relationship cannot be produced between just any actors. Only sympathetic groups will do. Given the homogeneity of media producers, this requires a certain type of advocate. Specifically it requires advocates who will be viewed sympathetically by a media elite that is, relative to the American population, very disproportionately white, male, rich, educated, politically Democratic, ethnically Ashkenazi Jewish, secular, and permissive on sexual matters.[35]

A powerful barrier to cooperation with the media elite is religiosity. The media elite, with its infrequent church attendance and liberal attitudes about sex, falls firmly into the secular camp in what has been described as the American culture wars between the "orthodox" and the "secular."[36] James D. Hunter describes America as being divided into two camps, and many major political battles, especially those involving sex, are the inevitable consequences of irreconcilable differences in the two groups' moralities. The "secular" camp considers individual freedom to be of paramount importance. The "orthodox" camp places ultimate value in traditional morality and the nuclear family. Since these two positions have radically different presuppositions, a compromise between them cannot be reached. Because the media are themselves secular, any group that advocates sexual morality grounded in traditional religion will tend to get an icier reception than groups with less traditional morality, such as homosexuals.

Race and ethnicity are less imposing barriers to cooperation with the media elite than religion. Although the media elite are themselves ethnically and racially homogenous, their views on race relations are more nuanced than their stark views on religion and sex. Although the media elite are loath to attribute black socioeconomic status to laziness (only 1% strongly agree) and most do not feel that black gains come at the expense of whites (97%), only 43% support preferential hiring for blacks.[37] This might suggest the media elite are tolerant, but unwilling to sacrifice their own prosperity and freedom for the benefit of out-groups. However, it could also signify that distrust for the ethnic other lurks beneath the surface. Almost 40% of the media elite fail to strongly disagree with the notions that blacks are shiftless and miscegenation is wrong. It is possible to interpret this as some form of media elite hostility to the ethnic other, but such hostility as may exist is definitely not as strong as the hostility the media elite holds for the religious right.

While the media elite's perspective on race seems to be somewhat ambivalent, their feelings on religion are strong and unambivalent in that they are actively opposed to conservative religious ideologies. These different levels of feeling suggest that the media elite's feelings toward various identity groups are not characterized by a strict dichotomy of sympathy versus disdain, but rather a trichotomy of sympathy versus ambivalence versus disdain. Groups closely aligned with the elite's ideology—such as homosexuals—receive sympathetic treatment. Those that the elite has no strong feelings for—such as various ethnic groups—receive ambivalent treatment. And those for whom the elite has active disdain—such as evangelical Christians—receive unsympathetic treatment. Because ambivalence is not a sufficiently strong feeling to prevent cooperation, the boundary between groups receiving sympathy and ambivalence is permeable; but disdained groups will remain so, barring radical change in the composition of the elite itself. Thus conservative religious advocates must inevitably be hostile, while groups representing other interests may be hostile or cooperative.

THE STRENGTH OF THE TYPES

Having described advocate tactics, it is now instructive to shift the unit of analysis from the tactic to the advocacy group to see how closely they adhere to my ideal types. Here I examine several media advocacy groups discussed elsewhere in this article to create a portrait of each group's tactics. Of course, no group perfectly embodied hostile or cooperative advocacy, but some very closely resembled one ideal type or the other.

The now defunct Action for Children's Television does not match either of my archetypes well, nor does it exactly fall between them. In fact, the group is quite unlike others in both its ends and means. Its unconventional modus operandi is largely due to the personality and philosophy of its founder, Peggy Charren. It should be noted that the group's unconventional behavior does not mean that it was unsuccessful. Arguably, ACT was among the most successful of advocacy groups; it won three lawsuits against the FCC in federal court[38] and is largely responsible for federal educational broadcasting requirements. ACT had a curious attitude toward state power. On the one hand, it was vehemently opposed to anything that resembled censorship or explicitly defined required content. On the other hand, it favored loose guidelines for broadcasters. Some tactics that ACT used fall under the hostile category (like FCC complaints), and others fall under the cooperative category (like giving awards). In short, ACT does not fit either of my ideal types even loosely.

The American Family Association appears to rely much more heavily on hostile than on cooperative tactics. The AFA frequently complains to broadcasters and advertisers, but does not seem to write complimentary letters to broadcasters (except when they yield to AFA threats). The AFA publishes long lists of offensive programs with explanations of why it found them offensive, and, to a lesser extent, positive programs and explanations as to why they are admirable. The AFA is well known for its high-profile boycotts, including its current boycott of Disney. The AFA also works with politicians, appearing 12 times in the Congressional Record for 1997-98. The AFA is a fairly close approximation of the hostile ideal type.

The Gay and Lesbian Alliance Against Defamation uses all of the cooperative tactics in my typology: letter writing, awards, cooperative promotion, friendly meetings, and free consulting. With the exception of the occasional critical letter and suggestion to constituents to write critical letters, GLAAD does not use hostile tactics. Although GLAAD does endorse legislation, the legislation does not impact the media, but rather regards other issues, such as gay marriage and hate crimes. Overall, GLAAD very closely resembles the cooperative ideal type.

The Catholic League for Civil and Religious Rights, which represents the interests of traditional Roman Catholics, is a nearly perfect example of a hostile media group, and consciously so. Its communications director told me that the League's purpose is to combat anti-Catholic discrimination, and it leaves praising pro-Catholic media content to others. The group uses letters, boycotts, and complaints to the FCC, although it tries to use the last two sparingly. Its sole departure from my idealization of a hostile group is that it does not encourage broadcasting regulations and generally tries to avoid involving the state, although it does occasionally contact the FCC. Reflecting its focus on the negative, the League publicly praises media in only two cases. The League will commend a media entity when it prints a retraction or apologizes for an offensive portrayal. It will also recommend positive media content that is truly exceptional, such as "The Prince of Egypt," a film that positively portrayed Judeo-Christian beliefs and whose creators contacted the League for advice while in production.

The Media Action Network for Asian Americans is an essentially hostile organization, although it does use some cooperative tactics. MANAA uses boycotts and hostile meetings with the media. It also gives awards and endorses desirable media, but these cooperative acts are secondary to MANAA's overall strategy of intimidating media producers who make offensive content.

The Christian Film and Television Commission (CFTVC), a conservative Christian group that publishes *Movieguide*, a magazine about the movies, very closely adheres to my description of a cooperative group. In fact the CFTC used the cooperative tactics of recommending desirable media to constituents, writing complimentary letters to the media elite, giving awards to desirable media portrayals, and holding friendly meetings with the media elite. With one exception it did not use any hostile tactics. The exception is that the CFTVC supports strong government broadcasting guidelines.[39] Overall, the CFTVC considers itself to be an "information service" and describes itself as a "ministry" that is about "focusing on the positive."

CONCLUSION

We have seen that although most advocacy groups combine both cooperative and hostile tactics, with the exception of ACT they tend to gravitate toward one pole or the other. Ideal typologies need not be perfect dichotomies; indeed,

Weber believed there were intermediaries (e.g., Anglicans) between the seemingly stark dichotomy of Protestants and Catholics.[40] Likewise, the fact that no advocate is perfectly cooperative or perfectly hostile does not dismiss the utility or validity of my typology. The fairly strong clustering about each pole, despite the existence of a continuum, is enough to support the typology.

While the data support my ideal typology of media advocacy groups, they also refute my suggestion that conservative groups will always be hostile. Given the secularism and sexually permissive attitudes of the media elite, we would expect it to be impossible for conservative advocates to behave cooperatively. My expectation that conservative Christian groups will always be hostile is clearly refuted by the existence of the CFTVC, which cooperates with the media but has a conservative ideology.

However, my analysis has not empirically assessed how effective different strategies, tactics, advocates, or campaigns are. Although I have demonstrated that a group's strategy is not necessarily contingent on its ideology, I have not shown what the *best* strategy is for each ideological orientation. That is to say, religious conservatives may be able to advocate cooperatively, but we do not yet know if they can do it successfully. To draw an analogy in the world of engineering, one can build an airplane with flapping wings, but it will not necessarily fly very well.

If we assume the world is peopled with rational actors, then each advocate will use tactics that are most effective in realizing his or her goals, given his or her situation. This is only an assumption, however, and our daily experience tells us that people often act irrationally. I leave it for future research to resolve the question of whether advocates' strategies optimally match their respective situations or whether it is possible for them to behave more effectively by changing strategies.

NOTES

1. The author would like to thank Ivan Szelenyi of Yale University for his extensive guidance on this paper when both he and the author were at the UCLA Department of Sociology.

2. Max Weber, " 'Objectivity' in Social Science and Social Policy," in *The Methodology of the Social Sciences*, translated by Edward A. Shils and Henry A. Finch (Glencoe, IL: Free Press, 1949), pp. 90-108.

3. Although it is standard procedure for ethnographers to disguise the identities of their informants, I felt this was unfeasible to do with GLAAD given the unique role of this organization. Fortunately, GLAAD has generously consented for me to identify it.

4. A dearth of portrayals is an amorphous target for criticism since one cannot seriously criticize a particular program for not portraying everything. One is instead forced to criticize television in general. The lack of specificity inherent in taking issue with a dearth of portrayals makes this a problem that is difficult for advocates to deal with. Gabriel Rossman, "In Response to Don Wildmon," in Michael Suman, ed., *Religion and Prime Time Television* (Westport, CT: Praeger, 1997).

5. Jonathan Kelley and M. D. R. Evans, "Class and Class Conflict in Six Western Nations," *American Sociological Review* 60 (April 1995), pp. 157-78.

6. Guy Aoki, "Strategies of the Media Action Network for Asian-Americans," in

Michael Suman and Gabriel Rossman, eds., *Advocacy Groups and the Entertainment Industry* (Westport, CT: Praeger, 2000).

7. Don Wildmon, "It Is Time to End Religious Bigotry," in Michael Suman, ed., *Religion and Prime Time Television* (Westport, CT: Praeger, 1997).

8. William Horn, "The Proactive Strategy of GLAAD," in Michael Suman and Gabriel Rossman, eds., *Advocacy Groups and the Entertainment Industry* (Westport, CT: Praeger, 2000).

9. Ted Baehr, *The Media-Wise Family* (Colorado Springs, CO: Chariot Victor, 1998).

10. ACT founder Peggy Charren takes a civil libertarian approach to media content. In her essay in this book she says that "too often children are used as an excuse for banning speech" and "being subjected to what some consider offensive is the price we pay for free speech." Peggy Charren, "Principles for Effective Advocacy from the Founder of Action for Children's Television" in Michael Suman and Gabriel Rossman, eds., *Advocacy Groups and the Entertainment Industry* (Westport, CT: Praeger, 2000). Mrs. Charren's organization has even gone so far as to sue the FCC in the D.C. Circuit Court for its attempts to sanitize speech on behalf of children in ACT v. FCC. ACT's rhetoric and action present a striking contrast to Ted Baehr, who writes that, in addition to media restraint and parental guidance, society needs "government enforcement of laws against obscene and indecent broadcasts." Ted Baehr, *The Media-Wise Family*, p. 164.

11. Although the League frequently attacked "Nothing Sacred" as anti-Catholic in its press releases, it took a more nuanced view in its annual report. The 1997 report says that "Nothing Sacred" is not "anti-Catholic in the usual sense of the term," but offensive because it promotes the objectionable idea that "dissident Catholics are better Catholics than loyal Catholics." That the League opposed the show for favoring dissident Catholicism clearly shows that the League regarded "Nothing Sacred" as likely to cause Catholics to assimilate into secular society rather than stigmatize Catholics. William Donohue, "Executive Summary," in *Catholic League's 1997 Report on Anti-Catholicism* (http://www.catholicleague.org/report97.htm).

12. Curiously, two popular current programs, "Dharma and Greg" and "The X-Files," feature mixed Jewish and Gentile couples and have not met the same high-profile ire as "Bridget Loves Bernie" did, although intermarriage remains a salient issue to Jews. This may well be because the Jewish characters in these shows are only ethnically, rather than religiously, Jewish. Dharma, as her name suggests, is a lotus Jew, i.e., an ethnic Jew who practices an Eastern religion. Likewise, agent Fox Mulder of "The X-Files" is an agnostic—and a possible romantic relationship with his Catholic partner is suspended in a perpetual purgatory of sexual tension anyway. However, it is interesting to note that neither Dharma's Eastern religion nor agent Mulder's agnosticism has spurred Jewish anti-assimilationist concern.

13. Guy Aoki, "Strategies of the Media Action Network for Asian Americans," in Michael Suman and Gabriel Rossman, eds., *Advocacy Groups and the Entertainment Industry* (Westport, CT: Praeger, 2000).

14. Ibid.

15. A basic explanation of reciprocal altruism can be found in Steven Pinker, *The Way the Mind Works* (NY: W.W. Norton & Co., 1997), pp. 402-406 and pp. 502-509.

16. Public opinion polls show that ethnic minorities typically have lower opinions of each other than whites do of them. National Conference on Christians and Jews, *Taking America's Pulse: The National Conference Survey on Intergroup Relations*, pp. 6-11. Cited in: Dinesh D'Souza, *The End of Racism* (New York: Free Press, 1995).

17. Catholic League, Press Release (November 20, 1997): "Petition Drive Against Disney Hits Million Mark." (http://www.catholicleague.org/ 97Press%20Releases/ pr04.htm).

18. "Pfizer, MCI, Glaxo Wellcome Top Sponsors of TV Trash," *American Family Association Journal*, October 1998, p. 5.

19. Kevin Kelleher, "Hip! Hip! Hooray! Anyone Remember Who We're Boycotting Today?" *Salon,* August 7, 1998, http://www.salon.com/ money/feature/1998/08/ 07feature.html.

20. Rex S. Heinke & Michelle H. Tremain, "Influencing Media Content Through the Legal System: A Less Than Perfect Solution for Advocacy Groups," in Michael Suman and Gabriel Rossman, eds., *Advocacy Groups and the Entertainment Industry* (Westport, CT: Praeger, 2000).

21. "FCC Contacted Over 'Histeria,' " *Catalyst*, December 1998.

22. Buddy Smith, "Personal Fouls: Reflections on a Not-So-Super Bowl," *AFA Action Alert* (email listserv), February 5, 1999.

23. The D.C. Circuit Court of Appeals recently prohibited the FCC from requiring licensees to have affirmative action policies in Lutheran Church-Missouri Synod v. Federal Communications Commission, Dkt. No. 971116A (D.C. Cir. April 14, 1998). An obvious caveat to this tactic is that it can be used only by advocates representing those constituencies that directly benefit from affirmative action, such as women and blacks.

24. In the summer of 1997 there was a widespread campaign led by conservative Christian groups in the United States and Canada to prevent the rock star Marilyn Manson from performing live at publicly owned concert venues on the grounds that his performance was legally obscene. Neil Strauss, "R-Rated Rock Concerts? Marilyn Manson and Mom?" *The New York Times*, December 1, 1997. Also in 1997 a local conservative Christian group convinced the Oklahoma City authorities to seize copies of the film "Tin Drum" from video retailers on the grounds that the film is obscene. Robert Butler, " 'The Tin Drum' is back—and beating loudly," *Kansas City Star*, July 18, 1997.

25. Joseph Lieberman, Press Release (March 12, 1998): "Lieberman Welcomes FCC Action Ushering in the Era of the V-Chip and Greater Parental Control of Television Viewing by Children." (http://www.senate.gov/member/ct/lieberman/general/ r031298b.html).

26. Ironically, Action for Children's Television has also opposed legislation hostile to the media's freedom, going so far as to sue the FCC three times over the issue. Action for Children's Television v. FCC, 852 F.2d 1332 (D.C. Cir. 1988). Action for Children's Television v. FCC, 932 F.2d 1504 (D.C. Cir. 1991). Action for Children's Television v. FCC, ___ F.3d ___, Dkt. No. 93-1092 (D.C. Cir. June 30, 1995) (en banc).

27. The fact that GLAAD encourages its constituents to write both positive and negative letters shows that their behavior is neither entirely hostile nor cooperative.

28. Other groups actively reject granting awards. William Donohue of the Catholic League says his group does not "go around here awarding people for not offending us." "League Targets 'Catholic-bashing,' " Associated Press article for April 19, 1998.

29. Robert Pekurny, "Advocacy Groups in the Age of Audience Fragmentation: Thoughts on a New Strategy," in Michael Suman and Gabriel Rossman, eds., *Advocacy Groups and the Entertainment Industry* (Westport, CT: Praeger, 2000).

30. Teresa Watanabe, "An Ecumenical 'Prince of Egypt,' " *Los Angeles Times*, December 12, 1998.

31. Examples for each group can be found on the Internet and/or in print: "The MANAA Video Guide," http://janet.org/~manaa/video_guide.html; "Gay Teen Angst Hits Capside High," *GLAADAlert* (http://www.glaad.org/ glaad/alert/990211/02.html); "The Good Stuff," *AFA Journal*, 2/17/99, p. 17; "Catholics Should Support 'The Prince of Egypt,' " Press Release: December 14, 1998 (http://www.catholicleague.org/ 98Press%20Releases/pr0498.html).

32. While some groups, such as GLAAD, are just as, if not more, enthusiastic about promoting content as they are about denouncing it, other groups, such as the Catholic

League, are much quicker to criticize than to praise. For example, the League vehemently criticized "The Practice" for showing a priest break the confessional seal. But the League failed to take notice when a few months later the same program showed a priest courageously refusing to exonerate himself by breaking the confessional seal to reveal the true perpetrator of a murder he was suspected of committing. The propensity of many advocates to criticize more than praise may be because most advocates rely on complaints from constituents rather than directly monitoring the media.

33. The mean moral acceptability score for 19 films reviewed on Baehr's Web site was 3.8 out of a possible 8. In Baehr's terminology this ranking means "caution." Of the films in my sample only one, the animated biblical epic "The Prince of Egypt," received the highest possible score, "exemplary." Likewise, only one, the teen horror film "The Faculty," received the worst possible rating, "evil." Ted Baehr, "Recent Films," *Movieguide* (downloaded January 21, 1999) (http://movieguide.crosswalk.com/ccn/movieguide.nsf/web+views/view_recent).

To obtain the mean score for films I converted Baehr's eight-level ordinal text ranking to a ratio variable ranging from 1 to 8. I then calculated the mean of this ratio variable and found it to be 3.8, which roughly corresponds to the fourth rank from the bottom on Baehr's scale, "caution."

34. John Dart, "Southern Baptist Delegates OK Disney Boycott," *Los Angeles Times,* June 19, 1997. (Also note that in November 1999 *Movieguide* had a very favorable review of the Disney film "Toy Story 2.")

35. Although this portrayal resembles a crude stereotype, it only reflects the extreme homogeneity of television elites. According to a respected, albeit somewhat dated, study: 99% are white, 98% are male, 63% earned over $200,000 a year in 1981, 75% are college graduates, about 75% vote for the Democratic candidate in a typical election, 59% were raised in Jewish homes, only 7% regularly attend worship services, and 51% condone adultery. Linda S. Lichter, S. Robert Lichter, and Stanley Rothman, "Hollywood and America: The Odd Couple," in *Public Opinion* (January 1983), pp. 54-58.

Anecdotal evidence suggests that in two decades the media elite has grown more demographically and religiously heterogeneous, both through recruitment (of women, minorities, and religious Christians) and revival (of secular Jews to active religious participation). Michael Medved, "Hollywood Makes Room for Religion," in Michael Suman, ed., *Religion and Prime Time Television* (Westport, CT: Praeger, 1997).

However, other anecdotal evidence suggests that the media elite is still largely secular. A personal anecdote is illustrative. I recently attended a lunch meeting of a politically conservative organization of Hollywood insiders. Despite the fact that many in attendance were Jews, including the group's founders, the meal (with no offered alternative) was chicken Kiev, a dish that mixes dairy products and meat and thus is not kosher. This suggests that even among politically conservative members of the Hollywood elite, religion is still not very strongly observed, if at all.

Recent survey data also suggest that while media producers are increasingly heterogeneous they are still much more secular and liberal than other Americans: 25% say attending religious services is important in contrast to the 82% who say eating right and exercising is important, 68% say they do not base their values on religion, only 17% support school prayer, 91% support legal abortion, 88% support sex education in public schools, 91% condone premarital sex, only 16% identify as politically conservative while 52% identify as liberal, only 17% are Republicans while 61% are Democrats, 71% attend church twice a year or less, and the respondents were four times as likely as respondents to the General Social Survey (1993) to say they do not believe in God. Unpublished survey data collected by the UCLA Center for Communication Policy in 1995. Unfortunately this survey is not directly comparable with the Lichter et al. sample, as the more recent sample is not drawn exclusively from the media elite but from media professionals, a somewhat larger group.

36. Hunter, James Davison, *Culture Wars: The Struggle to Define America* (New York: BasicBooks, 1991).

37. Lichter et al., "Hollywood ..."

38. ACT v. FCC I, II, and III.

39. Ted Baehr, *The Media-Wise Family*, p. 164.

40. Max Weber, trans. Talcott Parsons, *The Protestant Work Ethic and the Spirit of Capitalism* (New York: Scribner, 1958).

13

Advocacy Groups in the Age of Audience Fragmentation: Thoughts on a New Strategy

Robert Pekurny

During the past 20 years there have been major changes on the media horizon which have altered the economic structure and cultural impact of electronic media. A new environment has been created by a huge surge in the number of independent TV stations; the creation of the fourth, fifth, and sixth broadcast networks; the rapid adoption of VCRs; the even more rapid spread of direct satellite dishes; and the broad penetration of cable with its myriad basic and pay services. Yet, while the days of three major networks attracting 90% of prime time viewers are gone, many media advocacy groups employ the same strategies they used in those bygone days, days when the networks still constituted the core of their parent corporations.

This chapter will examine this new media ecosystem and suggest a new strategy which could increase the chances of media advocacy groups to achieve their goals.

PAST STRATEGIES: THE BOYCOTT OR THREAT THEREOF

One of the two major strategies employed by advocacy groups has been the threat of a boycott of advertisers who sponsor specific controversial shows and/or of the broadcast/media entity itself. Groups have leveled these threats through letter-writing campaigns and press conferences and at annual conventions. The latest wrinkle has been to cross-boycott a conglomerate, as evidenced by the Southern Baptist Convention's threat to boycott Disney/ABC because of allegedly pro-gay and anti-Christian broadcast programming content and the company's same-sex domestic partners policy. The Convention has aimed its boycott not only at the company's media operations, but also at its theme parks, merchandise, and other enterprises.

These threats have lost whatever power they may have once had for several reasons. First, most of the threats have failed to pan out. Second, there has been a significant increase in number of both advocacy groups and media outlets. Messages can not be as effectively delivered as there are too many voices making threats and so many media outlets that it is hard to reach them all. Third, the threat of economic loss has been minimized to acceptable levels due to audience fragmentation.

In regard to the third point, in today's electronic media environment, the fragmented audience is composed of people who have already self-selected themselves to watch or not watch certain potentially controversial programs. Threats to vote against a program by ceasing to be part of its audience are often made by those who are not or are perceived by the media entity under attack to have never been a part of the program's audience. Indeed, some classic cases of attacks (George Carlin's Seven Dirty Words on WBAI radio and the "Married with Children" dustup) were initiated by people who were channel surfing and not regular viewers or listeners. Thus, the actual loss of audience members who can be sold to advertisers is often negligible.

Recently a Tampa, Florida advertising executive said that "he wouldn't be surprised" if businesses in that area, which "tend to be a little more traditional . . ., had doubts about advertising on 'Ellen,' " but admitted that "he doesn't buy locally for 'Ellen' " because the show attracts too youthful a demographic.[1] Meanwhile, the promotion manager at Tampa's ABC affiliate admits that some local advertisers have refused to place spots on "Ellen," but that the situation is no worse than it was for "NYPD Blue." "Our ad time is always still sold out . . . it's not like we're having trouble selling it."[2]

Moreover, "Eisner and Associates, a Baltimore-based advertising agency, found that only three percent of 1,000 adults polled the week before Ellen's April 30th 'coming out' episode . . . would be less likely to buy products from advertisers who support the show."[3] And, " 'Those who would have a problem with companies advertising . . . aren't watching the show,' says David Blum, vice president of strategic planning for Eisner. 'Those that advertise only get the benefits, because the people watching are disposed to thinking well of advertisers supporting the show.' "[4]

Indeed, boycotts can be counterproductive. "Married with Children's" ratings grew significantly as a result of Michigan housewife Terry Rakolta's much publicized boycott campaign against the show. More recently, "Ellen's" ratings peaked with the coming out episode when "(m)ore than 36 million people tuned in . . . exceeding the average audience for television's top-rated programs, 'ER' and 'Seinfeld.' Ratings stayed above average the next two weeks, exceeding 16 million viewers."[5] "In October, after the new TV season began, 'Ellen' averaged 15.3 million viewers a week. . . . The show's ratings have declined rapidly since then. During calendar-year 1998, 'Ellen' has drawn 10.6 million viewers a week, giving up 5.5 million people or 34%" of its lead-in's audience."[6] The first burst of controversy and threats of boycotts apparently gave a major boost to the series' ratings.

On a corporate level, Disney, whose Touchstone studio produces "Ellen" and whose ABC network airs it, has felt little effect from boycotts. Disney is currently being boycotted or petitioned by the following groups (with membership figures and area of dispute indicated where available):

- Southern Baptist Convention (15.7 million members): upset by Disney's gay-friendly

policies for gay partners of employees and its "rejection" of family values
- Concerned Women of America (500,000 members): doesn't like Disney's depiction of such curvy, seductive female characters as Pocahontas
- King for America (conservative group led by niece of Martin Luther King Jr.): upset by Disney's "anti-family themes"
- The Assemblies of God (1.4 million members): wants Disney to "return to the values that strengthen and build this nation"
- The American-Arab Anti-Discrimination Committee upset by the portrayal of Arabs in Disney movies such as "GI Jane" and "Kazaam"
- The Catholic League (350,000 members): conducted a petition drive to get ABC to drop "Nothing Sacred" and boycotted Miramax in 1995 over the film "Priest"
- American Family Association (circulates a magazine to 400,000 people): boycotting over Disney's policy on domestic partners' benefits
- National Federation of the Blind (50,000 members): petitioned Disney to stop production of the movie "Mr. Magoo"

Also recently considering boycotts of Disney were Catholics United for the Faith, Coral Ridge Ministries in Fort Lauderdale, Presbyterian Churches of America, and the Family Research Council.[7]

According to Richard Land, president of the Southern Baptist Convention's Christian Life Commission, the Convention's boycott has met with overwhelming approval. Moreover, he said that "Disney is going to find out just how many regiments and just how many divisions of Godly people Southern Baptists have."[8] Yet, according to a recent survey, "[a]mong Baptists who said their views are represented by the Southern Baptist Convention, 15.8% said they strongly agreed with the boycott and 14.3% said they agreed with the boycott. But 28.7% said they strongly disagreed with it and 26.7% said they disagreed with it."[9]

And the effect of these boycotts on Disney? "Disney and ABC said . . . that boycotts were having no impact; Disney's 4th-quarter earnings for [the] period ending Dec. 31 were up 18% to $755 million on [a] 6% revenue increase to $6.34 billion."[10] Disney Chairman Michael Eisner said that the Southern Baptist boycott "hasn't had any financial impact."[11] This despite the claims of Richard Land of the SBC, who said that Disney will eventually pay attention because "Southern Baptists are . . . heavily disproportionate users of Disney items. Think about who's looking for family-oriented entertainment. Compared to the regular population they're more married, have children more and have intact families more. So this is the heart and soul of the Disney customer base in revolt."[12]

If a threatened boycott of 15.7 million members of the heart and soul of Disney's customer base has no effect, what threat can any other advocacy group convincingly make? Experience would indicate that media programmers have little reason to fear loss of audience or revenues as a result of boycotts or threats thereof.

GOVERNMENT INTERVENTION AND REGULATION OF PROGRAM CONTENT

Since the inception of television as a mass medium, there have periodically been government hearings and threats of intervention. The two major areas of controversy over the decades have been sex and violence in programming and most particularly their potential effect on children. Government hearings have often been spurred by advocacy groups, sometimes by national events such as the 1968 assassinations, and, at other times, some think, to give politicians a soap box. These hearings have usually amounted to nothing more than saber-rattling, that is, threatening the governmental regulation of program content, either through some unspecified program standards or through nonrenewal of broadcast licenses. The usual outcome has been that broadcasters merely modify their self-regulation, for example, by crackdowns on violence or introduction of the Family Viewing Hour.[13] This has been enough to head off dreaded government intervention which, in those rare instances when it has occurred (e.g., safe harbor regulations for television), has usually been struck down by the courts.

This pattern, however, changed in recent years when Congress and the President, pressured by advocacy groups, were not satisfied with the media's self-regulation of violent content. This led to the adoption of program advisory ratings by most cable and broadcast networks, as well as legislation mandating the V-chip so that parents can block programs carrying a rating of which they do not approve.

Nevertheless, NBC, the current leader in the ratings, has thus far refused to go along with the same ratings system used by all the other broadcast television networks. Despite thinly veiled threats from members of Congress and from the advocacy groups that lobbied for the advisory system and V-chip, NBC has not changed its position and has not suffered any economic consequences. Indeed, NBC recently reported a record profit of over $1 billion, up 22 % from the previous year.[14] It seems as though NBC's decision about how to replace "Seinfeld" will have more effect on its future than any actions by the government or advocacy groups.

In short, even government action to regulate content has lost its impact on at least one major media entity.

WHY NEW STRATEGIES ARE NEEDED

So the boycott and government-intervention strategies no longer work, if they ever did. As discussed above, this, in part, is related to the fact that audiences have become specialized and self-selected. Audiences today are also usually smaller than audiences of old. There are only a few programs on television today that command the truly mass audience 30 shares (as measured by the Nielsen rating system) of yesteryear, and these seem immune to the boycott strategy due to either their popularity or their program content.

Moreover, media organizations have become more broadly based. Each of the major networks and most of the major studios are owned by corporations with international holdings in a wide range of entertainment and nonentertainment entities. Just as the audiences for individual programs have become smaller and therefore less important to a media organization's bottom line, so has the fragmentation of these corporations' interests become so extreme that one unit's fate, for example, a broadcast network's, no longer accounts for as large a part of that corporation's total revenues, profits, and assets. Moreover, if you are offended by ABC's programming, maybe you will watch a program on another network which is produced by Disney. Or maybe you will watch sports on ESPN, also owned by Disney. Or perhaps you will watch a video or pay-per-view of a Disney product or the Disney Channel. Are you unhappy with Time Warner's TBS? Maybe you will watch CNN or read *Time* magazine or see a Warner Brothers movie on video or at a theater. A disgruntled viewer will have to work hard to avoid any of the media outlets of NBC/GE, Disney/ABC, Viacom, and Time-Warner.

Another reason new strategies are needed is that media corporations have two audiences beyond the one they sell to advertisers. First, they have their stockholders. As the stock market has zoomed to new record levels, media organizations have had to compete with other corporations for investors' dollars. "Hollywood stocks, after coming to life in 1997 following years as laggards, outperformed the broad market in the first quarter [of 1998] amid the continued run of the nearly eight-year bull market."[15] As the bottom line has become all important, being able to point to higher revenues and profits, despite multiple, simultaneous boycotts, assuages investors and allows corporate executives to continue doing what they deem best for their companies.

Another audience that may at times have greater influence than the viewing or subscribing audience is the creative community. As the number of media outlets and the number of hours of content needed have proliferated, media organizations have had to pay increasingly higher fees to increasingly less experienced creative personnel. Media organizations need to meet and exceed one another's bids not only in terms of dollars but also in terms of other tangible and intangible matters.

Thus, Disney's granting of health benefits to same-sex partners, the target of several of the boycotts listed above, was a business decision made by the corporation. Other entertainment companies had long before granted these benefits. Disney found itself at a competitive disadvantage by lagging in this area. While advocacy groups threatened boycotts, Disney had to weigh whether its corporate policies, which did not include same-sex benefits, would one day be responsible for it not attracting or keeping on board creative personnel who might create its next hit sit-com or compose the score for its next animated musical. The possibility of losing some Southern Baptists at its theme parks must have been viewed as an acceptable risk when compared to losing the creative force behind its next big television or film hit.

Furthermore, studio and network support for "Ellen's" lesbian story lines or "Nothing Sacred's" frank take on religious issues does not go unnoticed in the creative community. A studio or network that will schedule and support such programs is one that is more likely to attract writing and producing talent than an organization that is viewed as closed to new ideas or quick to drop a series at the first sign of controversy. Indeed, when NBC was third in the ratings, programmer Brandon Tartikoff was asked at an industry luncheon why a program creator should come to NBC first. After joking, "[b]ecause we have plenty of free parking," he pointed out that his network had stood behind quality, cutting-edge, and controversial programming, giving it a chance to grow and find its audience.

Michael Eisner, in a letter accompanying Disney's annual report, stated, "In each of our divisions . . . we seek to be in business with the best and most creative people we can find. . . . We then try to give them freedom to do their best work. We try not to censor them, and I will always defend the right of the talented artists who work for us to push the limits of their imagination."[16]

Having the first shot at the best creators and their ideas is something each studio and network wants. In this light, keeping a show like "Nothing Sacred" can help a network. Standing up to the threat of a boycott can actually benefit a company's bottom line.

Given that media organizations are ignoring boycotts and governmental threats and, in so doing, are in part demonstrating to their stockholders and the creative community that commercially viable visions will be nurtured and protected, new strategies are needed if individuals or groups wish to change the content of the media.

NEW STRATEGIES IN THE NEW WORLD

Given the above arguments, I propose that advocacy groups abandon threats of boycotts, as well as mass letter-writing campaigns to media corporations, advertisers, and the government. Instead, I suggest the use of specific, targeted, individual or small-group efforts that concentrate on positive approaches and rewards for those who produce programming.

Just as the large media organizations have realized that their fortunes lie in attracting and cultivating the individuals who actually create television programs and feature films, so must advocacy groups realize that it is at this "creative grassroots" level of producers and writers that they must focus their efforts.

In television, the writer-producer is king. It is the "show runner," the highest-ranking writer-producer, who sets the overall tone and makes specific decisions about casting, dialogue, stories, and other matters.

Writers pride themselves on being thoughtful and the brightest people in the creative process. However true this may or may not be, advocacy groups need to deal with this self-perception. And rather than rejecting outright what writers and producers create, such groups must learn of the processes, values, pressures, and reward structures involved in the creation of programming. Advocates must demonstrate an understanding and appreciation of the challenges creators face to show that they warrant admission to the marketplace of ideas in the production process.[17]

Once "at the writing table," advocates need to educate creators about the issue at hand, never forgetting that in most cases the issue they are presenting is only one in a constellation creators face each day. Advocates need to steer away from absolutes as much as possible, realizing that the creative process is a subjective one. While they seek to raise creators' awareness of the issue at hand, advocates also need to appeal to the creators' sense of taste, appropriateness, and what is most dramatically or comedically effective. They should not seek to supplant the subjective judgments of the creators. All of this should be done in the name of effecting the changes in content the advocates seek.

These suggestions can be successfully implemented. In fact, they have been in many ways over the years.

In the 1960s NBC stars Johnny Carson and Dean Martin regularly made "Bruce" jokes in which the person so named was gay. Two mothers, writing individually to the network, asked if the network and, by extension, the stars were aware of the angst they caused their young sons, named Bruce, in grade school each day. With the power of this argument the network convinced the stars to drop the Bruce jokes, though they kept doing "gay" jokes by using "hairdresser" as the new code word. It would take more years and societal change for a major reduction of this category of joke in general.[18]

On a personal experience level, I have several times, as a member of a situation comedy's writing staff, argued for changes in what I felt were antisocial jokes or lines. While working on "Happy Days," on several occasions I agreed with the staff that the joke in question was funny. But I would then ask if anyone at the table minded, for example, that thousands of young kids who wear dental braces would feel hurt when they heard Fonzie say a particular line. Bringing the matter down to the level of an individual viewer's response—a response many of the writers who were parents could empathize with—led to changes in the lines in question.

While working on another series, I pointed out that we were repeatedly writing jokes about people shooting each other with guns. In one instance, the fact that the most recently created joke was to be delivered by a character belonging to a racial minority added to my argument that perhaps we should spend five minutes to see if we could come up with a different category of joke. This was suggested not because we feared letters of protest, but because I thought we had gotten lazy creatively—and by using a joke that was not the most socially beneficial. Moreover, we could come up with something different if we just spent a few extra minutes. Taking this as a creative challenge, we changed the joke and broke free from the "gun joke" pattern.

While conducting a study of the production process of "Saturday Night Live," I observed a rehearsal at which Dan Aykroyd said that he had problems with a joke about a retarded person because he had a brother with that condition. Guilt-stricken, the writer immediately changed the line, in part because the potential effect of his joke on an individual viewer had been brought home to him. (I later asked Aykroyd if he really had a brother who was retarded and he told me that he did not. But he knew, he said, that this would be the most effective way of changing a joke he did not like.)[19]

Thus, specific comments about how a specific joke, topic, or issue might cause problems for a reasonable individual viewing the program for entertainment purposes seem to be very effective. Along these lines, advocates for change also need to be aware that under the pressure of production deadlines writers might be able to address specific problems in a focused manner, but have neither the time nor the inclination to ponder big social agendas. Arguing about masses of generic, unspecified viewers whose faces and lives the writer cannot conjure up in his or her mind will have less effect than painting a picture of one individual reacting as a human being. Writers create specific characters in defined settings reacting individually. When advocates can frame their arguments in regard to viewers along these same lines, their chances of success are greatly enhanced. As the writing community ages, more of the creators are also parents who are sensitive to the possible negative effects of media content on children. Potentially, advocates and creators could communicate effectively on a concerned-parent-to-concerned-parent level.

As for the appropriate forum for such a dialogue, advocates could meet face-to-face the writers of a specific program. Here an advocate would do well to contact people who are below the "show runners," but who are still writer-producers. Such people, whose names can be read off of a show's credits, are not the ones who receive network and studio notes and therefore are less likely to be burned out by "nonwriters" telling them how to do their job. In addition, they tend to receive less mail and other attention and are more likely to agree to meet with an advocate or respond to a well-written letter. A request for a meeting over lunch, which requires only a limited time commitment from the writer-producers, is most likely to receive a positive response.

Advocacy groups can also conduct workshops and seminars or send out mailings to the Writers Guild of America membership. In addition, especially useful for writers are contact numbers and persons who can quickly supply answers to specific questions. These numbers can be included in the WGA's monthly magazine *Written By* or on the Guild's Web page.

Advocates can also provide positive reinforcement via an awards or other honors event that recognizes programs that distinguish themselves in the advocates' eyes. Writers and producers like awards and honors for purely human, ego-driven reasons. Beyond that, beginning staff writers may find that an award from a given organization will allow their agent to negotiate a better deal for them on the current or a different series. Any distinction that will allow an agent to set her or his client apart from the pack is valued. As pointed out earlier, the increased need for programming for the expanded number of media outlets has compressed the time it takes to go from "beginning writer" to "show runner." Thus, an award to a beginning writer this year may give him or her a boost to the position of show runner for years to come.

Such awards have in the past led writers, who have to come up with 22 specific stories a year, to pitch ideas, characters, and stories they might not have otherwise put into the creative mix, leading to many "special episodes" of series that have addressed various social and medical issues. It would therefore seem that spending a few thousand dollars for publicity and a plaque as means of positive reinforcement could be worthwhile.

CONCLUSIONS

An argument was made that advocacy groups with negative agendas of boycotts, letter-writing campaigns, and threats of government intervention greatly reduce, if not completely destroy, their chances of achieving the changes in media content they seek. This has been true historically and is even the case in the present age of audience fragmentation and the vertical and horizontal expansion of media corporations. The mega-corporations of this new generation are virtually too large and diversified to even worry about advocacy groups or even governmental threats.

What these new mega-corporations do value is the creative personnel who produce the content for their many channels. As these writer-producers become increasingly valuable to media corporations, it is these people who actually create the content who must be engaged by advocacy groups if they wish to change program content. What has proven historically effective is presenting to these writer-producers well reasoned arguments, including those seasoned with "seat of the pants" logic and individual, personal experiences.

If advocacy groups, social scientists, or media policy experts wish to change program content, they will find their time, money, and efforts most effectively spent by appealing to individual writer-producers' senses of taste and responsibility. Advocates and others should express their experiences and concerns, but then respect the creative community's experience, talent, and ability to incorporate useful input in future program content. It is these members of the creative community who will produce future program content, not advocacy groups, researchers, or government officials. As bothersome as that fact may be, the recognition of it will make everyone's best efforts more effective.

NOTES

1. " 'Ellen' on Hiatus, but Controversy Isn't," in *St. Petersburg Times*, March 11, 1998, p. 1D.

2. " 'Ellen' on Hiatus."

3. " 'Ellen' on Hiatus."

4. " 'Ellen' on Hiatus."

5. "Ratings, Not Sexuality, Steer Future of 'Ellen,' " in *Los Angeles Times*, March 11, 1998, Section F, page 1.

6. "Ratings, Not Sexuality."

7. "Sex, Violence, Religion Unite Diverse Groups Against Disney," in *Orlando Sentinel*, August 31, 1997, p. A1.

8. *Television Digest*, Notebook Section, June 23, 1997.

9. "Most Baptists Disagree with Denomination's Disney Boycott," in *San Diego Union-Tribune*, October 24, 1997, p. E-5.

10. *Communications Daily*, Mass Media Section, March 31, 1998.

11. *Television Digest*, Notebook Section, November 24, 1997.

12. "Disney in Their Sights," in *Dallas Morning News*, October 25, 1997, p. 1G.

13. Robert G. Pekurny, "Broadcast Self-Regulation: A Participant-Observation Study of the National Broadcasting Company's Broadcast Standards Department," Ph.D. dissertation (Minneapolis: University of Minnesota, 1977).

14. "NBC Boosts GE," in *Television Digest*, January 26, 1998.

15. "Hollywood Stocks Score a First-quarter Bull's-eye," in *Hollywood Reporter*, April 1, 1998, p. 1.

16. "Eisner Takes on Critics in Letter to Shareholders," in *Orlando Sentinel*, January 6, 1998, p. B6.

17. For an overview of the organizational factors at play here, I refer readers to Robert Pekurny, "Coping with Television Production," in James S. Ettema and D. Charles Whitney, eds., *Individuals in Mass Media Organizations: Creativity and Constraint* (Beverly Hills: Sage Publications, 1982).

18. Pekurny, "Broadcast Self-Regulation."

19. Robert G. Pekurny, "The Production Process and Environment of NBC's 'Saturday Night Live,' " in *Journal of Broadcasting* 24 (Winter 1980), pp. 91-99.

14

Interest Groups and Public Debate

Michael Suman

Interest groups are a vital component of our democratic system. They wield influence in many realms of society, including those of the arts and entertainment. The chapters in this volume outline many contributions interest groups have made in relation to the world of television. In both television and beyond, many interest groups have played a key role in educating and informing the American public about significant issues, and in doing so they have served to stimulate important public debate. Unfortunately, the influence of interest groups is not always positive. Today there is evidence that some of these groups stifle, prevent, and distort public debate of significant issues, rather than encourage it. Add this to the fact that powerful economic forces discourage open debate in our society, and you have cause for concern.

That interest groups are having negative effects on debate is evident outside the realm of the mass media. For example, museums are now subjected to an unprecedented amount of scrutiny and pressure from interest groups. Many groups now insist on exerting their influence at the earliest stages of planning a show, and more and more are successful at getting their points of view incorporated. Some have even been successful at closing a show altogether. The Library of Congress hastily dismantled an exhibition about the architecture of slave quarters because of complaints by African Americans that some of the images presented of slaves and slave quarters were offensive. The Smithsonian drastically altered an exhibit on the Enola Gay and the bombing of Hiroshima after receiving complaints from groups of military veterans such as the American Legion. The groups were upset that the Japanese were shown as victims and that the bomb was not credited with ending the war. The result was a bland commemoration, devoid of interpretation so as to avoid any possible offense. Clothing industry lobbyists objected to another Smithsonian exhibit, this one on the history of sweatshops, because it featured a model of a sweatshop in which clothing, as opposed to some other type of product, was produced. Similar activities are evident in the realm of theater. A recent example involved the Catholic League for Religious and Civil Rights' campaign against the initially unseen and unfinished Terrence McNally play "Corpus Christi" because the play follows a group of gay men who reenact Christ's spiritual journey. After failing to get the author to amend his script, the League raged against its opening through news releases, pickets, and demonstrations.

In the realm of television, the focus of this book, some of these debate-quashing interest groups have been especially active. For example, last season the National Puerto Rican Coalition and the Hispanic Association on Corporate Responsibility angrily objected to a "racist" episode of "Seinfeld" in which a Puerto Rican flag was accidentally set on fire by one of the show's bumbling characters, Kramer. The Coalition demanded nothing short of a total apology during the following week's episode for this "unconscionable insult" to the Puerto Rican community. In another example, Mexican American groups objected to the presence of a talking Chihuahua on Taco Bell commercials. The Tampa chapter of the League of United Latin American Citizens, among others, urged Hispanics to boycott Taco Bell for its "criminal insensitivity."[1] Last season, prominent African Americans and even the Los Angeles City Council denounced the short-lived sit-com "The Secret Diary of Desmond Pfeiffer" because it featured a black character in the context of slavery times. The city council, fearing that the show could "fan racial discord," unanimously passed a resolution directing the Los Angeles Human Rights Commission to investigate it. The Beverly Hills-Hollywood branch of the NAACP marched on the show's producer and broadcaster, Paramount, to protest the show's alleged trivialization of slavery. The groups demanded nothing short of immediately pulling the show off the air. And a number of interest groups, including the Coalition Against Black Exploitation, have protested and called for a national boycott of the Fox animated series "The PJs," a comedy about an inner-city housing project. Activist Najee Ali complained that the show is "very unbalanced" and "is offensive to anyone who has lived in the projects, in poverty, or has had an alcohol or drug problem." The opponents have demanded that Fox pull the show and rework it into a more positive look at life in inner-city projects. In response, Fox released a statement that referred to its belief that "the true measure of any show lies in its ability to raise important cultural issues rather than avoid them."[2]

Unfair and stereotypical portrayals do still appear on television and elsewhere, and groups protesting them certainly have some legitimate complaints. But at times it appears that some of these protesting groups are being a bit thin-skinned. And many of them seem to believe that they alone know how the matters which they hold dear should be presented and portrayed. When these groups are successful at wielding influence, significant debate may, in some cases, actually be curtailed.

Groups are certainly free to protest anything they want. We have a First Amendment in this country that guarantees us freedom of speech. But as with any right, it can be used wisely or it can be abused. When any particular group is upset at a portrayal, the ideal solution to the problem would be to debate the issue at hand, bringing out all sides of the matter to the degree that this is possible. Get your grievance out in the open and let's all talk about it. Sadly, many, if not most, interest groups are not interested in this solution. For example, those protesting "The Secret Diary of Desmond Pfeiffer" seemed to have no interest in discussing the issue of setting comedies in tragic historical periods, which could have included, in regard to the Nazi era, dissections of the BBC miniseries "Genghis Cohen," the Italian film "Life Is Beautiful," and the television sit-com "Hogan's Heroes." Similar discussions could have included references to the Bolshevik-era comedies "Children of the Revolution" and Mel Brooks' "The Twelve Chairs"; the sit-com "F-Troop" and the film "Little Big Man," both set in the era of the attempted genocide of American Indians; and the Korean war movie and sit-com "M*A*S*H." Instead, nothing was acceptable to the protestors but immediately pulling the show. Jesse Jackson demanded that the show be taken "off the air." Danny Blakewell, head of the Brotherhood Crusade, announced that he and his allies would "not allow any comedic characterizations that trivialize our suffering and pain, distorts (sic) and exploits (sic) our history and denigrates (sic) the bones of our ancestors."[3] They were not interested in talking; they merely wanted capitulation to their demands.

This absolutist, debate-quashing stance seems to be part of a larger tenet held by many of these groups that no one should ever be allowed to offend any group, racial, ethnic, religious, or other, in any way. And never should a group's collective beliefs or its members' behaviors be subject to criticism, either. This is actually part of the cultural environment of what has been labeled "identity politics," according to which individuals relate to each other as members of competing groups, defined by social categories such as race, religion, gender, and sexual orientation.[4] In the competition it is strategically advantageous to be designated as victimized or disadvantaged, so group members are always on the lookout for opportunities to be so designated.

This raises some important questions. In this environment, will anyone in television be so bold as to take artistic chances that may rile some advocacy group ready to pounce on what may be defined as a victimizing portrayal? And if not, what type of fare will fill our television screens? Brian Lowry addressed these issues in a recent *Los Angeles Times* article in which he posed the following question: "Could 'All in the Family,' rightfully heralded as one of the best sit-coms ever, find a place on network television in the hypersensitive 90s, when everything of a topical nature seems to offend somebody?"[5] He argues that one result of writers avoiding the headaches involved with tackling issues that could offend some identity group might be the pervasiveness of innocuous sexual humor on television. Writers turn to sex jokes because they are not as likely to alienate any particular group. These jokes do upset some organized groups, particularly those of the religious right, but this is outweighed by the fact that at the same time these jokes appeal to the youth audience in which advertisers, and thus the media industries, are so interested. The result is that many important issues go begging and the audience gets a lot of cheap sex jokes. What we end up with is nothing but a formula for pabulum, with the only social controversy involved being an assault to the religious right's Puritanical sensibilities.

In this age of identity politics a related corollary to the offend-no-one idea is the belief that if one is offended, one should respond with all available legal force. Thereby debate can be cut off as quickly as possible, hopefully even before it begins, through the means of demonstration, vigorous denunciation, pickets, and even occupation.

The lengths to which interest groups will go to quash debate were illustrated recently when the conservative Claremont Institute and the National Association for Research and Therapy of Homosexuality set out to hold a conference in Los Angeles titled, "Making Sense of Homosexuality." The National Association contends that homosexuality is a developmental disorder that can be cured. Civic leaders, such as Joe Hicks, executive director of the Los Angeles Human Relations Commission, denounced the conference, and advocates bombarded the Beverly Hilton, the site of the conference, with hundreds of protest calls. In response, the hotel dropped the event. The morning after the hotel bailed out, all 15 members of the Los Angeles City Council signed a resolution condemning the conference. Subsequently, the conference organizers tried to rent space in another hotel, the Biltmore, for the occasion. In response, State Assembly Speaker Pro Tem Sheila Kuehl said that she would have a discussion with Art Torres, chairman of the California Democratic Party, about the possibility of canceling some post-election victory parties scheduled to be held at the Biltmore. So much for the right of free expression of those who wanted to host the conference. So much for an open debate on homosexuality.

Ideally, matters of public importance should be subject to a full airing of all sides of the issue at hand. Then, after hearing all viewpoints, the public can make informed decisions on the matter. But all too often today, interest groups are jumping in to pull the plug on debate before it can really get started.

The Catholic League entered the arena of public debate when it vigorously criticized the ABC dramatic series "Nothing Sacred," which chronicled the life of a priest in an inner-city parish. It began its opposition before the show was even on the air. The League contended that the show portrayed traditional Catholicism in a very bad light and was ultimately anti-Catholic. According to the League the series was "nothing more than a political statement against the Catholic Church. The goal is to put a positive spin on Catholic priests who prefer Hollywood's libertine vision of sexuality to the moral teachings of the Church. This propaganda is fodder for dissenting Catholics and anti-Catholic bigots alike." This "sick look at priests" is "an insult to most Catholics." Everyone should have supported the Catholic League in exercising its right to make these criticisms of the show. Unfortunately, the League was not satisfied with just adding its voice to a public debate. In fact, it attempted to silence the voice of the show's creators by pressuring Disney and ABC to pull the program, principally through a boycott campaign of the program's corporate advertisers. The League was initially successful in scaring away some of the show's sponsors. Nine of the original 14 national advertisers, including Kmart, Isuzu, Sears, Weight Watchers, and Red Lobster, withdrew in the first few weeks. If the League disagreed with "Nothing Sacred's" take on Catholicism it definitely should have made this public as part of an ongoing debate which would be healthy not only for the arts, but also for society in general. The League should also support mass media and artistic portrayals from its own perspective. (In fact, this may be preferable to using negotiations, threats, or other means to get one's own point of view included in a given presentation, which can result in a mishmash of watered down positions.) But here, as is all too common with interest groups today, the League ultimately chose to try to stifle debate rather than promote it.[6]

As one can see from the aforementioned examples, this cautious, debate-quashing cultural climate is fostered by groups of every stripe and ideological predisposition. And, again, often these groups feel that they are the only ones whose opinion counts when it comes to issues regarding their group and its interests. Howard Rosenberg of the *Los Angeles Times* wrote a column arguing that the UPN sit-com "The Secret Diary of Desmond Pfeiffer" was not racist. A reader responded with a letter to the editor. "By what authority or experience does Rosenberg presume to define what constitutes racism for many in the African American community? . . [W]e are the ones who claim both the right and the responsibility to cite racism when we experience it. . . . So Rosenberg should understand that it is racist because African Americans say it is racist, because many African Americans experience it as racist. Period!"[7] Do certain groups own exclusive rights to portrayals of their members and the historical periods in which they have suffered? Can the judgments of advocacy group members never be questioned by outsiders? What about debate and discussion?

Furthermore, how far is the game of victimization to go? Can an outsider never suggest that the accusers are being unreasonable? In this light, is every criticism of a member of a racial minority racism? Is every criticism of the Catholic Church anti-Catholicism?

In part the tendency to offend no one has been fostered in America by an increasing tolerance of differences in belief, creed, and lifestyle over the last several generations. In 1924 when the entire high school population of Middletown was interviewed for the now famous study conducted by the Lynds, 94% agreed with the statement that "Christianity is the one true religion and all people should be converted to it." When the same statement was presented to a comparable population over half a century later only 38% agreed.[8] This tolerance, which has replaced knee-jerk dismissals of other beliefs and opinions, is fostered, in part, by the fact that the United States has increasingly become a more diverse society. But we might also ask if it is possible that this tolerance is, in some cases, interfering with critical evaluation and reasoned judgment.

The current climate I have been discussing has no doubt led to a good deal of self-censorship and prevented our public debate from being as robust as it might be. But does this mean that television, the focus of this book, has become a sterile wasteland, so incredibly bland as not to offend anybody?

Women claw and hit and throw chairs at one another on the "Jerry Springer Show." Mentally disabled people compete in a "Frankenstein beauty contest" on CBS's "Howard Stern's Radio Show." Primary school children swear like sailors and engage a piece of talking excrement on "South Park." A high school teacher has an affair with one of her students on "Dawson's Creek." Ally McBeal salivates over a well-endowed nude male model. Teenagers talk about anal and oral sex on MTV's "Loveline." There certainly does seem to be a lot of offending going on as television routinely delves into areas that would have been unthinkable just a few years ago.

In terms of censorship, self- or otherwise, this is certainly not the worst of times. In the 1950s there were black lists and standards and practices departments that did not let Lucy say that she was "pregnant" with little Ricky or allow Rob and Laura Petrie to sleep in the same bed. Much of this simply reflects changes in society—changes that many interest groups bemoan. These changes have also been going on for some time as reflected in earlier shows such as "All in the Family," "Maude," and "Soap." The explicitly covered Clinton sex scandal is only the most recent and blatant example of the changing standards.

Beyond the changing culture, economics must always be considered the major causal factor when analyzing television content. Economic factors play into the equation of what programming will end up on the screen in a number of ways. Ultimately CBS did not allow the middle-aged Mary Richards on the "Mary Tyler Moore Show" to be divorced, not because they were afraid of getting on the wrong side of Catholic interest groups, but because they believed that such a portrayal would have driven away numerous viewers who found the idea of divorce to be scandalous. What most determines what ends up on television is the bottom line. And going too far in terms of violence, sexual content, political messages, or other controversial content can, if it drives away viewers, limit a show's financial prospects. But financial pressures can work the opposite way as well. In the increasingly competitive television market there is pressure to present subject matter that is different or risque or edgy in order to stand out in the crowd. Not only are there so many more television channels—with Fox, UPN, the WB and the 200 or so cable services—but there are also so many more media in general. And as for competition on television, cable, which is subject to less government regulation, has long taken the position that its programming can be more risque because viewers must sign up for the service and know what to expect. So broadcast television has changed, in part, to compete.

The changes in television content have been fought tooth-and-nail by interest groups. The American Family Association decried and organized boycotts in reaction to Billy Crystal's recurring homosexual character in "Soap" and David Caruso's bare behind in "NYPD Blue." But the juggernaut toward the more risque and revealing continues relatively unabated. And paradoxically, "successes" by the interest groups attempting to control television content may even prove counterproductive. The new television labels, which advocates hoped would stanch the flood of television raunch and titillation and will soon be used in conjunction with the much vaunted V-chip, may actually serve as an invitation for producers to make more envelope-pushing material. Comedy Central places a TV-MA rating on "South Park" and is secure in believing that it has acted responsibly, even if millions of young kids are watching the program. Pressing matters in the same direction, advertisers are increasingly not worried about cutting-edge material slapped with a variety of labels because it attracts the young adult demographic in which they are most interested. Moreover, one cannot deny that this type of programming will freeze the thumb of the increasingly restless channel-surfer. What young man can breeze by the slightly pixelated stripper on the Springer or Stern shows?

But does this move toward cheap sex jokes and titillation really represent television's move toward fostering an open and robust debate of important and significant social issues? Obviously not. This subject matter is routinely trivial, superficial, and devoid of any meaningful substance.

Interest group pressure opposed to this programming can be ignored because these shows are very profitable. But the networks' defiance of angry interest groups disappears when the subject matter at issue is not so economically promising.

When subject matter does have potential for threatening the bottom line, we can still expect television to bring out the muzzle. And this seems to be the case especially with controversial points of view in regard to politics, religion, or social issues. Ironically, it is these very issues that are most significant and important for public debate and which are of primary concern to most interest groups. On these issues television seems to fear the interest groups and the possible influence they can have on viewership levels or in getting corporate sponsors to withdraw support, whether these fears are well founded or not. The result is that the slimy, salacious, and sleazy (that, as Lowry argues, are increasingly delivered by writers) may slither past the network censors, but when "Ellen" wants to deal with homosexuality or "Nothing Sacred" raises issues about AIDS or abortion in the context of religion, the standards and practices departments get busy. "Ellen" was kept in harness on a number of occasions, and an episode of "Nothing Sacred" featuring a priest with AIDS was never aired.

Television's fear of potentially controversial subject matter that could potentially damage the bottom line influences programming decisions even when interest groups are not directly involved. This was the case when Fox shelved a drama dealing with the sexual harassment charges against Clarence Thomas. Similarly, NBC's "Saturday Night Live" excised a skit making fun of the fact that the networks are owned by large conglomerates.

This last example also brings to mind the current dominance of the likes of Disney/Cap Cities, News Corporation, Viacom, and Time Warner in the entertainment industry. The effects of the concentration of power and control in the hands of a few huge conglomerates are, and will increasingly be, far reaching. To get a taste of this dominance, let me list the media interests owned by just one of these conglomerates, Time Warner: the CNN News Group, including Cable News Network, CNN Headline News, CNN International, CNNfn, CNN/SI, CNN en Español, CNN Airport Network, CNNRadio, CNNRadio Noticias, and CNN Interactive; Turner Broadcasting System, Inc., including TBS Superstation, Turner Network Television, Cartoon Network, Turner Classic Movies, TNT Europe, Cartoon Network Europe, TNT Latin America, Cartoon Network Latin America, TNT & Cartoon Network in Asia Pacific, Cartoon Network Japan; New Line Cinema, including New Line Cinema, Fine Line Features, New Line International, New Line Home Video, New Line Television; HBO and Cinemax; Time Inc., including *Time, People, Sports Illustrated, Fortune, Life, Money, Parenting, In Style, Entertainment Weekly, Cooking Light, Baby Talk, Coastal Living, Health, Hippocrates, People en Español, Progressive Farmer, Southern Accents, Southern Living, Sports Illustrated For Kids, Sunset, Teen People, This Old House, Time for Kids, Weight Watchers, Your Company, Asiaweek, Dancyu, President, Wallpaper, Who Weekly,* Time Life Inc., Book-of-the-Month Club, Warner Books, Little, Brown and Company, Oxmoor House, Leisure Arts, Sunset Books, and Time Inc. New Media; Warner Bros., including Warner Bros. Pictures, Warner Bros. Television, Telepictures Productions, Warner Bros. Television Animation (Looney Tunes and Hanna-Barbera), MGM Library, Castle Rock Entertainment, The WB Television Network, Warner Home Video, Warner Bros. Domestic Pay-TV, Cable, and Network Features, Warner Bros. Consumer Products, Warner Bros. Studio Stores, Warner Bros. International Theatres, Warner Bros. Recreation Enterprises,

DC Comics, Mad Magazine; Warner Music Group, including The Atlantic Group, Elektra Entertainment Group, Sire Records Group, Warner Bros. Records, Warner Music International, Warner/Chappell Music, WEA Inc., Ivy Hill Corp., WEA Manufacturing, WEA Corp., Warner Special Products, Warner Custom Music, Alternative Distribution Alliance, Giant Merchandising, and part of Columbia House; and 34 cable clusters. Moreover, as this book comes to press, there are plans for America Online to merge with Time Warner, and for Time Warner, with its Warner Music already one of the five dominant record companies in the world, to acquire another of the top five music companies, the EMI Group. What effect will such huge entities have? For one thing, with television, and media in general, increasingly controlled by fewer and larger corporations, the influence of the bottom line will become ever stronger. Moreover, concentration of media ownership also points to less diversity of opinion.

So in the end, we are faced with a double whammy—interest groups working to limit public debate and economic considerations propelling television in the same direction. Let us hope that countervailing cultural and economic forces that foster vigorous and open debate will emerge.

NOTES

1. *The Seattle Times*, March 8, 1998.

2. *Los Angeles Times*, January 6, 1999.

3. *Los Angeles Times*, October 2, 1998.

4. James B. Jacobs and Kimberly Potter, *Hate Crimes: Criminal Law and Identity Politics* (New York: Oxford University Press, 1998).

5. *Los Angeles Times*, October 13, 1998.

6. We might also do well to remember George Bernard Shaw's observation that "all great truths begin as blasphemies."

7. *Los Angeles Times*, October 8, 1998.

8. Theodore Caplow, *American Social Trends* (Orlando, Florida: Harcourt Brace Jovanovich, 1991), p. 69.

IV

Articles by Industry Representatives

Advocacy Groups Confront CBS:
Problems or Opportunities?

Carol Altieri

It is fall 1972. Five prominent New York rabbis enter the office of Thomas J. Swafford, vice president of program practices at CBS, demanding that a new situation comedy entitled "Bridget Loves Bernie" be expunged from the airwaves. Mr. Swafford, a man of enormous charm and intelligence, listens closely to their concerns about the comedy program which features two young people who embark on an interfaith marriage. The show deals with how the couple and their respective families cope with the differences in their cultural backgrounds. One of the rabbis, outraged, exclaims, "Take this blasphemy off the air or YOU will be responsible for finishing the work that Adolph Eichmann started."

It is fall 1973. CBS is deluged with 500,000 pieces of mail in a two-week period as a result of an organized letter-writing campaign launched by a Southern preacher who has accused CBS of "putting X-rated movies on television." The film, directed by Luchino Visconti, was entitled "The Damned." It chronicled the slow, steady moral decay of the German elite in the early days of the Third Reich as experienced through the lives of a prominent Berlin family. Conveniently ignored by the good Reverend was the fact that the movie was scheduled for 11:30 P.M. and had been so heavily edited that it could easily have been retitled "The Darned."

It is spring 1974. The CBS program practices staff meets with the Gray Panthers, who complain that the only commercials they ever see featuring seniors depicts them as either constipated or addle-brained. "We have a LIFE!" said Lydia Bragger, then director of the organization. "I'm 70 years old and the fires definitely have not burned out yet!"

Between 1971 and 1974, I was Tom Swafford's executive secretary at CBS in New York, and I am glad I paid attention. I learned about "pressure groups," "special interest groups," or, as they are now called, "advocacy groups" at the foot of a master who knew virtually everything there was to know about every facet of broadcasting. While he was extremely sensitive to the diversity of America and to "hyphenated" sensibilities, he was, and to this day remains, a self-described "militant" broadcaster. He believed that broadcasters *of course* have a sobering responsibility to their constituencies and they must serve the public interest, convenience, and necessity. *But*, don't anyone *dare* try to keep something off the air simply because it may run counter to his or her own particular value system. I recall Tom's incredulity as he would read some piece of mail or emerge from a meeting with a certain group. Many of these encounters were replete with invective and threats, and many of the arguments presented were full of sheer hypocrisy. Most of the arguments included a statement such as the following: "I'm not concerned about my *own* family because I monitor what *my* children see, but I *am* fearful for all those *other* families who do not pay attention to the damage that is being done to minds everywhere by today's television programs." Such a statement really nettled CBS's chief censor.

Twenty-five years ago the three networks were virtually the only games in town, and there was nowhere near the number of viewing choices that are available today. Cable as we know it today did not exist. I recall a prescient moment during this period when Fred Silverman, then programming head at CBS, walked past me with a little plastic box in his hand. He held it out to me and said, "Carol, do you know what this is?" "No," I replied. Fred looked at me, held it up, and said, "This, my dear, is the *future*." What Fred was referring to was the videocassette. Since that time various technologies have given birth to an explosion of viewing alternatives, which, in turn, have influenced our perceptions, our communities, and our culture in a variety of ways.

As the current vice president of program practices at CBS in a multinetwork, 500-channel universe, part of my role is to participate in a dialogue with advocates of myriad causes, and I welcome opportunities to do so. As a shaper of entertainment content policy, I and my staff cannot pretend to have full knowledge of all the serious problems facing society, such as violence, abortion, teenage sexuality, drug addiction, and HIV infection. Nor can we pretend to have complete understanding of all the diverse customs and cultures of all the various ethnic and racial groups constituting American society. When we put something on the air, we want to be responsible and informative. The only way to do that is to take reasonable steps to ensure the accuracy and veracity of what we are depicting, even in works of fiction. Those steps often include retaining the services of qualified experts in a given field or independently researching the topic in question. Then we work with writers and producers to mold the acquired information to the imperatives of the script. I have also hosted seminars featuring various advocates for the benefit of CBS executives so that our collective consciousness could be raised in hopes of avoiding mistakes that could alienate our audience.

Our efforts do *not* include asking a specific advocacy organization to consult on a project in order to gain its seal of approval, or to curry favor with the gadfly du jour, or to simply cover our posteriors. While this may seem glib, it is important to note that the advocacy group universe is so fragmented and splintered that just when you think you have come to an agreement, a different "chapter" or "region" decries the settlement, arguing that *its* membership was not consulted. So if it seems that networks are not responsive to advocacy group concerns, it is not because we are ignoring them, but rather because we cannot listen to every fragmented and splintered entity that calls something to our attention, each of which requires—or demands—a different response. And more often than not, television executives *are* responsive, especially when the issue at hand touches virtually every citizen. And we should also remember that television has often been proactive in influencing public awareness on issues such as seatbelt use, the dangers of smoking (why do you think Kojak sucked on a lollypop?), drug abuse, alcohol abuse, the existence of contraception options, ways to avoid the spread of HIV, and the perils of driving while intoxicated.

It is prudent for advocacy groups to convey their concerns not just to network executives, but to the creative element as well, such as members of the Writers Guild or the Caucus for Producers, Writers, and Directors. The writers and producers who create the programs are, overwhelmingly, people of talent, reason, and benign purpose, although there are times when a writer's fondest idea or strongest story element collides with higher obligations and responsibilities. There may never be a "guarantee" that a certain point of view or manner of ethnic portrayal will find its way into a program, but reaching beyond the distributor to the originators of the controversial material does assure that most, if not all, of the bases have been covered. From there, extended dialogue among all the players can identify problems and determine what specific and meaningful steps can be taken to address, if not solve, them.

Some situations are more easily and swiftly handled than others. For example, it is far simpler to advise producers of how we want them to treat cigarette smoking in a script than it is to ensure balance and fairness in presenting points of view regarding abortion or birth control. In the first case, we tell them that featured, reappearing, and/or sympathetic characters should not smoke and, if they do, a specific story line should be explored showing how the character decided to quit and then does so. Alternatively, other substantive characters in the program should have lines that berate the smoker in ways which leave no doubt about the severe consequences of the habit. In dealing with issues like birth control, so much depends upon whose story we are telling. In the case of a program dealing with birth control, whose point of view are we addressing: that of an expectant mother or father, that of a doctor who wrestles with a personal moral dilemma, that of a teenager who wants to become sexually active but feels she cannot confide in her parents about getting on the pill? Depending on whose story we are telling, the treatment of the issue changes to illumine that particular character's journey toward decision.

But here we open ourselves up to criticism. If the character is a devout Catholic and does not even consider abortion or contraception as an option, various women's groups are outraged that we are "caving in" to religious factions. If the same character does not raise religious concerns in the course of deciding which road to take, invariably we are accused of preempting God from the process, and we incur the wrath of those who believe abortion or birth control to be intrinsically, and under any and all circumstances, wrong.

In response to letters or phone calls from advocacy groups about a certain characterization or treatment of a given issue, I always make the point that this was a specific story about a specific person with a specific point of view within a specific set of circumstances. Such a characterization or treatment is not meant to create the impression that it is representative of all people, everywhere. Often, groups ask me to make that point in an opening or closing legend. There are times when such information deserves inclusion to clarify a possible misunderstanding by the viewer.[1] But in the overwhelming number of cases, program practice has taken great pains to ensure inclusion of different viewpoints within the body of the program if this can be accommodated by the dramatic or comedic imperatives of the script.

When we as viewers choose to involve ourselves in a television program, we bring with us our own set of parameters and sensitivities which make the experience completely subjective. If the story is substantial and the execution is successful, the piece will stand on its own merits, leaving each of us to draw differing inferences and/or insights from what we have just seen. And at its best, television engages us mentally, emotionally, and spiritually, and might even push us to consider something we might otherwise not have.

Obviously, television cannot be everything to everybody, although some think it should be. There is now a movement afoot insisting on balance in regard to controversial issues not just in the context of an entire schedule or within the unfolding story of a movie or series arc, but within a scene or exchange of lines. If this is the requirement, we may succeed in enumerating 15 different points of view, but none of them will be examined in the depth each may deserve. Such narrow thinking is obviously antithetical to creative expression. And it is this perceived threat that so many writers and producers rail against in this age of political correctness.

We all want to feel empowered, to believe that as thinking, reasonable contributors to society, each of us can make a difference. And each of us wants to be a part of this medium of television, reflected in all our glory and in all our various permutations. In a perfect world, all of this would be so. Unfortunately, ours is not a perfect world. While there have been many attempts by Hollywood writers and network executives to create series featuring Asians, Latinos, Italians, and other ethnic groups, it is apparently difficult for us to "get it right." Even when popular actors and comedians like Pat Morita and Paul Rodriguez appear weekly, there always seem to be objections about their characters' ethnic behaviors and portrayals. Perhaps the continuation of workshops and other programs that the networks have been offering in an effort to develop new and exciting opportunities for minority writers and show runners will help alleviate the problems. We hope so. Everyone acknowledges there is still much to be done and that progress is incremental.

In this context, the "I'm mad as hell and I'm not going to take it anymore" approach advanced by Howard Beale in "Network" is not the most effective strategy for advocacy groups today. And as media-savvy as many groups have become, there are still those who believe that confrontation is the only way to make themselves heard. And that is too bad, because contrary to former Vice President Dan Quayle's label of "media elite," most of us in television do listen and are aware that we play a significant role in our evolving popular culture. Advocacy groups help us to carry out that role and even contribute to the success of our business by helping to keep us in touch with all segments of the viewership. What is more, they help us to meet the commitment we have made to serve the public interest, regardless of how many "publics" that interest includes.

NOTES

1. For a television movie entitled "Murder: By Reason of Insanity," CBS ran the following advisory:

"This story is based on the tragic lives of Adam and Ewa Berwid. Adam's violent behavior is not intended to be a general reflection of the mentally ill, the vast majority of whom never commit a violent act. Indeed, they are not more prone to violence than the non-mentally disordered."

Dealing with Advocacy Groups at ABC

Alfred R. Schneider

The role of special interest groups in the television programming process became an issue during the development of the medium in the 1960s and 1970s. Over time each of the participants in the broadcasting business—the station, the network, the advertiser and his or her agency, the screening service, the program producer—faced off and sometimes found an accommodation with one or more of the many special interest groups that tried to exert influence.

Those of us who were responsible for the review of programs prior to broadcast tried to remain neutral and objective as our nation experienced significant social and political change in the 1960s and 1970s. During this tumultuous period we were responsible for putting out ideas that were discussed and digested, accepted or rejected. It was not an easy job. Why did we not show more moments of religious observance such as grace at meals or prayers before bed? Why did we not show that homosexuality was a perversion and adultery a sin? Why did we always show big corporations as evil and taking advantage of the common man? Why were most of the victims that were portrayed women? Why were there no positive black or Latino role models? When were we going to stop showing the stereotypical evil Arab in white sheets and burnoose? Why was the killer always a psychopath and mental illness depicted as leading to criminality? Why were the Polish people in "Winds of War" portrayed as participants in carrying out Nazi atrocities in the concentration camps? Why couldn't Petula Clark kiss Harry Belafonte?

The first special interest advocate I encountered was not a group but an individual, a most influential individual, Isabelle Goldenson, wife of the president of the American Broadcasting Company. She objected to jokes that Jerry Lewis, on a comedy variety show in 1963, directed at her husband, Leonard Goldenson. She felt that these jokes were embarrassing and demeaning to the struggling president. On Yom Kippur eve, a Saturday night in October, I was told by Oliver Treyz, president of the ABC Television Network, to use a switch to block any further "Lennie" references that Lewis might utter. That night I believe that I missed one and got one, but it was the last time Lewis told a "Lennie" joke.

Over the next 30 years, issues rather than taste became our primary concern as we dealt with the special interest groups.

Born of frustration on the one hand and the need to proselytize on the other, special interest groups proliferated in the 1960s and 1970s. Each group, whether its cause was ethnicity-, religion-, race-, gender-, health-, or child-oriented, believed that it had to set the record straight, to oppose the way that television portrayed it and/or its cause, and to tell America what it should believe or think about the issue at hand. Responding to these pressures was difficult for television. It was not clear what role television should play. Should it be an objective informant or a passionate propagandist? The licenses issued to stations required them to serve the public interest—and this implied that they should take no sides. The lexicon of guideposts contained the words "objectivity," "fairness," "balance," and "equal opportunity." But each advocacy group had its own vision of what the content of television should look like. Blacks, Indians, Hispanics, Italians, Jews, Christians, and Asians—to list just a few categories—all believed, and with good cause, that they were not fairly represented, that they were stereotyped, that their culture was misrepresented or ignored. And to make matters worse, they had been granted no hearing.

In the 1980s advocacy groups really hit their stride. During this period NBC ran into buckshot with the television miniseries, "Beulah Land." At ABC we also became deeply involved with issues surrounding the portrayal of the American Indians. With "Mystic Warrior" (Brandon Stoddard's follow-up to "Roots") we were caught up in an intraracial controversy within the American Indian community between those who favored assimilation and those who saw merit in accurately portraying for the first time on television the roots and traditions of Native American culture.

The seeds of this interest group activity were planted some decades before. In the 1950s a fervently anti-Communist grocery store chain owner visited advertisers and their agencies in New York City to "advise" them about whom to hire or not to hire for the programming they sponsored.[1] During the same period the American Business Consultants, which consisted of three former FBI agents, issued a newsletter entitled "Counterattack" and produced a series of monographs. In 1950 it published "Red Channels: The Report of Communist Influence in Radio and Television." This work contained 200 pages of detailed background information on 151 broadcast personalities whom it suggested were, at the very least, sympathetic to communism. It avoided outright accusation, but through innuendo and guilt by association it identified those who were "undesirable." Advertisers, agencies, and networks soon set up a system of security checks to ensure that no one who was "tainted" would be hired. In some instances loyalty oaths were required for new employees. In addition, several conservative members of the American Federation of Television and Radio Artists, along with individuals with American Legion and advertiser connections, formed Aware Inc. Aware "cleared" performers until 1955.[2] This entire system was not broken until John Henry Faulk won a libel case against Aware Inc. in 1962.

It was in that year that an advertiser attempted to influence network news reporting. This action had a significant chilling effect on the industry. Jim Hagerty, vice president in charge of ABC network news and public affairs, and I traveled to Los Angeles to try to assuage Patrick J. Frawley, chairman of Eversharp, Inc., the parent company of the Schick Safety Razor Company. We were directed to attempt to get him to reverse his decision to cancel a $1 million advertising contract between Schick and ABC involving the shows "Combat" and "Stoney Burke." Frawley, a staunch supporter of the Christian Anti-Communism Crusade, had sent a cancellation telegram to ABC in response to Mr. Alger Hiss's appearance on Howard K. Smith's news program "The Political Obituary of Richard M. Nixon," which followed Nixon's defeat for the office of governor of California. Mr. Nixon was a member of the House Un-American Activities Committee which raised perjury charges against Mr. Hiss. On Smith's program Hiss accused Mr. Nixon of being "politically carried along" and of "molding appearances to a point of view that he began with" in the investigations. On the same program, Gerald R. Ford, Jr., then a Republican representative in Congress from the State of Michigan, presented a well-articulated contradictory point of view.

Frawley's telegram seeking the cancellation stated that "we are shocked at the extreme poor taste and judgment shown by the ABC network in presenting a convicted perjurer involved in the passing of United States secrets to the Communists as a critic of the former Vice President of the U.S." Schick's action was followed by the Kemper Insurance Company's refusal to continue its sponsorship of the "ABC Evening Report." In addition to these actions, a number of ABC affiliates failed to carry the Smith program.

Here ABC, and the industry as a whole, was faced with the first major confrontation in which economic coercion was used to effect editorial decision making, putting journalistic integrity at risk. Of course there had been attempts to influence politically charged programming in the past.[3] One of the most memorable examples was the American Gas Association's requesting removal of all references to gas chambers in the Studio One rendition of "The Nuremberg Trials." And ABC had problems early in its history with Walter Winchell's Sunday night programs. But until the Smith incident no advertiser had attempted to suppress the news.

At that time ABC was just beginning to build its news departments and could ill afford outside attempts to influence its journalistic judgment, not to mention economic reprisals. ABC did garner support from the press and the television industry. Dick Salant, then president of the news division of CBS, said that he was "distressed at the pre-broadcast efforts to suppress any part of the Howard K. Smith broadcast and at the post-broadcast actions by advertisers and others to punish ABC." He argued that such actions "struck at journalistic independence, including the right to be wrong and to present unpopular views."

LeRoy Collins, president of the National Association of Broadcasters, said that the broadcast was within "the range of sound journalism," and Newton Minow, then chairman of the FCC, spoke out against advertisers who try to influence radio and television broadcasts "through commercial reprisals."[4]

The Smith incident was but a harbinger of troubles to come.

Our trip to Los Angeles to meet with Mr. Frawley was the first of many such endeavors. In the 1960s and 1970s society was grappling with controversial issues of sexuality, civil rights, and violence. Dramatic fare, including many made-for-television movies as well as situation comedies such as "All in the Family," "Maude," and "Soap" began to deal with these controversial matters. As issue-oriented programming emerged so did many more special interest groups. Entertainment programming soon became the target of those seeking to influence public perception.

It was on the trip to meet Mr. Frawley that Jim Hagerty and I formulated policy on how to deal with special interest groups and advertiser defections. We decided that we would meet and dialogue with those who felt offended, frustrated, wronged, or misrepresented by our television offerings. But it was also determined that while we would try to learn by listening and discussing, we had to remain masters of our own house. Control had to remain with the broadcaster. As Hagerty put it in regard to news (though his basic point applies to entertainment programming as well), "To yield to prior censorship and the pressure of personal attack and economic boycott is to surrender the basic right of freedom of the press. This right we will never surrender—or compromise. To do so would be to betray our responsibility as a news medium. If we are weakened, you (the public) are weakened, for if through fear or intimidation we fail to provide all the news—good or bad, favorable or unfavorable—then you, the citizens of the nation, cannot be properly informed." And that is basically what we said to Frawley. We also informed him that we would not let him out of his contract, which was the main message that management had sent us to deliver. But we were also told to listen and to explain our role as communicators in our democratic society, our intention not to be propagandists, and our need to present balanced and objective reporting. We also explained how it was our job to decide what is newsworthy and what is not. In this role sometimes we would make errors in judgment, but we must be allowed to make these mistakes as this is part of the process. On November 15, 1962, after some eight hours of meetings, breaking bread, shouting, and listening, Frawley issued a statement that his firm would live up to its legal commitments, but would do so reluctantly and under protest.

I specifically adopted the policy that was initially formulated for news to entertainment programming that was coming under fire from pressure groups. The first tactic adopted by these groups was direct confrontation. But soon they attempted the strategy of economic boycott, that is, encouraging viewers and constituents to threaten advertisers so they would withdraw sponsorship from television programs.

One early attempt at direct confrontation involved the program "The Untouchables." The leadership of the Italian-American community in New York expressed concern over Mafia portrayals in the program. While meetings were being held to discuss the problem, we learned that longshoremen on the docks of New York City were dumping Lucky Strike cigarettes into the water. Lucky Strike was a major sponsor of "The Untouchables." Saner heads prevailed once it was made clear that our discussions could be impeded if this action was not halted, and soon the longshoremen were reloading the cigarettes.

In the 1970s criticism of and related actions directed at television's role in influencing society's ideas, attitudes, and mores were not carried out solely by the Moral Majority and the fundamentalist religious right. In fact these elements may have adopted some of the tactics of the special interest groups that they abhor the most, those representing the gay community.

The explosive debate over media depiction of gays and lesbians began shortly after the telecast of the first two-hour movie dealing explicitly with homosexuality, "That Certain Summer."

Early in January 1973 some 25 members of the New York-based Gay Activist Alliance, including its director Ron Gold, staged a sit-in in Leonard Goldenson's office on the 39th floor of the ABC Building. They were upset about the program "Marcus Welby, M.D." The gay community had recently succeeded in having the American Psychiatric Association remove homosexuality from its list of mental illnesses. It now sought to use the media in its struggle for recognition and acceptance of homosexuality as normal and natural. In this light, two Welby episodes caused a major confrontation. This confrontation manifested itself first in the aforementioned sit-in and then in a national protest that resulted in an eventual liaison between the network and the Gay Media Task Force.

We were aware of the relevant issues and tried to be sensitive to them. After internal review the first Welby episode, which concerned a married man seeking Welby's help in dealing with his homosexual tendencies, was broadcast with only a few changes. But the second episode, entitled "The Outrage," was, after review, subjected to a number of changes. This episode dealt with the molestation of a young teenage boy by a male school teacher. After much discussion as well as consultation with Dr. Melvin S. Heller, clinical professor of psychiatry and director of the Institute of Law and the Health Sciences at Temple University, we made it clear in the episode that the physical assault of the youth was a result of the perpetrator's extreme emotional problems and not his homosexuality. All overt references to homosexuality were removed, and we made efforts to make the public, our affiliated stations, and the advertisers aware that it was not our intention in this episode to cast homosexuality in a negative light. But the gay community was not convinced, and the aforementioned protests and demonstrations followed. From this time on we participated in an ongoing dialogue with the gay community that we hoped would enable us to fairly and objectively present homosexual characters to the television audience without taking sides in the religious and social controversy.

The issue of homosexuality arose again with what some criticized as a stereotypical character on the show "Barney Miller," the long-running comedy that parodied police work. We were also criticized for the recurring homosexual character on "Soap." Not only was the gay community offended by Billy Crystal's comedic portrayal, but also the religious community objected to the character as proselytizing for homosexual acceptance. The program "Soap," first telecast in the fall of 1977, probably raised more ire than any other program up until that time and gave the religious right a platform for protest and pressure.

Thinking that society had changed significantly in regard to the issue of homosexuality, in the 1990s we aired an episode of "Thirtysomething" in which two homosexuals were shown in bed together, holding hands and discussing relationships and the tragedy of AIDS. But we found that the advertising community, fearing negative viewer reaction, was still sensitive to the presentation of such behavior. The gay community applauded us for the matter-of-fact way in which the encounter was handled, but several fundamentalist groups sent out letters to advertisers and constituents threatening and advocating boycott tactics. In keeping with our policy of exposition not advocacy, we saw no problem with the two adults in bed. After all we were in the "reality period" of television. And we did remove a kiss between the two men which was in the original script. Unfortunately, the network lost over $1 million in revenue as sponsors defected from the program. So much for social change.

After these experiences, in January 1984 we published a workbook entitled "Sexuality, Television and Broadcast Standards" written by Dr. Melvin S. Heller. In part, this was a product of Heller's discussions with our editors, Dr. Philip Sarrel and Dr. Lorna Sarrel, Yale professors and consultants to ABC, concerning the consequences, emotional impact, and societal perceptions of the proposed sexual content in our programming. This monograph set forth our policy and guidelines for handling homosexual behavior and other aspects of sexuality.

The subject, content, and depiction of sexual activity were at the heart of the Moral Majority's and later the Reverend Donald Wildmon's concerns and boycott campaigns against advertisers.

The Reverend Jerry Falwell's role as prime spokesman for Christian fundamentalist special interest groups was taken over in the 1980s by the Reverend Donald Wildmon of Tupelo, Mississippi. First through a group called Christian Leaders for Responsible Television and later through the American Family Association, Wildmon called for consumer boycotts of advertisers who sponsored shows containing sex, and violence and profanity as well.

The creative community was extremely concerned with Wildmon's and related activities. They feared the creation of a climate that would effectively chill their ideas, harm their product, and decrease their profits. In 1981 at the urging of David Wolper and other leaders in the community, the Academy of Television Arts and Sciences and the Caucus of Producers, Writers, and Directors convened a symposium in Ojai, California for the express purpose of "develop(ing) more thoughtful and coherent means of responding to the pressure groups, so that we may learn from our critics while resisting censorship." In a word, they sought to give backbone to the networks and advertisers and prevent a "blanding out" of the medium. They concluded that diversity of thought is healthy, that pressure groups are natural and acceptable but many of their methods are not, and that stations and networks should have strictly enforced guidelines to deal with these groups' complaints.

Advertisers and their agencies responded to the advocacy group situation by setting up screening services. These services screened every prime time program and reported back to the agency or the advertiser on those matters that might cause some special interest group to object. The advertiser or agency representative would then contact the sales department of the network and ask to be moved out of the program. While in most instances the commercial could be replaced with that of another advertiser, this invariably led to a diminution of revenue and monetary loss for the network. Advertisers realized that the boycotts' effect in terms of numbers of potential consumers not buying the product was insignificant, but they still did not want to have negative publicity associated with their company or image. Accordingly a "chilling effect," though difficult to measure in real terms, emerged, which resulted in a temperance of those programs that did not command a major audience. On the other hand, for those programs that commanded a sizable audience, little change was apparent. For example, when Terry Rakolta spoke out against "Married with Children," an on-the-edge sexually oriented situation comedy on the new Fox network, sponsors reacted, but very few, if any, changes were made in the program, and it continued to draw a significant, and even larger, audience.

Another element in this situation that should be mentioned is the fact that, at times during the last 30 years, television and print news reports of advocacy group activities have played a role in promoting the rhetoric of passion and anger over the dialogue of reason. They have given the forces of intimidation undue attention. And by overreporting their size and actual strength the press has, at times, increased advocacy groups' impact and triggered excessive reaction.

CONCLUSION

Clearly, a rational dialogue must be maintained between the television industry and special interest groups. Special interest groups that we at the networks have dealt with have been concerned with almost every imaginable issue: children, sexuality, ethnicity, stereotyping, civil rights, mental health, drug addiction, animals, the family, guns, even waterbeds. Their concerns vary widely, but all share the desire to introduce their opinions to the television audience, to influence others' perceptions of them, to persuade other people to adopt their cause, and to increase awareness of social problems they have selected as most significant. The airing of a diversity of opinion is essential for a responsible democracy. And through airing their opinions these interest groups have made countless contributions to our political, social, and economic development.

Given the pervasiveness of the medium, the sheer volume of television programming, and its impact on society, it is no wonder that television attracts advocates. However, television should not be held responsible for solving all of society's social problems—redressing grievances, halting crime on the streets, reducing divorce rates, and feeding the hungry. While it can raise the consciousness of the nation, it should not be considered as the major vehicle for social relief or altering behavior. Television does offer role models and influence people's understandings. But viewers must ultimately take responsibility for their own behavior. All that television can ultimately do is strive to be committed to diversity, fairness, and balance.

The airing of diverse opinions is of crucial importance. Without diversity we have sameness, blandness, maybe even totalitarianism. There is no surer route to decadence and self-destruction than the exercise of repressive control over thought. We must strive to enable the many divergent interests in our society to carry on a meaningful dialogue that results in their being heard.

While encouraging dialogue we must discourage certain methods and means selected by some advocacy groups to accomplish their goals. When the tactics used are those of intimidation, coercion, or organized boycotts, the fires of experimentation can be dampened, ideas can be chilled, and the free flow of ideas can be hampered.

Special interest groups will be with us forever. The industry must continue to meet, talk, and listen—and change. But outside special interest groups cannot be allowed to superimpose their beliefs, ideas, and standards to achieve their special objectives and goals, any more than the broadcasters can allow the creative community, a particular advertiser, or even the broadcasters themselves to impose their own special interests on the product presented in a medium that serves all. And the viewer *individually* must make the ultimate choice of what to watch and listen to.

NOTES

1. Kathryn C. Montgomery, *Target: Prime Time: Advocacy Groups and the Struggle over Entertainment Television* (New York: Oxford University Press, 1989), pp.13-14.

2. Christopher H. Sterling and John M. Kittross, *Stay Tuned: A Concise History of American Broadcasting* (Belmont, CA: Wadsworth Publishing, 1978).

3. In regard to the struggles of CBS news, see Sally Bedell Smith, *In All His Glory: The Life of William S. Paley, the Legendary Tycoon and His Brilliant Circle* (New York: Simon and Schuster, 1990).

4. "Minow Supports Amnesty to Hiss" in *The New York Times*, November 19, 1962.

17

Television and Pressure Groups: Balancing the Bland

Lionel Chetwynd

"You should be happy with this. This should work well for you." The speaker whom I shall call R.I. was a self-styled "children's advocate"; the venue was a PBS special devoted to discussing the V-chip and other forms of outside intervention into the process by which popular entertainment is created and then delivered to the American people. She had no way of understanding how arrogant her words seemed to those of us on that panel who daily fight the war in which commerce and art are married to produce American popular culture. And no matter what one might think of the quality of that popular culture, the fact is, it travels the world, capturing the imaginations of billionsn and, not incidentally, earning more export dollars for this country than any other industry.

Some consider that international projection of our national personality a bad thing; but they should remember that the availability of programs like "Kojak" and "Dallas," often ridiculed at home, nonetheless presented images of civilian restraints on police and everyday freedoms that were instrumental in bringing down the Berlin Wall.

But back to R.I., who was high-handedly explaining to us what was good for us, what was best for us in the entertainment industry. If all she represented was the foolishness of the uninformed then one might be merely amused; unfortunately, she represents one of the most destructive forces in American life today: the self-assured, self-righteous, indignant scold.

(Parenthetically, more often than not these people are less interested in shaping what the creators of television do than they are in securing a seat for themselves at the creative table. It has not been unknown for failed writers, unsuccessful actors, and would-have-been producers to seek the credential of spokesperson for a pressure group to become part of a process into which they could not otherwise gain entrance.)

Why would one describe such a well-meaning person as a seriously destructive force? Part of it has to do with technology. Before television, the dominant mass entertainment was film, and this was policed by the Hays Code, a detailed (and obligatory) set of rules that determined what behavior and social ethos motion pictures would project. Frequently derided in our day and age as excessively restrictive and puritanical, it should be remembered that the Hays Code did not stand in the way of what is considered Hollywood's Classic silent era, or its Golden era, a period spanning roughly 30 years from the advent of sound in the late 1920s.

But with the coming of television, the motion picture industry gradually came to believe that it would have to distinguish itself from the small screen by offering types of entertainment that were not acceptable on a television service that actually went into people's homes and bedrooms. So in time the industry set up the MPAA ratings system in which anything goes as long as a film has an appropriate sticker.

Through the 1950s, 1960s, and most of the 1970s television in America was the property of three networks which, for most of this time, were partners with advertising agencies. In such an environment there were a few pressure groups and special interest groups, but for the most part this type of organization had little reason for being. There was, in that day, a more broadly accepted notion of who we were as a people and what was suitable for our families.

But by the time we had lived through the polarization of Vietnam, the cynicism-inducing Watergate years, and the serious recession of the late 1970s, television had changed its shape entirely: cable had begun to proliferate and the era of the 500-channel universe was upon us.

It was this technological change that freshly empowered pressure groups and gave them a place in the process that was unearned and frequently unintelligently occupied. The coming of an infinite number of channels accessed by a remote control in every home meant that a television broadcaster was forced to grab the attention of a potential viewer immediately—or the remote control would click and a competitor would get his chance. In such an environment, the power of pressure groups was magnified. With pressure groups threatening to discourage a large block of viewers from watching a show, the broadcaster was facing a diminished audience and thus reduced odds that he could hold a large enough audience for long enough to make a program succeed.

With attracting a sizable audience the goal for both broadcaster and narrowcaster, they found themselves forced to compete by pushing the envelope whenever they could—all without treading on the interests of the powerful pressure groups.

The television industry also learned that views of censorship and content had a political component. Liberals tended to be angered by violence, conservatives by sex. And to this day, these two groups are often in disagreement about what they consider suitable. But it is an uneven battle, one in which the liberal view consistently predominates. That is because the community that produces the popular culture is decidedly liberal and tends to embrace liberal causes. Whether from coffee cups given to writers by the Sierra Club that list ten ecological facts they should include in their scripts or attending the obligatory fundraiser for liberal causes, fresh entrants to the Hollywood community quickly learn that the politically correct is the professionally adept.

So liberal pressure groups are commonly found working inside the industry. The doors of the power structure are open to them, and the creative community embraces them. It is relatively simple for them to ensure that their message is embodied and embedded in the popular culture.

This liberal bias in the industry is frequently unconscious, since for most people in Hollywood defining themselves as liberal is less a statement of a set of political choices they have made than it is a proclamation of their credentials as good human beings. One good example of the result of this bias is the way television tends to treat clergy—rarely as people of faith, but usually as social workers in clerical collars who end up pushing a liberal agenda.

Conservative pressure groups are often more widely visible since they must work from the outside. They tend to use public national campaigns aimed at inspiring consumer boycotts and frightening local affiliates away from programs they deem inappropriate. Frequently, these economic pressures are serious and cause great concern in the executive offices of the industry. Network programmers therefore find themselves trapped between the clamor of conservative consumers on one hand and the cacophony of the creative community on the other. Somehow they must bridge the gap between the two.

The result has been a change from the old view of "balanced programming" to the newer "balance within a program." That is to say, once upon a time, a broadcaster could present a program with a strong point of view on any subject (abortion, for example), providing they made an attempt to present another program presenting a different point of view. The result was often edgy and exciting programming. Pressure groups have put an end to all that. Broadcasters anxious to keep an audience watching ensure that any point of view will be quickly countered by the opposite opinion, thus making sure that the program is internally balanced. The result has been, for the most part, a terrible blanding of television and the slow undermining of truly provocative programming, the kind of programming that helps a society define itself and understand the many differing groups of which it is composed.

Steven Bochco and David Kelley aside, the notion that television can enlighten as well as entertain is slowly disappearing under the enormous burden of pressure groups. This is not to say that citizens should not be heard and not be allowed to join together to increase the volume of their voice. On the contrary, that is an essential aspect of democracy. But what they must understand is that theirs is but one point of view, no more and no less right than that held by the group across the street. Pressure groups and special interest groups must be reminded that our national motto is E Pluribus Unum. And television must reflect a freely interactive society, not a politically correct one.

They must be heard. They must be listened to. But they should not be given a seat at the table. Those seats belong to the people in the arena who should ultimately be controlled by the on-off switch and the judgment of their fellow citizens as to what they will watch and how they will spend their hard-earned income.

Unfortunately, too many pressure groups disagree with this notion. And in doing so these pressure groups have become industrial as what was already described as a wasteland is now being strip mined by every group of three people or more who think they know best.

V

Epilogue

18

A Millenarian View of Artists and Audiences

Nicholas Johnson

This collection of essays offers the reader a wide-ranging discussion of the possible, and the appropriate, involvement of the audience in shaping the content of entertainment and journalism. It is a fitting and useful update to Kathryn C. Montgomery's seminal work, *Target: Prime Time: Advocacy Groups and the Struggle over Entertainment Television.*[1] Many essays, such as Michael Suman's "Interest Groups and Public Debate," contain a rich source of data and anecdote about individual advocacy groups and their activities. Together they represent a variety of opinions as well.

At one extreme there are the activists and moralists who seek to prevent, or at least minimize, what they see as the antisocial and immoral consequences of the media.

- Ted Baehr's piece, "How Church Advocacy Groups Fostered the Golden Age of Hollywood," and William Donohue's "A Catholic Look at the Entertainment Industry" provide us a history of the role of organized religion in this cause.
- Guy Aoki ("Strategies of the Media Action Network for Asian Americans") explains the need for, and tactics of, media advocacy from a racial, or ethnic, perspective.

At the other end of the spectrum is an uneasy coalition from the worlds of commerce and the arts that desires, often for inconsistent reasons, to preserve its "freedom" to create—and to maximize profit.

- Carol Altieri ("Advocacy Groups Confront CBS: Problems or Opportunities?") offers a view from CBS's program practices department, as Al Schneider does in his revealing and useful history from inside ABC ("Dealing with Advocacy Groups at ABC").
- Mickey Gardner's call to arms against advocacy ("Public Policy Advocacy: Truant Independent Producers in a Federal City Fixated on a 'Values Agenda' ") carefully details, and candidly expresses, his frustration with *any* interference in the creative

process.

- Gabriel Rossman ("Hostile and Cooperative Advocacy") expressly recognizes, and analyzes, advocacy groups' use of both "cooperative" and "hostile" tactics. Rossman's analysis is consistent with Al Schneider's belief that "at times . . . advocacy group activities have played a role in promoting the rhetoric of passion and anger over the dialogue of reason."
- Lionel Chetwynd, less restrained, believes media advocates are "one of the most destructive forces in American life today: the self-assured, self-righteous, indignant scold" ("Television and Pressure Groups: Balancing the Bland"). Michael Suman agrees, and asserts the efforts of these "thin-skinned" critics who "believe that they alone know" how to manage media yield a "cautious, debate-quashing cultural climate."

Many of the authors reveal experience on more than one side of the issues. That has been my fate as well.

I have represented the industry as a lawyer, regulated it as a Commissioner of the Federal Communications Commission, and worked in it as a host and editor (PBS's "New Tech Times," NPR commentaries). I have criticized the industry as an author (*How to Talk Back to Your Television Set*) and nationally syndicated columnist ("Communications Watch"), and tried to reform it (as Chair, National Citizens Committee for Broadcasting, which arguably produced one of the few periods of *reductions* in levels of televised violence). I now lecture and teach about it in law schools ("Law of Electronic Media") and elsewhere.

By design, I have no economic interest in these issues. I do not work for, represent, own stock in, or otherwise speak for any telecommunications, mass media, or related industry or company. That does not make me right. It just means that any misinformation or faulty analysis you find here is mine alone.

My bias, to the extent I have one, favors artistic freedom and diversity—while respecting the views of everyone in our democracy. I fought censorship as an FCC Commissioner (including my public attacks on the censorship efforts of President Nixon and Vice President Agnew). I have been associated ever since with Project Censored (which produces an annual "Ten Best Censored Stories") and many other organizations similarly inclined. I value my friendships within the creative community that I have had over the years.

That said, what sense can we make of the range of views represented by this book's authors?

For starters, there is a need to listen, carefully, to those with whom we disagree. We who value diversity, investigative journalism, artistic freedom, and creativity would better serve our cause by being more aware of how rare and recent is our view. That is not to say we are not right. It is only to say we are taking on thousands of years and hundreds of cultures.

Next to the biological preservation of our species, few drives are stronger than the desire to protect and perpetuate (and for some, even proselytize for) one's culture. Parents, as well as priests, feel strongly about their responsibility, as well as their right, to socialize their tribe's next generation according to the values of the last. Early twentieth-century "country folk" resisted their children's attraction to "evil city ways." The Amish even turn their backs on *agricultural* modernity—thereby avoiding such concerns as "Y2K"! Indigenous peoples around the world (including our own Native Americans) struggle to hold, and pass on, ancient customs. This desire extends throughout all socioeconomic classes. Some families place a very high value on children practicing, and marrying within, the family's religious faith. Others are equally insistent on their children preparing for designated professions through attendance at particular prep schools and colleges. Tradition!

It was not, after all, very long ago in human history that any heretical deviation from the dominant church's theology was considered to be blasphemy—a crime. (Indeed, *heresy*, used as a pejorative, is derived from the Greek word *hairesis*, meaning "to choose for oneself." So much for individual creativity!) Severe punishments, including painful death, were among the risks assumed by those who deviated from the politically correct views of the religious right of those times. Criticism of government officials was punishable as sedition. Much like with broadcasting licenses in early 20th century America, only loyal and trustworthy printers were granted the licenses necessary to engage in the mass media of their day.

But before we engage in a unanimous sigh of relief over the fact that we are no longer living in such times, reflect for a moment on the extent to which we still are. From baby radio's first squawking cries, most countries assumed, with little or no debate, that radio would be, as a matter of course, under the exclusive control of public corporations or the government. (Turning ours over to the Navy was a serious early option.) Not only was it unthinkable (in the literal sense) to permit radio's commercial exploitation, all countries assumed that any force with this much potential for shaping society required some form of societal responsibility and control.

Nor are these concerns merely matters of history, however recent. The kinds of political and artistic freedoms we take for granted are unknown in many countries in the world even today. How many of the world's six billion citizens have the opportunity to subject their leaders to the kind of media assault President Clinton endured during the Monica Lewinsky scandal (or, for that matter, throughout his entire presidency)? How many would permit, as we do, everything from defamatory political commentary to embarrassing ridicule by stand-up comedians? By contrast, in how many countries would the perpetrators quickly find themselves confronting the kinds of punishments meted out in merry old England?

There is still a near-universal resistance to cultural forces from outside one's "tribe"—whether racial, religious, ethnic, or other community. But the cultural control formerly (and, to some extent, still today) exercised by kings and tyrants has, in democracies, been passed to the body politic.

There has been a three-dimensional explosion in the spread of democracy—that is, a presumed *right* of "the people," and each individual, to influence, if not control, the things that matter in one's life. The three dimensions are:

1. **Persons.** Voting in America was originally limited to white, male landowners over 21 years of age. It was gradually expanded to include non-landowners, African

Americans and other racial minorities, women, and persons between 18 and 21.

2. **Places.** Whether you associate democracy with ancient Athens or modern America, it is clearly continuing to expand its *geographic* reach over time.

3. **Realms of Life.** Originally limited to "government," the principles of democracy have been extended to people in many other areas of life—from family members to a corporation's shareholders, from a union's rank and file to a student council.

In fact, Thomas Streeter ("What Is an Advocacy Group, Anyway?") expressly recognizes the extension of democratic principles to media when he asserts that advocacy group pressure is "a peculiar and attenuated variation on representative democracy characteristic of our corporate-centered age." (Even Lionel Chetwynd ["Television and Pressure Groups: Balancing the Bland"], who is extremely *critical* of media "pressure groups," acknowledges "that citizens should . . . be heard and . . . allowed to join together . . . [as] an essential aspect of democracy.")

"Dilbert" notwithstanding, distributive decision making, rewards for suggestions, protections for "whistle-blowers," and innumerable legislative protections have even brought a measure of worker participation to private corporations. Although libertarians and conservatives may take a different view of the matter, for the most part Americans also accept the notion of public ownership—with its attendant democratic control—of highways, schools, libraries, and parks.

This is not a diversion from our subject. I mention these trends because we are living at a time, and in a country, in which Americans assume that "things that matter"—from the street light on our corner to the curriculum taught by our child's third-grade teacher—should reflect, at least to *some* degree, their own concerns and desires. Which brings us to the entertainment media. For among the "things that matter" few, if any, matter more than the media.

As Bernard Cohen has observed, even if television doesn't tell us what to *think*, it certainly tells us what to *think about*.[2] We see its influence in speech patterns, hair and clothing styles, and, as the advertising industry persuades manufacturers, buying patterns. Teachers report the shortened attention span of students from kindergarten on—not to mention the problems television helps create for teenage girls, poignantly described in Mary Bray Pipher's *Reviving Ophelia*. Public health officials bemoan television-induced obesity in children and a variety of self-induced illnesses and diseases in their parents. Others are concerned about stereotyping (for example, of race, gender, or age), declining moral values, and crime and violence.

Al Schneider ("Dealing with Advocacy Groups at ABC") acknowledges that "[t]elevision does offer role models and influence people's understandings." He sees "its impact on society." However, he also believes that "television should not be held responsible for solving all of society's social problems."

Given television's influence and consequences, the remarkable fact is not that there are advocacy groups (and individuals) in our democracy that want to reform the mass media. The wonder is why there are not more of them. (When building media reform coalitions, I used to insist to other organizations' leaders, "Regardless of what your first priority may be, your *second* priority simply has e smoking."[4]

l Curtin ("Gatekeeping in the Neo-Network Era") quotes, with seeming
ent, John Leonard's belief that television is "pro-gun control and anti-death
. . . alert to child abuse, spouse-battering, alcoholism, . . . [and] medical
ctice . . . and celebrate[s] the integration of the races."

any of these positions square with my own ideological orientation is,
be, irrelevant. As a public health person of sorts, I have tracked, and
Sonny Fox's (and others') use of the soap opera format in third world
to impart population control and other information ("Using Soap
Confront the World's Population Problem") and Jay Winsten's public
rts ("Harvard Alcohol Project: Promoting the 'Designated Driver' ").
point—scarcely controversial by now—is simply that mass media do,
y, tend to reflect the conscious and unconscious values and interests of
ors and owners.

ot clear whether Mickey Gardner means to challenge this assertion or
lic Policy Advocacy: Truant Independent Producers in a Federal City
a 'Values Agenda' "). If not, his attack on a "values agenda" is very
targeted. He is clearly opposed to the nation's "values" being affected
y by democratically elected representatives. On the other hand, there is
tion that he finds troublesome the "values agenda" of nonelected,
executives being foisted upon the American audience.

ere exceptions to the mass media reflecting the values and interests of
e behind the media?

ael Curtin contrasts Murdoch's censorship (not too harsh a word) of Chris
n's Hong Kong memoirs to serve Murdoch's corporate interests in China with
corporations' release of such films as "Seven Years in Tibet," "Kundun," and
Corner"—presumably equally harmful to their future corporate profits in
a.

, of course, the drumbeat of conservative criticism of the "liberal media"
nues. Lionel Chetwynd ("Television and Pressure Groups: Balancing the
d"), speaking of the entertainment industry, asserts as a given that there is a
ral bias in the industry." So here we have an industry controlled by large
orations airing "liberal" messages that might seem to run counter to their
ests.

the fact remains that there is a great measure of truth in the current
sticker: "The media are only as liberal as the conservative businesses
them."[5]

in says he is "not convinced that ownership of a media conglomerate
s centralized control." With respect, I disagree. Even Mickey
—for the most part "proindustry"—believes that "the media
lation and increased vertical integration . . . raise the serious prospect of
hed program diversity." And consider Al Schneider's story ("Dealing
vocacy Groups at ABC") regarding the influence of the ABC president's
abelle Goldenson. Michael Suman ("Interest Groups and Public Debate")
"concentration of media ownership also points to less diversity of

to be media reform.")

Thomas Streeter ("What Is an Advocac
importance of democratic pressure. He
envision a society in which the organizatior
full, open, public debate. . . . [T]here i
democratic control of media organization."

When a high school class picks a band
soloist (or minister), there may or may
performer, but there is tribal control. So long
or publication takes place *within* the tribe, i
stress. The tribe, through whatever its formal
may be, will have a measure of consensus al
The "*tribal* marketplace" really *is* an adequate

In short, "media" are not the problem. It i
creates the conflict; it is the invasion of forn
causes the problem. When a sound truck can l
a television station's programming reaches
covers a continent, tribal control is lost.

It is a problem illustrated by the dilemma
Confront CBS: Problems or Opportunities?")
It is somewhere between very difficult and vi
programming that simultaneously passes mu
minority and is still of sufficient interest t
economically viable. At best, it leaves the crea
Severeid once described (from the perspective
sensation of being eaten by ducks.

And Michael Curtin's thoughtful portra
three-network economy to a marketplace of mu
distribution systems ("Gatekeeping in the
necessarily support his assertion that television
However many channels there may be—and n
"Ellen" and "TV Nation"—tribes are still, for the
mention powerless) with programming that m
network programs (or programs modeled on them

Though tribal control may be lost, the desire f
"you have not converted a man because you ha
you convert by cacophony.

A broadcaster once told me, "You're not pa
enemies." Similarly, today's tribal spokespersons,
their values really are being challenged by televisi
the details in "A Catholic Look at the Entertai
Catholics' values, traditions, and culture—as we
persons—*are* being eroded by mass media.

The content of mass media cannot be value neu

- Carol Altieri ("Advocacy Groups Confront CBS: Pr
us how she and her department "advise producers

opinion."

There may be exceptions (before someone is fired); there may be a corporate decision that, for this time and place, the appearance of openness to self-criticism and diversity, or of editorial boldness, is of greater value than short-term profit (or avoidance of loss). But it is clear that—however management may choose to define it—maximizing the global media conglomerate's corporate profit ultimately will be what drives content decisions. As Michael Suman has observed, "What most determines what ends up on television is the bottom line."

Unfortunately, bottom lines do not always respond to highest values. Consider Gabriel Rossman's interview of William Horn, speaking for the gay and lesbian organization GLAAD (and Al Schneider's report of ABC's response to gay and lesbian pressure). They review the history, and continuing need, for such an organization. Why is it still needed? Because a producer who is on the fence about the treatment of a fictional homosexual in a script written in West Los Angeles may end up affecting the treatment of an actual homosexual on the fence in the Wild West of Wyoming.

It is not enough to remind such a victim (if they are still alive) that the television set has an "on-off" switch, that an individual does not *have to* watch a program she finds distasteful, that parents should control their children's television diet. John Prine once wrote a song advising us to "blow up your TV." But even those who accept his counsel continue to live in a televised society in which most of their fellow citizens' experiences and beliefs have been, at least to some extent, mediated. In short, even if Congress had not put the phrase into the Communications Act of 1934, there is, inherently, a "public interest" in the content, and consequences, of our entertainment industries' products.

Of course, even if describing a problem is a good beginning, it does not constitute a solution. How *can* we balance these seemingly irreconcilable drives of (a) tribal integrity, (b) artistic freedom in the mass media, and (c) global multimedia conglomerates' need to profit maximize? With great difficulty.

Let me review some of the approaches discussed by this book's authors and utilized over the past 30 or 40 years.

GOVERNMENT REGULATION

Whatever may have been the wisdom, integrity, and possibility of government regulation of program content when the three networks' affiliates *were* "television" for most viewers, such regulation is no longer possible today.

Rex Heinke and Michelle Tremain ("Influencing Media Content Through the Legal System: A Less Than Perfect Solution for Advocacy Groups") have done a thorough job of laying out the history, law, and reasons why. They conclude that "the courts are an increasingly inhospitable place to address the concerns of those wishing to change the way the world views them." So I will just add a few words of my own.

There are administrative as well as legal hurdles to government regulation of 500 channels (what Michael Curtin calls "a blizzard of options"). In the 1960s "*the* networks"—which were not, after all, "licensed broadcasters"—were regulated by the FCC by virtue of (a) the network "owned-and-operated" stations (which were, of course, licensed) and (b) the legal two-step of regulating the contract terms entered into by station licensees. This is not to say that a rationale could not be found, perhaps, for governmental regulation of, say, ESPN or the Comedy Channel. It is only to say that a *program supplier* is not, per se, a "broadcaster" required to be licensed under the terms of the 1934 Communications Act.

Law, wisdom, and ideology aside, the prospect of an FCC trying to regulate program content in a 500-channel world strikes me as an administrative nightmare—if not, indeed, an impossibility.

And we have, so far, assumed that what we are talking about is "television"—albeit a form of video entertainment that may come to us from the Internet, telephone company, communications satellite, coaxial cable, or optic fiber, rather than conventional over-the-air broadcast. But "convergence" is more than a buzzword. Video is, today, not only a commercial import to our television screens in real time. It may be a rented (or owned) videotape—or output from our own video camera. It may come from a CD-ROM or DVD disk—or off the Internet. Indeed, video distribution via the Internet may, someday, render obsolete much of what we write here today, navigating as we are by a rearview mirror focused on our experience and expectations regarding "television" and "cable." It is already possible to watch regular cable television on our computer screens (not to mention the video clips we can download from the Web). To complete the circle, we can also, if we wish, get a device to view our Web surfing on our conventional television screen. And all of this can be miniaturized into shirt-pocket or wristwatch-sized devices—or wall-sized screens in home entertainment centers.

We will not even begin here to describe the additional range of games and other entertainment played and viewed on independent devices, or television screens, or stand-alone computers—and those involving Internet-connected players. When one considers the full range of what would need to be "regulated" in order to minimize the adverse effects of the media, most broadly defined, regulation becomes an even more impossible task.

Finally, it is not clear why the FCC would bring any more enthusiasm to this task than it has to any past issue involving a conflict of public and corporate interests.

As a part of an overall strategy media reform advocates will want to continue to include letters, proposed regulations and legislation, and litigation. The example of Peggy Charren's accomplishments with Action for Children's Television is reason enough to fight on. Decades after "deregulation" there are still *some* regulations, and public-minded officials, in place. Using them may at least attract the attention of industry management (and possibly journalists) in ways that may promote reform.

But these tactics alone are unlikely to be adequate.

BOYCOTTS

Robert Pekurny's piece ("Advocacy Groups in the Age of Audience

Fragmentation: Thoughts on a New Strategy") paints a pretty gloomy picture of the utility of boycotts. I will not repeat his arguments here, most of which I find persuasive. (But see Al Schneider's description, from within ABC, of the impact of advertiser pressure.)

My own experience in the 1970s, however, with the National Citizens Committee for Broadcasting, was that: (a) monitoring programs for levels of violence, as defined by Dr. George Gerbner, (b) matching the most violent programs with their advertisers, and then (c) announcing to the world the nation's "ten bloodiest corporations" *did* have an impact on corporate management, the corporations' advertising agencies, and, ultimately, the studios, networks, and producers. The levels of violence in the programs they televised did decline.

Even if the boycott, as such, has relatively little effect on revenues, the publicity it engenders may move a public-relations-sensitive executive to action—and also help an organization build membership.

Toward the end of Michael Curtin's piece ("Gatekeeping in the Neo-Network Era"), Curtin offers an innovative approach to what might be called a "reverse boycott" that any media reformer would do well to ponder.

PICKETING, STREET THEATER, AND OTHER CREATIVE CHANGE STRATEGIES

It is not necessary or appropriate to review here all the techniques developed over the years by community organizers and social change artists. There is a body of literature on the subject. The range is limited only by one's imagination, experience, talent, courage, and budget. If properly conceived and executed there is no reason to suspect such strategies could not have an impact in any age.

LETTER WRITING

It is true that postal rates continue to climb. But they still have a long way to go before reaching the levels of many corporations' multimillion-dollar budgets for advertising, public relations, and lobbying. So long as you do not expect too much from a letter, envelope, and stamp, the time and money spent can have a disproportionate impact. If your e-mail is free, and your recipient can receive it, the benefit-cost ratio of this avenue is even more favorable. At a minimum, most recipients at least keep a tally, and occasionally an individual letter is read and moves an executive to action. More extensive letter-writing campaigns, like any other technique, will benefit from strategic thought and planning.

MEETINGS AND CONFERENCES

For those with the necessary ability, money, time, and access, the kinds of individual meetings with writers and producers described by Robert Pekurny ("Advocacy Groups in the Age of Audience Fragmentation: Thoughts on a New Strategy") can, of course, be most effective.

If it is possible for individuals with a common interest to find each other and organize, they may be able to afford to have their own "ambassador to Hollywood." As a practical matter, however, such personal contact is not a realistic option for most members of the television audience.

Certainly Pekurny's suggestion of *positive* re-enforcement and awards can not do any harm. This conclusion can also be drawn from Gabriel Rossman's analysis of "cooperative" tactics ("Hostile and Cooperative Advocacy").

For what it is worth, over the course of my lifetime, to the best of my recollection, I have always begun with the cooperative approach in all of the dozens of situations in which I have found myself responsible for trying to effect change. It is my favorite strategy. It is sensible. It saves time, effort, stress, and money, and is an all-around more civilized way to proceed. Sadly, however, I have all too often found myself confronting administrators and adversaries on the other side of the table with whom cooperative strategies simply do not work.

It has been said that a successful administrator "needs gray hair so as to look wise and hemorrhoids so as to look concerned." But all too many show evidence of neither. They may display arrogance or avoidance, complacency or control, defensiveness or duplicity, elusiveness or evasiveness, feigning or fear, ignorance or indecisiveness—or all of the above. They may be manipulative and myopic, resistant and repressive—need I complete this alphabetical list? Maybe you have encountered one or two such individuals yourself. So many are simply unwilling to try the administrative strategies of cooperation, fairness, inclusion, justice, openness, and responsiveness.

In fairness, it may well be that this is simply their reaction to being consistently overworked, the target of irrational and hurtful criticism, and repeatedly disappointed by the individuals they have treated with kindness, reason, and trust. Whatever the case, my suspicion is that a good many of the organizations Rossman describes as using the tactics of "hostility" may, like I, not be using them as a matter of first and favored choice. It is just that having tried the cooperative approach with such people, one soon—however reluctantly—comes to the conclusion that the only ways to bring about change with them are boycotts, lawsuits, legislation, regulation, shareholder actions, and embarrassing media attention.

ORGANIZATIONS

Although relatively obvious, it should perhaps be mentioned that the successful impact of many to most of the activities just described require (or will at least substantially benefit from) organizations of one kind or another. Peggy Charren has offered us some very useful "Principles for Effective Advocacy from the Founder of Action for Children's Television." And note that an "organization" can gather leverage from coalition efforts as much as, if not more than, from its own "members."

When I chaired the National Citizens Committee for Broadcasting (NCCB) in the 1970s we were successful in getting the television networks to reduce levels of violence in entertainment programming. We used direct mail to build a membership base and fund our activities. But I always found that my influence with Congress increased substantially when I could walk into a congressional hearing room with "the other NCCB" (National Conference of Catholic Bishops) on one arm and the AFL-CIO on the other.

It is not just a matter of the "numbers" of persons affiliated with the organizations. In my experience the more broadly representative a coalition is (for example, in terms of politics, socioeconomic class, ideology, gender, or race/ethnicity), the more it will be listened to.

EDUCATION

Given the proliferation of available media, described above, I sometimes think the only truly effective, long-term strategy is education—as Michael Curtin ("Gatekeeping in the Neo-Network Era") puts it, "to help citizens make sense of the options available to them." If it is important that increasing numbers of audience members eschew the trivial and the tawdry, and prefer the virtuous to violence, developing individuals with the education and inclination to do so voluntarily may be the last best hope.

Is this a perfect solution? Of course not. One might as well try to educate the fish in the sea about the virtues of life on a dry land they have never seen and cannot survive. Changing attitudes and tastes about the mediated environment through which *we* swim, while we are swimming in it, is kind of like trying to change a flat tire on a moving car. But if it *could* be done it would provide a solution that would have the virtue of elevating media taste and utility while maintaining, indeed enhancing, the individual freedom of creators and audience alike.

So, what else might we do?

A NEW MODEL

There is no magic solution. As described above—indeed, throughout this book—the best strategy is multiple strategies. But there is an additional idea I would like to throw into the mix—not as an alternative, but as a supplement: an organization to which individuals and organizations can take their complaints about the media.

The Hutchins Commission, and others over the years, have proposed something analogous called a "News Council" for complaints about newspapers. Where tried (Minnesota at one point) it has had mixed success. Similarly, Great Britain has the Broadcast Standards Commission.

There is enough to this idea that we ought to consider it for the entertainment industry. It is a way of turning down the volume on the sort of behavior that Gabriel Rossman ("Hostile and Cooperative Advocacy") describes as "hostile" strategies and which Michael Suman ("Interest Groups and Public Debate") fears will produce self-censorship. It is an effort to balance respect for tribes with creative freedom.

It does that, for starters, by avoiding the use of "government"—of great concern to Mickey Gardner ("Public Policy Advocacy: Truant Independent Producers in a Federal City Fixated on a 'Values Agenda' ") and others. It also avoids funding, and control, by "the industry." It might be funded, for example, by one of our nation's public-spirited and well-endowed foundations.

The "council" and its supporting staff would be made up, presumably, of "the good, the true, and the gray"—that is to say, prominent individuals who have not been identified with, and are not perceived to be, spokespersons either for the industry or media advocacy groups. Indeed, they would be chosen as individuals, not as representatives of *any* organization. Of course, they should represent, to the extent possible, the demographics of America. To relieve the creative community's anxieties the organization would have no legal or other power to enforce its will.

Once adequately promoted by the news media, so that the audience knew it existed, the council could perform the role of an entertainment industry ombudsperson. That is, it would be the place that critics of the entertainment industry could go with their letters, e-mail, phone calls, and surveys. Academics could contribute relevant research. Sometimes the council would simply count letters—not unlike what networks have always done. At other times it might request (not demand) a visit with a studio or network executive, producer, or writer. With proper funding, it could also do surveys and other research. When complaints warrant it, the council could make an effort at fact finding (without any right of subpoena) and issue such reports as it deems useful and appropriate. Its impact on the industry, however, would rest solely on the persuasiveness of the data, the reasoning in its reports, and the news media's willingness to cover their activities.

Some of our authors have described the lengths to which industry representatives now go to gather public input. Norman Lear had an assistant who functioned as, in effect, an ambassador to the outside world of various special interests. The producers of "Prince of Egypt" consulted with hundreds of representatives of various religions. Properly perceived, the council—although not controlled by the industry—could serve the creative community in constructive ways as well. It could provide, in a totally unbiased and nonideological way, a type of public input that the industry appears to seek anyway. Moreover, it could organize that input, put it in context, and make sense out of it. It could help the industry avoid dealing with what Lionel Chetwynd ("Television and Pressure Groups: Balancing the Bland") characterizes as "every group of three people or more who think they know best"—while giving voice to the three people who do. More importantly, it would provide *some* opportunity for democratic input—although not control—by an audience that often feels marginalized, trivialized, and helpless in dealing with global media conglomerates.

Media can be "pushed" or "pulled." Conventional television and radio programming is "pushed"—that is, made available, as broadcast, when a receiver is tuned to the station. Books, videotapes, and the results of Internet search engine research are "pulled"—that is, they are brought into our lives, and consciousness, because we have selected them, at the moment we want them. To the extent that future technology, and media education, turn our mediated lives into a media economy that is increasingly "pull" rather than "push," the demand for audience control will diminish proportionately. Until that happens, however, the struggle between artist and audience, democratic control and artistic freedom, will continue.

NOTES

1. Kathryn C. Montgomery, *Target: Prime Time: Advocacy Groups and the Struggle over Entertainment Television* (Oxford University Press, 1990, paper ed.).

2. Bernard Cohen, *The Press and Foreign Policy* (Princeton, N.J.: Princeton University Press, 1963), p. 13.

3. Morley, John Morley, viscount, "On Compromise" (1874).

4. Although, I might note, my own nonscientific impression is that there is a lot more unnecessary product placement of tobacco in TV and film entertainment than there used to be.

5. Northern Sun Merchandising.

Selected Bibliography

Baehr, Ted. *The Media-Wise Family*. Colorado Springs, Colo.: Chariot Victor, 1998.

Bagdikian, Ken H. *The Media Monopoly*. Boston: Beacon Press, 1992.

Barnouw, Eric. *A Tower in Babel: A History of Broadcasting in the United States to 1933*. New York: Oxford, 1966.

Caplow, Theodore. *American Social Trends*. Orlando, Fla.: Harcourt Brace Jovanovich, 1991.

Choper, Jesse H. *Consequences of Supreme Court Decisions Upholding Individual Constitutional Rights,* 83 Michigan Law Review 1, 58 & n. 371, 1984.

Classen, Steven Douglas. "Southern Discomforts: The Racial Struggle Over Popular Television," in Lynn Spigel and Michael Curtin, eds. *The Revolution Wasn't Televised: Sixties Television and Social Conflict*. New York: Rouledge, 1997.

———. "Standing on Unstable Grounds: A Reexamination of the WLBT-TV Case," in *Critical Studies in Mass Communication* 11, Spring 1994.

———. *Watching Jim Crow: The Struggles Over Mississippi Television, 1955-1969*. Durham, N.C.: Duke University Press, forthcoming.

Cohen, Bernard. *The Press and Foreign Policy*. Princeton, N.J.: Princeton University Press, 1963.

Curtin, Michael. "Connections and Differences: The Spatial Dimension of Television History," in *Film and History*, in press.

———. "On Edge: Culture Industries in the Neo-Network Era," in Richard Ohmann, Gage Averill, Michael Curtin, David Shumway, and Elizabeth G. Traube, eds. *Making and Selling Culture*. Hanover, N.H.: University Press of New England, 1997.

Davis, James A. *General Social Survey Codebook*. Chicago, IL: National Opinion Research Center, 1994.

Department of California Highway Patrol. "A compendium for the implementation of the designated driver program." Sacramento, Calif.: Office of Public Affairs, 1992.

Donohue, William. "Executive Summary," in *Catholic League's 1997 Report on Anti-Catholicism*. http://www.catholicleague.org/report97.htm.

Epstein, Edward J. *News from Nowhere: Television and the News*. New York: Vintage

Books, 1973.

Federal Communications Commission. "Public Service Responsibility of Broadcast Licensees." Washington, D.C.: Government Printing Office, 1946.

———. "Fairness Doctrine Obligations of Broadcast Licensees," 50 Federal Register 35, 1985.

———. Report on Editorializing by Broadcast Licensees. Washington, D.C.: Government Printing Office, 1949.

Gans, Herbert J. Deciding What's News: A Study of CBS Evening News, NBC Nightly News, Newsweek and Time. New York: Vintage Books, 1980.

Gieber, W. "News Is What Newspapermen Make It," in L.A. Dexter and D. Manning White, eds. People, Society and Mass Communications. New York: Free Press, 1964.

Gitlin, Todd. Inside Prime Time. New York: Pantheon, 1983.

Habermas, Jürgen. Legitimation Crisis. Boston: Beacon Press, 1975.

Harvey, David. The Condition of Postmodernity: An Inquiry into the Origins of Cultural Change. Cambridge, Mass.: Basil Blackwell, 1989.

Herman, Edward S., and Robert W. McChesney. The Global Media: The New Missionaries of Corporate Capitalism. Washington, D.C.: Cassell, 1997.

Hirsch, Paul. "Processing Fads and Fashions: An Organization-Set Analysis of the Cultural Industry Systems," in American Journal of Sociology 77, 1972.

Hunter, James Davison. Culture Wars: The Struggle to Define America. New York: BasicBooks, 1991.

Jacobs, James B., and Kimberly Potter. Hate Crimes: Criminal Law and Identity Politics. New York: Oxford University Press, 1998.

Janowitz, M. "Professional Models in Journalism: The Gatekeeper And The Advocate," in Journalism Quarterly 57, 1975.

Kelly, Jonathan, and M. D. R. Evans. "Class and Class Conflict in Six Western Nations," American Sociological Review 60, 1995.

Kittross, John. "A Fair and Equitable Service or, A Modest Proposal to Restructure American Television to Have All the Advantages of Cable and UHF Without Using Either," in Federal Communications Bar Journal 29, 1976.

Media Action Network for Asian Americans. "MANAA Video Guide." http://janet.org/~manaa/video_guide.html.

Medved, Michael. Hollywood vs. America: Popular Culture and the War on Traditional Values. New York: HarperCollins, 1992.

Miyoshi, Masao. "Borderless World? From Colonialism to Transnationalism and the Decline of the Nation-State," in Rob Wilson and Wimal Dissanayake, eds. Global/Local: Cultural Production and the Transnational Imaginary. Durham, N.C.: Duke University Press, 1996.

Montgomery, Kathryn C. Target: Prime Time: Advocacy Groups and the Struggle over Entertainment Television. New York: Oxford University Press, 1989.

Mothers Against Drunk Driving (MADD). Position statement: "Responsible marketing and service of alcohol." Dallas, Tex.: MADD, 1990.

National Conference of Christians and Jews. Taking America's Pulse: The Full Report of the National Conference Survey on Inter-Group Relations, conducted by L H Research, 1995.

Patten, Chris. East and West: China, Power, and the Future of Asia. New York: Times Books, 1998.

Pekurny, Robert G. "Broadcast Self-Regulation: A Participant-Observation Study of the National Broadcasting Company's Broadcast Standards Department." Ph.D.

dissertation. Minneapolis: University of Minnesota, 1977.

———. "Coping with Television Production," in James S. Ettema and D. Charles Whitney, eds. *Individuals in Mass Media Organizations: Creativity and Constraint.* Beverly Hills, Calif.: Sage Publications, 1982.

———. "The Production Process and Environment of NBC's 'Saturday Night Live,' " in *Journal of Broadcasting* 24, Winter 1980.

Pinker, Steven. *The Way the Mind Works.* New York: W.W. Norton & Co.: 1997.

Roper Organization, The. *The Social Climate for Drinking: A Roper Analysis Prepared for the House of Seagram.* 1990.

———. *A special report to Anheuser-Busch by the Roper Organization.* 1991.

Rothman, Stanley, and S. Robert Lichter. "Hollywood and America: The Odd Couple," in *Public Opinion,* January 1983.

Schiller, Herbert I. *Mass Communication and American Empire.* Boulder, Colo.: Westview, 1992.

Shoemaker, P.J. *Gatekeeping.* Newbury Park, Calif.: Sage Publications, 1991.

Smith, Sally Bedell. *In All His Glory: The Life of William S. Paley, the Legendary Tycoon and His Brilliant Circle.* New York: Simon and Schuster, 1990.

State Farm Insurance Companies. "Be a good neighbor, be a designated driver." Bloomington, Ill.: State Farm Insurance Companies, 1991.

Sterling, Christopher H., and John M. Kittross. *Stay Tuned: A Concise History of American Broadcasting.* Belmont, Calif.: Wadsworth Publishing, 1978.

Streeter, Thomas. *Selling the Air: A Critique of the Policy of Commercial Broadcasting in the United States.* Chicago: University of Chicago Press, 1996.

Suman, Michael, ed. *Religion and Prime Time Television.* Westport, Conn.: Praeger, 1997.

Tuchman, Gaye. *Making News: A Study in the Construction of Reality.* New York: Free Press, 1978.

Weber, Max. *The Methodology of the Social Sciences,* translated by Edward A. Shils and Henry A. Finch. Glencoe, Ill.: Free Press, 1949.

———. *The Protestant Ethic and the Spirit of Capitalism,* translated by Talcott Parsons. New York: Scribner, 1958.

Index

ABC, 4, 24, 59, 71, 95, 105–109, 118, 131–133, 135–136, 145, 148, 150–151, 153

abortion, 121, 126–127, 141

Academy Awards, 34

Academy of Television Arts and Sciences, 136

Action for Children's Television, 9–10, 57, 79, 88, 92, 97–98, 152, 154

Addison, Anita, 35

advertising, 4, 15, 25, 30, 32–33, 47, 54–55, 57–58, 69–70, 80, 83, 89–90, 94–95, 97, 105–106, 109–110, 117–118, 120, 132–136, 140, 148, 153. *See also* promotion

advisories, 24

advocacy groups, 15, 19, 20–21, 27, 30, 37, 46–47, 49, 50, 55–57, 61, 65, 69, 73, 77, 79–83, 85–91, 93–95, 97–99, 105, 107–110, 112–113, 115, 117, 119, 125–128, 132, 136–137, 145–146, 148, 156. *See also* names of specific organizations
cooperative, 85, 89, 92–96
effectiveness of, 94, 99
hostile, 89, 91–92, 94–96
membership of, 88–90
as promoters of desirable content, 65, 155
publications of, 94. *See also* Gay and Lesbian Alliance Against

Defamation, *GLAADAlert*; *Movieguide*

affirmative action, 91, 96
in issuing broadcast licenses, 82

agenda setting, 31

agnosticism, 68

AIDS, 15, 28, 121, 135

Ali, Najee, 116

"All in the Family," 117, 120, 134

"All My Children," 16

"Ally McBeal," 119

American-Arab Anti-Discrimination Committee, 32

American Business Consultants, 132

American Family Association, 27, 87, 90–92, 94–95, 97–98, 107, 120, 136

American Federation of Television and Radio Artists, 132

American Legion, 115, 132

American Psychiatric Association, 135

arranged marriage, 13

Asian Americans, 29–36, 66, 73, 88–89, 115, 117

Assemblies of God, 107

assimilation, 87–88, 132

audiences, 5, 10, 13–15, 20, 23–24, 26, 37, 39, 60, 66–73, 80, 93–94, 106–109, 112, 117, 126, 135, 137, 140–141, 145, 149–150, 155–156
fragmentation of, 70, 106, 108, 112
self-selection of, 106

Augustyne, Sonya, 34
awards, 92–93, 97–98, 112, 154
Aware Inc., 132
Aykroyd, Dan, 111

"Babe," 39
"Babyface," 37
balance, 86, 89, 94, 127–128, 132, 137,
    141, 151, 155
Bandura, Albert, 13
"Barney Miller," 135
"Basic Instinct," 26
BBC News, 66
Beatles, 70
Beatty, Warren, 68
Bells of St. Mary's, 21
"Beulah Land," 132
"Beverly Hillbillies," 73
"Beverly Hills 90210," 15
Bikel, Ofra, 68
birth control, 127
Blakewell, Danny, 117
Blum, David, 106
Bochco, Steven, 141
boycotts, 24–26, 33–34, 43, 82, 89–92, 94,
    97–98, 105–110, 112, 116, 118, 120,
    134, 136–137, 141, 153–154
Bragger, Lydia, 125
brand names, 73, 94
"Bridget Loves Bernie," 88, 125
"British invasion" of pop music, 70
broadcast requirements, 108
Broadcast Standards Commission, 155
broadcasting, 4, 11, 13–16, 35, 43–45, 47–
    49, 54, 56–61, 65, 69–71, 73, 79–82,
    91–92, 97–98, 105, 108, 120, 125,
    131–133, 135, 147, 152, 156
Brooks, Mel, 117
Brotherhood Crusade, 117
"Bulworth," 68, 74
Business Executives' Move for Vietnam
    Peace, 44

cable television, 28, 57, 58, 66, 69, 71, 73,
    83, 91, 105, 108, 120, 122, 140, 149,
    152
Canby, Vincent, 38
Carlin, George, 106
Carson, Johnny, 110
Caruso, David, 120
Catholic League for Religious and Civil

Rights, 20–21, 88, 90–91, 94–95, 98,
    107, 116, 118
Catholicism, Roman, 19–21, 37, 85, 88,
    90–91, 94–95, 98, 107, 116, 118–120,
    127, 145, 149
Caucus for Producers, Writers, and
    Directors, 127, 136
Cayetano, Ben, 35
CBS, 4–5, 16, 34–35, 44, 59, 119–120,
    125–126, 133, 145, 149
CBS v. Democratic National Committee,
    44
censorship, 9–10, 43, 48–49, 57, 68, 83,
    97, 110, 119, 126, 134, 136, 140, 146,
    150. See also creative freedom; First
    Amendment;   freedom   of   speech;
    standards and practices
Center for Health Communication, 3
Centre for Media Studies of India, 14
channel surfing, 70, 106
Charren, Peggy, 9, 97, 152, 154
"Cheers," 5
children, 5, 9–11, 13, 17, 20, 38, 54–57,
    79, 80, 82, 87–88, 94, 107–108, 111,
    119, 120, 126, 137, 139, 146, 148, 151
"Children of the Revolution," 117
chilling effect, 45, 119, 155
China, People's Republic of, 14, 66, 73,
    150
China Population Information Service, 14
Christian Anti-Communism Crusade, 133
Christian Film and Television
    Commission, 39, 93–94, 98–99
Christian right. See religious right
Christianity, 38–39, 85, 87, 90–91, 93–94,
    98–99, 105, 107, 119, 133, 136. See
    also Assemblies of God; Catholicism,
    Roman; church film offices; religious
    right; Southern Baptist Convention;
    United Church of Christ.
church film offices, 37, 39
Church of Satan, 38
cigarettes, 82, 127, 150
civil rights movement, 9, 19, 25, 81
Civil War, American, 89, 91
Claremont Institute, 118
Classen, Steven, 81
clergy, 20, 141
Clinton, Bill, 53, 54, 57, 60, 68, 120, 147
CNN, 31, 73, 109, 121
Coalition Against Black Exploitation, 116

coalitions, 11, 31, 36, 89, 91, 145, 148, 154, 155
Cohen, Bernard, 148, 157
Collins, LeRoy, 133
"Coming Out With Ellen" (GLAAD campaign), 94
Committee Against Anti-Asian Violence, 31
Communications Act of 1934, 43, 151
communism, 66, 132, 139
Concerned Women of America, 107
Conference on Advocacy Groups and the Entertainment Industry, 20
conglomeration, 67, 70–71, 73, 78, 121, 151, 156
Congress, 44, 46, 53, 55–58, 60, 79, 91–92, 108, 133, 151, 154
Congressional Record, 98
conservatism, 20, 85, 87, 90, 95, 97–99, 107, 118, 132, 141, 150
constituencies of advocacy groups, 81, 87–89, 93, 94, 107
consulting, 92–93, 98, 110, 126
consumer welfare (as basis of lawsuits), 81
content guidelines, 91, 92
convergence, technological, 152
Cook, Fred J., 45
cooperation, 14–15, 66, 74, 85, 89, 92–99, 146, 154
corporations, 5, 25, 69, 70, 77–79, 82, 90, 105, 108–110, 112, 122, 131, 147–148, 150, 153
"Corpus Christi," 116
"Cosby Show," 5, 59
"Counterattack," 132
Court of Appeals, Fifth Circuit, 48
creative freedom, 95, 109, 126
Crichton, Michael, 30
critics, 65–68, 70, 72–73, 94, 136, 146, 156
Crystal, Billy, 120, 135

Dachau concentration camp, 30
Dalai Lama, 67
"Dallas," 139
"Damned," 125
"Dead Man Walking," 39
"Death of a Princess," 47, 49
defamation, 43, 49–50, 88, 132
democracy, 9–11, 66, 77–78, 80–81, 83, 115, 134, 137, 141, 146–149, 156

Democratic National Committee, 44
deregulation, 54, 58, 60, 70, 152
designated driver, 3–6, 26, 127
"Die Hard 2," 38
direct satellite service, 105
"Dirty Dozen" (list of advertisers), 90
disclaimers, 127
discrimination, 9, 19, 26, 36, 47, 68, 98
Disney. *See* Walt Disney Company
diversity, 23, 34–35, 54, 57–59, 61, 68, 79, 83, 86, 119, 122, 125, 136–137, 146, 150–151

E! Channel, 31
East and West: China, Power, and the Future of Asia, 66–68
Eco, Umberto, 82
economics, 4, 45–46, 67, 70, 82, 91, 105–106, 108, 115, 122, 133–134, 137, 141, 146
"Ecstasy," 37
educating the public, 115
Educational Television Requirement, 10, 82, 92
effects of the mass media, 69
Eichmann, Adolf, 125
Eisner and Associates Advertising Agency, 106
Eisner, Michael, 107, 109
"Ellen," 24–27, 71, 74, 94–95, 106, 109, 121, 149
Enola Gay, 115
Equal Protection Clause (of the 14th amendment), 47
Equal Time Rule, 44
ethnicity, 19, 49, 71, 81, 96, 132, 137, 155. *See also* race
ethnography, 85
executive, 5, 15, 30, 71, 81, 106, 118, 125, 141, 153, 156
"Eyes on the Prize," 68

fads and fashions, marketing that deals with, 72
Fairness Doctrine, 44–46, 82
Falwell, Jerry, 27, 136
family planning, 13–15
family values, 107
Family Viewing Hour, 108
"Fantasy Island," 86
Faulk, John Henry, 132

Federal Communications Commission, 43–46, 50, 54–60, 78–80, 91, 97–98, 133, 146, 152
complaints filed with, 44, 97
feminism, 19
film, 20, 23, 25–26, 28–32, 37–39, 48–49, 67–68, 71, 73, 78, 86–87, 93, 98, 107, 109, 117, 125, 140, 157. *See also* movies
First Amendment, 32, 44–45, 47–49, 53–58, 60–61, 116
Ford Foundation, 16
Ford, Gerald R., 133
foreign, perception of ethnic groups as, 29, 32–33
Fox, 13, 15, 30–32, 59, 68, 71, 73, 91, 116, 120–121, 137, 150. *See also* Newscorp
Frawley, Patrick J., 133
Freedman v. Maryland, 48–49
freedom of speech, 9–10, 48, 54, 67, 79, 116
freedom, creative, 68, 95, 155
"Fresh Prince of Bel Air," 72
"Frontline," 68
"F-Troop," 117
Fung, Dennis, 32

gatekeepers, 65, 67, 69–70, 72–73, 78
Gay Activist Alliance, 135
Gay and Lesbian Alliance Against Defamation (GLAAD), 23–28, 85–87, 92–94, 98, 151
GLAADAlert, 93
Monitoring & Response Committee, 92
Gay Media Task Force, 135
gays and lesbians. *See* homosexuality and homosexuals
General Social Survey, 26
genocide, 117
Gerbner, George, 153
Gere, Richard, 67
"Genghis Cohen," 117
Glazer, Nathan, 19
Gold, Ron, 135
golden age of Hollywood, 37, 140
Goldenson, Leonard and Isabelle, 131, 135, 150
Goldwater, Barry, 45
Gomez, Jaime, 34
Gore, Albert, 53

government, 3–5, 7, 10, 15, 19–20, 30–32, 43–49, 53, 55, 57–60, 65–66, 68–69, 74, 78–79, 82–83, 86–87, 91, 108, 115, 118–119, 121–122, 126–128, 132–135, 141, 146–156. *See also* Federal Communications Commission
government hearings, 91, 107
Gray Panthers, 125

Hagerty, Jim, 133–134
Handel, Bill, 33
haole, 35. *See also* whites
"Happy Days," 111
Hargis, Billy James, 45
HarperCollins, 66, 68
Harvard University, 3, 10, 26, 150
Harvey, David, 71
Hawaii, 29, 34–35, 87
"Hawaii Five-O," 34–35
Hawaiian pidgin, 35
Hayashi, Dennis, 30
health, 3, 5, 13–16, 82, 109, 118, 132, 136–137, 148–150
Heller, Melvin S., 135–136
heresy, 147
Hicks, Joe, 118
Hiroshima, 115
Hirsch, Paul, 72
Hispanic Association on Corporate Responsibility, 116
Hispanics. *See* Latinos and Latinas
Hiss, Alger, 133
Hollywood, 3, 5, 19–21, 32, 37–39, 53–55, 67–68, 71–72, 78, 94, 109, 116, 118, 128, 140–141, 145, 154
"Hollywood Uncensored," 37
Hollywood v. America, 21
Hollywood v. Catholicism, 21
homogenization, cultural, 70
homosexuality and homosexuals, 21, 23–27, 86, 93, 98, 105, 107, 109–111, 116, 118, 120–121, 131, 135–136, 151. *See also* "Ellen;" Gay Activist Alliance; Gay and Lesbian Alliance Against Defamation; Gay Media Taskforce; Heller, Melvin S.; Human Rights Campaign; National Gay and Lesbian Task Force; National Association for Research and Therapy of Homosexuality; "Making Sense of Homosexuality" (conference)

Hong Kong, 29, 66, 150
Honolulu Advertiser, 35
"House Party" (radio program), 32–33
House Un-American Activities
    Committee, 133
"Howard Stern's Radio Show," 119–120
human rights, 67
Human Rights Campaign, 27
Hundt, Reed, 54–55
Hunter, James Davison, 96
hunters, 49
Hutchins Commission, 155
hypersensitivity, 21, 116–117, 128, 146

ideal types, 85–86, 96–98
identity group, strength of attachment to,
    88
identity politics, 117
immigration, 29, 32
India, 13–14, 17
Indians, American, 19–20, 117, 132, 147
interest groups. See advocacy groups
Islam and Muslims, 49
Ito, Lance, 32

Jackson, Jesse, 34, 117
Jackson, Mississippi, 81, 83
Japanese American Citizens League, 30
Jennings, Peter, 4
"Jerry Springer Show," 119–120
Johnson, Lucy, 16
Johnston, George, 30
Joseph Burstyn, Inc. v. Wilson, 48
Judaism and Jews, 21, 30, 37, 96, 125

Kasem, Casey, 32
Kazungu, Tom, 15
Kennedy, John F., 9
Kenya, 15, 17
KFI-AM, Los Angeles radio station, 33
King for America, 107
KKBT, Los Angeles radio station, 32–34
Koop, C. Everett, 5
Kordus, Marie, 33
Ku Klux Klan Act of 1871, 47
Kuehl, Sheila, 118
"Kundun," 67, 150
Kwan, Michelle, 33

"L.A. Law," 5
Lamar, Hedy, 37

Land, Richard, 107
Latinos and Latinas, 34, 116, 131
lawsuits, 37, 44, 48–49, 89, 91
Le Vey, Anton, 38
League of United Latin American
    Citizens, 116
Lear, Norman, 156
legal system, 43, 50
legislation, 55–56, 58, 89, 91–92, 98, 108,
    152, 154
legitimation, 78
LeMasters, Kim, 35
Leonard, John, 68–69, 150
letter writing and petitions, 15, 33, 89–90,
    92, 98, 105, 109–110, 112, 119, 125,
    153
Lewinsky, Monica, 147
Lewis, Jerry, 131
liberalism, 20, 38, 74, 88, 96, 140, 150
Library of Congress, 115
license renewal (broadcasting), 81, 91
Lichter, S. Robert, 20
Lieberman, Joseph, 91–92
"Life Is Beautiful," 117
"Little Big Man," 117
Liu, Lucy Alexis, 34
lobbyists, 38–39, 55–56, 69, 78–79, 91,
    115, 153
London, John, 32
Los Angeles City Council, 91, 116, 118
Los Angeles City Human Relations
    Commission, 30, 116
Los Angeles Times, 4, 31, 117, 119
"Loveline," 119
Lowry, Brian, 117

"Making Sense of Homosexuality"
    (conference), 118
"Marcus Welby, M.D.," 135
Marin, Cheech, 34
market failure, 82, 83
marketplace of ideas, 45, 48, 110
markets, 5, 16, 25, 45, 48, 53–54, 58, 59–
    61, 65, 66, 70–73, 78, 79, 81–83, 89,
    90, 93, 109–110, 120, 149, 156
"Married with Children," 106, 137
Martin, Dean, 110
"Mary Tyler Moore Show," 120
"M*A*S*H," 117
Massachusetts Restaurant Association, 4
"Maude," 120, 134

Mayeda, Daniel M., 32–33, 92
McNally, Terrence, 116
media, conservative orientation of, 67
media, liberal orientation of, 68, 140, 141, 150
Media Action Network for Asian Americans, 29–34, 87–89, 92–94, 98, 145
media elite, 5, 53–54, 57, 60–61, 89, 91–99, 109–110, 112–113, 128, 136, 138, 140, 146, 156
media portrayals, 49
    assimilating, 87–88
    child-corrupting, 87–88
    desirable, 93, 118
    diminishing, 59, 86–87
    offensive, 89, 93, 95
    poor role models, 86–87
    stigmatizing, 86–88
media professionals, 25, 28, 67
medical problem, social issues cast as, 82
Medved, Michael, 21
meetings (between advocates and broadcasters or advertisers), 89, 92
"Melrose Place," 15
"Men in Black," 72
mergers, 70
Miami Herald Publishing Co. v. Tornillo, 46–47, 82
"Middletown" study, 119
minorities, ethnic, 9, 34–36. See also African Americans; Asian Americans; discrimination; ethnicity; Judaism and Jews; Latinos and Latinas; miscegenation; race
Minow, Newton, 133
miscegenation, 29, 88, 96, 125
Mizuhara, Theo, 33
model minority, 32, 34
moguls, 65
monopolies, 69
Montgomery, Kathryn C., 145, 157
Moonves, Les, 34–35
Moore, Michael, 71
Moral Majority, 134, 136
morality, 9, 14, 20, 26, 37–39, 53–55, 57–58, 60, 66, 68, 79, 92–94, 96, 107, 146, 148–151
Morita, Pat, 128
Mothers Against Drunk Driving, 3, 5
Motion Picture Association of America, 38

Motion Picture Code, 38, 39
Movieguide, 39, 93, 94, 98
movies, 10, 21, 23–24, 26–27, 37–39, 43, 48–49, 58, 67–68, 90–91, 98, 107, 125, 134. See also names of specific movies
Moyers, Bill, 68
Moynihan, Daniel Patrick, 19
Muir v. Alabama Educational Television Commission, 48
Murdoch, Rupert, 59, 66, 68, 73, 150
museums, 115
"Mystic Warrior," 132

Nader, Ralph, 82
Nakamura, Michael, 35
narrowcasting, 70
"Nash Bridges," 34
National Association for Research and Therapy of Homosexuality, 118
National Association for the Advancement of Colored People, 93, 116
National Association of Broadcasters, 4, 38, 133
National Citizens Committee for Broadcasting, 146, 153–154
National Coalition for Redress and Reparations, 30
National Conference of Catholic Bishops, 155
National Designated Driver Campaign, 3, 5
National Federation of the Blind, 107
National Gay and Lesbian Task Force, 27
National Highway Traffic Safety Administration, 5, 6
National Lesbian and Gay Journalists Association, 25
National Puerto Rican Coalition, 116
NBC, 4–5, 24, 59, 71, 108–110, 121, 132
neo-network era, 65, 71–72, 74, 105, 140, 151
network era, 65, 70, 72–73
networks, 4–5, 13, 15, 21, 38, 59, 61, 65–66, 69, 70–73, 80, 82, 86, 91, 106, 108–112, 117, 121, 127–128, 131–133, 135–137, 149, 152, 156
networks, new, 105
New York Post, 25
New York Times, 4, 11, 25
Newscorp, 65–66, 121. See also Fox
Nickelodeon, 20

Nigeria, 49–50
norms. *See* morality
Norwalk Japanese Cultural Center, 30
"Nothing Sacred," 88, 90, 95, 107, 109–
    110, 118, 121
"Nuremberg Trials," 133
"NYPD Blue," 106, 120

"Object of My Affection," 24
obscenity, 38, 91
Ohio University, 14
oligopoly, 69, 78, 109, 112, 121
ownership of the mass media, 67, 108–110

Pan American Health Organization, 17
Paramount, 68–69, 71, 73, 116
Patten, Christopher, 66, 68, 73, 150
"Pearl," 29, 34
Pearl Harbor, 29
Perlman, Rhea, 34
personal attack rule, 44–46
petitions. *See* letter-writing and petitions
picketing, 25, 116, 117
Pipher, Mary Bray, 148
"PJs," 116
pluralism, 27, 55, 80, 83, 115–122, 135,
    146–147, 149
"Pocahontas," 107
policy, 6, 10, 14, 33, 44, 47, 53, 55, 58, 60,
    65, 69, 77, 79–80, 82, 105, 107, 113,
    126, 134, 136
political campaigns, 44, 46
political correctness, 21, 116–117, 128,
    146
political editorializing rule, 44–45
"Political Obituary of Richard M. Nixon,"
    133
Population Communications International,
    13–17
Population/ Family Life Education
    Program in Tanzania, 15
"P.O.V.," 68
Power 106, Los Angeles radio station, 33–
    34
prejudice, 9, 19–21, 26, 36, 38, 68, 118
Prime Time Access Rule, 59, 82
"Priest," 21, 107
"Primal Fear," 21
"Prince of Egypt," 93, 98, 156
print media, 4, 24, 30, 43, 46–47, 50, 73,
    92, 94, 137, 155

prior restraint (on free speech), 92
producers, 16, 33, 53–55, 89–90, 110, 116,
    131, 151, 156
Proffit, Stuart, 66
promotion, 4–5, 14, 31, 72–73, 92, 94, 98,
    106, 118
protest, 31–32, 34, 95, 111, 116, 118, 134–
    135
public interest, 45, 57–58, 69, 79, 82, 91,
    126, 128, 132, 151
public relations, 4, 15, 78, 86, 153
public service announcements, 4
public television, 10, 47–48, 74, 83, 139,
    146

Quayle, Danforth, 128

race, 29, 33, 68, 81, 96–97, 117, 132, 148–
    150, 155. *See also* ethnicity;
    miscegenation
racism, 26, 31, 34, 81, 82, 90, 116, 119
    institutionalized, 36
radio, 4, 13–15, 30, 32–33, 45, 60, 69, 78–
    79, 88–90, 92, 106, 133, 147, 156
Rafu Shimpo, 30–31
Rainbow Coalition, 34
Rakolta, Terry, 106, 137
"Rambo III," 38
reasonable access rule, 44
reciprocal altruism, 89
recruiting   membership   of   advocacy
    groups, 90
"Red Channels: The Report of Communist
    Influence in Radio and Television,"
    132
"Red Corner," 67, 150
*Red Lion Broadcasting Co. v. Federal
    Communications Commission*, 45–46
regulation, 79, 147
REI (retail chain), 74
Reiner, Rob, 16
religion, 16, 19, 21, 37–39, 49, 87, 96–97,
    117, 119, 121, 127, 132, 145, 147, 149
religious right, 97, 117, 134–136, 147
responsibility of the press, 46
"Rising Sun," 30–32
Rodriguez, Paul, 128
romance (in the media), 29
Rothman, Stanley, 20
Rubin, Alvin B., 48

Salant, Dick, 133
satellites, 58, 66, 69, 71, 149, 152
"Saturday Night Live," 111, 121
Saudi Arabia, 47
scarcity argument, 44, 47
Schick Safety Razor Company, 133
Screen Actors Guild, 5
"Secret Diary of Desmond Pfeiffer," 91,
    116, 119
secularism, 88, 96
sedition, 147
Seeger, Pete, 9
"Seinfeld," 73, 106, 108, 116
"Sense and Sensibility," 39
"Seven Years in Tibet," 67, 150
sex, 10, 20, 26, 38, 80, 86–88, 91, 96, 105,
    107, 109, 117–121, 126, 133, 136–137,
    140
Sex in America, 26
"Sexuality, Television and Broadcast
    Standards" (manual), 136
"Shadowlands," 39
Shalala, Donna, 16
Sherman, William Tecumseh, 89
Sierra Club, 140
Silverman, Fred, 126
Simpson, O.J., 32
single parenthood, 16
slavery, 89, 91, 115, 116
Smith, Howard K., 133
Smith, Will, 72
Smithsonian Institute, 115
Sniffen, Elsie, 35
"Soap," 120, 134, 135
soap operas, 13–15, 17, 150. *See also* "All
    My Children;" "Beverly Hills 90210;"
    "Melrose Place;" "Party of Five;"
    Population Control International; Soap
    Summit; "Twende na Wakati;" "Tinka
    Tinka Sukh;" *Ushikwapo Shikamana*;
    telenovellas; "Young and the Restless"
Soap Summits, 15–16
social expectation theory, 3, 86
social learning theory, 13
social norms, 3–4, 7
sociology, 19
Sony, 67
Southern Baptist Convention, 25, 43, 91,
    105–107, 109
"South Park," 119–120
"Spin City," 24
standards and practices, 38, 80, 119, 121,

125, 145
Stanford University, 13
Stanton, Frank, 5
Star Bulletin, 35
"Star Trek," 72
STAR TV, 66, 73
Steinem, Gloria, 10
Stephen J. Cannell Productions, 35
stereotypes, 86–88
Stern, Howard, 119
Stoddard, Brandon, 132
strategy of advocacy groups, 3, 6, 10, 24,
    36, 69, 71, 73, 89, 96, 99, 105, 108–
    110, 153–155. *See also* tactics
    cooperative, 85, 89, 92, 96, 110, 140.
    See also advocacy groups, cooperative
    hostile, 89, 92, 128, 141, 154. *See also*
    advocacy groups, hostile
"Studio One," 133
Sullivan, Ed, 70
Supreme Court, 43–46, 48, 56, 82
Swafford, Thomas J., 125

Taco Bell, 116
tactics (of advocacy groups), 24–25, 33,
    79, 85, 89, 91–92, 94–99, 134, 136,
    137, 145, 146, 152, 154
Tagawa, Cary, 34
Tanzania, 13–15
Target: Prime Time, 145, 157
telenovelas, 17
television, 3–5, 9–11, 13–14, 16, 20–21,
    23–31, 34, 37–39, 43, 46–49, 53–61,
    65–66, 68–73, 78, 80, 82, 83, 85–88,
    90–92, 95, 106–110, 115–117, 119–
    122, 125–128, 131–137, 139–141,
    148–154, 156
television networks. *See* ABC; cable
    television; CBS; Fox; NBC; neo-
    network era; networks; Nickelodeon;
    UPN; WB
television series. *See* specific names of
    television series
"That Certain Summer," 135
theater, 109, 115
Thomas, Clarence, 121
Tibet, 67
Time Warner, 68, 73, 78, 109
"Tinka Tinka Sukh," 14
Tinker, Grant, 5
tolerance, 119
"Tongues Untied," 68

Torres, Art, 118
"Touched by an Angel," 27
"Toy Story," 39
Toyota, Tritia, 32
Treyz, Oliver, 131
tribal control, 149
"Truman Show," 68
"TV Nation," 71, 74, 149
"Twelve Chairs," 117
"Twende na Wakati," 14

UNICEF, 17
United Church of Christ, 81–82
United States of America, 5, 15, 17, 29–
    30, 36–37, 39, 49–50, 53–55, 58–59,
    65, 67, 70, 74, 78, 83, 96, 107, 119,
    121, 125, 132–133, 140, 147, 148, 156
University of Houston, 47
University of Nairobi, 15
University of New Mexico, 15
"Untouchables," 134
UPN (television network), 119–120
U.S. Center for Substance Abuse
    Prevention, 6
Ushikwapo Shikamana, 15

values. See morality
V-Chip, 54–55, 57, 80, 92, 108, 120, 139
VCRs, 71, 126
veterans, military, 115
Viacom, 72–73, 109, 121
victimhood (as morally superior), 119
villains, 29
violence, 10, 16, 37–38, 57, 80, 87, 91,
    107–108, 120, 126, 133, 136, 140, 146,
    148, 153–155
Visconti, Luchino, 125
volunteering, 9

"Wag the Dog," 68
Wakabayashi, Ron, 30
Walt Disney Company, 25, 43, 59, 67, 73,
    90, 94, 98, 105–107, 109, 118, 121.
    See also ABC; boycotts
Washington Post, 4
Watching Jim Crow, 81
WB television network, 120–121
Weber, Max, 85
Westinghouse, 4, 59, 79
whites, 23, 29, 34–36, 83, 88, 91, 96, 131,
    147. See also haole
Whole Earth Catalogue, 74
Wilbraham, Craig, 32–33
"Wild Bunch," 38
Wildmon, Donald E., 27, 87, 136
"Will and Grace," 24, 86
Winchell, Walter, 133
Wiseman, Frederick, 68
WLBT-TV, 81, 82
Wolper, David, 136
Wong, Russell, 35
Woo, Mike, 32
World Health Organization, 17
World War II, 30
writer-producers, 110, 112–113
Writers Guild of America, 5, 29, 112, 127
Written By, 112

Yamaguchi, Kristi, 33
"Year of the Dragon," 32
"Young and Restless," 16

Zedong, Mao, 66
Zelnick, Strauss, 30
Zemin, Jiang, 67

About the Editors and Contributors

CAROL ALTIERI joined CBS in 1969 as a secretary in the Press Information Department. Five years later she became a program practices editor, responsible for children's programs, feature films, specials, sports, and series development. Altieri was transferred to Los Angeles in 1979 as senior editor and was primarily responsible for acquisition and editing of feature films and screenplay pre-buys. After serving as manager of administration for two years, she became director of prime time programming standards, dealing with network series, movies for television, mini-series, theatricals, and drama development. In August 1984, Altieri was named West Coast vice president for program practices, overseeing the clearance of programs originating on the West Coast, as well as the administration of television program labeling and other content policy issues.

GUY AOKI is cofounder and president of Media Action Network for Asian Americans, the only organization solely dedicated to monitoring the media and advocating positive and balanced portrayals of Asian Americans. Aoki has led campaigns against a variety of media portrayals of Asian Americans in film, television, and radio. Aoki writes a biweekly column in the *Rafu Shimpo* newspaper, "Into the Next Stage," about media images and Asian Americans.

TED BAEHR is chairman of the Christian Film and Television Commission and publisher of *Movieguide*, a family guide to the movies based on Judeo-Christian values. As past president of the Episcopal Radio-Television Foundation, he served as executive producer and host of the weekly PBS television program "Perspectives." Baehr has authored a number of books, including *The Christian Family Guide to Movies and Video*, Vols. 1 and 2, *Getting the Word Out*, *Hollywood's Reel of Fortune: A Winning Strategy to Redeem the Entertainment Industry*, and *The Media-Wise Family*. He received his J.D. from New York University School of Law.

PEGGY CHARREN is the founder of Action for Children's Television (ACT), a national child advocacy organization established in 1968. Ms. Charren is also a visiting scholar at the Harvard University Graduate School of Education, where she serves on the Technology Council. Among numerous other honors, she was awarded the Presidential Medal of Freedom in 1995, a Peabody Award in 1992, and an Emmy in 1988. She is a member of the board of trustees of public television station WGBH in Boston and the White House Advisory Committee on Public Interest Obligations of Digital Television Broadcasters. She has advised numerous government agencies and private foundations. Ms. Charren is author or coauthor of *The TV-Smart Book for Kids*; *Television, Children and the Constitutional Bicentennial*; and *Changing Channels: Living Sensibly with Television*.

LIONEL CHETWYND, writer, director, and producer, graduated valedictorian from Sir George University in Montreal and later attended Trinity College of Oxford University. Chetwynd wrote the motion picture screenplay for "The Apprenticeship of Duddy Kravitz," for which he received an Academy Award nomination for best screenplay adaptation. Among his other credits are the Emmy-nominated "Sadat," which received an NAACP Image Award nomination; "Miracle on Ice," which was honored with the Christopher Award; and the television movie "Johnny, We Hardly Knew Ye," for which he received the Freedom Fund's George Washington Honor Medal. Chetwynd has been a member of the faculty of New York University's Graduate Film School and has lectured on screenwriting at both the Frederick Douglass Center in Harlem and UCLA.

MICHAEL CURTIN received his Ph.D. in communication arts at the University of Wisconsin-Madison. He is an associate professor in the Department of Communication and Culture and the director of the Cultural Studies Program at Indiana University. Curtin has been a visiting scholar at Wesleyan University and the Chinese University of Hong Kong. He is currently residing in Taiwan finishing research for a book that he is writing about the transnational trade in film and television. Curtin is the author of *Redeeming the Wasteland: Television Documentary and Cold War Politics* and is coeditor of *Making and Selling Culture* and *The Revolution Wasn't Televised: Sixties Television and Social Conflict*.

WILLIAM A. DONOHUE is president and CEO of the Catholic League for Religious and Civil Rights, the nation's largest Catholic civil rights organization, and the publisher of the Catholic League's journal, *Catalyst*. Donohue, a Ph.D. in sociology from New York University, is an adjunct scholar at the Heritage Foundation and serves on the board of directors of the National Association of Scholars and its New York State chapter board. He is the author of three books, including *Twilight of Liberty: The Legacy of the ACLU*, and many articles. Donohue serves on the board of advisors of the Washington Legal

Foundation, and on the boards of the Howard Center for Family, Religion, & Society; the Educational Freedom Foundation; and the Society of Catholic Social Scientists. He appears as a frequent guest on television and radio, speaking on civil liberties and social issues.

IRWIN SONNY FOX has moved from performing, producing, and an executive career in television to become senior vice president of Population Communications International. PCI uses the mass media around the world to modify attitudes and change behavior of its audiences on matters relating to family planning, women's health, and violent behavior, among others. Its choice for the most effective means to convey these messages in a meaningful way is serial dramas, commonly known in America as "soap operas." Research has proven the efficacy of this strategy in China, Kenya, Tanzania, Mexico, Brazil, and India. In the United States PCI works with the creative community through its "Soap Summits" and "Prime Time Summit." Fox is the author of four books.

MICKEY R. GARDNER is an attorney in Washington, D.C. who manages a communications entertainment law firm. The firm, founded in 1990, specializes in policy and regulatory aspects of domestic and international communications law, as well as entertainment law. The firm represents corporations and associations involved in new technologies, programming, broadcasting, telephone, and cable interests before the Federal Communications Commission, Congress, and agencies of the federal government. Gardner has also served as the pro bono chairman of the United States Telecommunications Training Institute, a nonprofit international training initiative which he founded in 1982. He is currently an adjunct professor at Georgetown University, where he teaches a course entitled "The Modern American Presidency."

REX S. HEINKE is a partner in the law firm of Gibson, Dunn & Crutcher LLP and is cochair of its Intellectual Property Group. He received his J.D. from Columbia University School of Law in 1975. Heinke specializes in trial and appellate litigation with particular emphasis on First Amendment issues such as defamation, privacy, and prior restraint. Among the clients he has represented are the *Los Angeles Times*, NBC, Paramount, the *Wall Street Journal*, Fox, *The New York Times*, and *Newsweek*. Heinke is the author of *Media Law*, a leading treatise on the legal problems of journalists and the media. He is also a member of the Editorial Advisory Board of the *Media Law Reporter*.

WILLIAM HORN is the assistant entertainment media director for the Gay and Lesbian Alliance Against Discrimination (GLAAD). He works with the entertainment media to ensure positive portrayals of the lesbian, gay, bisexual, and transgender community in television and other media.

NICHOLAS JOHNSON is a former FCC commissioner and now teaches at the University of Iowa College of Law. He is the author of *How to Talk Back to Your Television Set*. He has been a host and editor (PBS's "New Tech Times," NPR commentaries) and a nationally syndicated columnist ("Communications

Watch"). Johnson was also chair of the National Citizens Committee for Broadcasting.

ROBERT PEKURNY received his Ph.D. in speech-communication from the University of Minnesota. His dissertation was based on a participant-observation study of NBC's "censors." He also conducted research on the television program production process, including studies of "Saturday Night Live," "Happy Days," and "Mork and Mindy." He spent 14 years as a professional staff writer on a half dozen situation comedies. He then returned to university teaching and currently heads the Media Production Program at Florida State University.

GABRIEL ROSSMAN was formerly a research assistant at the UCLA Center for Communication Policy and is currently a graduate student in sociology at Princeton University where he specializes in the sociology of culture. He contributed an article to and assisted in editing *Religion and Prime Time Television* (Greenwood, 1997). He is assistant editor of the present volume.

ALFRED R. SCHNEIDER retired in 1991 from the position of vice president of policy and standards at Capital Cities/ABC, a post he had held since 1983. He is a graduate of Harvard Law School. As an adjunct professor at Fordham University's Graduate School of Business Administration at Lincoln Center, New York, he taught a course on broadcasting and social policy, and another on the press, the law, and the corporation. An executive with 35 years of experience in the broadcasting business, Schneider possesses particular expertise in policy, administrative, and legal matters.

THOMAS STREETER, an associate professor of sociology at the University of Vermont, studies the institutions, laws, and policies of the electronic media in the context of culture. His *Selling the Air: A Critique of the Policy of Commercial Broadcasting in the United States* won the 1996 Donald McGannon Award for Social and Ethical Relevance in Communication Policy Research. Streeter, who holds a Ph.D. from the University of Illinois, has taught at the University of Wisconsin and University of Southern California, and has published essays on cultural and critical theory, copyright, free speech, and competition in the electronic media.

MICHAEL SUMAN is research director of the UCLA Center for Communication Policy. He has served as project coordinator of the center's television violence monitoring project and has coauthored several nationwide surveys, including the center's current panel study on the social impact of the Internet. Suman, who received his Ph.D. in sociology from UCLA, has taught sociology, anthropology, and communication studies in Japan, Korea, China, and the Marshall Islands. He is now a member of the faculty in the Department of Communication Studies at UCLA. He is editor of *Religion and Prime Time Television* (Greenwood, 1997) and senior editor of the current volume.

MICHELLE H. TREMAIN joined the Los Angeles office of Gibson, Dunn &

Crutcher LLP in 1996. She currently practices in the Litigation Department with a concentration on copyright, right of privacy, and First Amendment matters. Tremain received her law degree in 1996 from the UCLA School of Law, where she was elected to the Order of the Coif.

JAY A. WINSTEN is associate dean and director of the Center for Health Communication at the Harvard School of Public Health. The center's mission is to mobilize the power of mass communication to motivate positive behavior and contribute to informed public policy. The center's best-known initiative is the Harvard Alcohol Project, conducted in collaboration with Hollywood studios and leading television networks. Launched in 1988, the project represented the first large-scale effort to incorporate health messages in the dialogue of Hollywood scripts. A new initiative, with ABC, CBS, and HBO as initial partners, uses the mass media to recruit mentors for at-risk adolescents. Winsten received his Ph.D. in molecular biology from the Johns Hopkins University.

ISBN 0-275-96885-5

HARDCOVER BAR CODE